Heartbreaking, breathtaking, and incredibly raw, Tubbs draws you into his very heart and soul. His brutal honesty tears away at any preconceived notions you may have of life as a gay man. Yet the lessons he learns, and the trials he powers through can and will strike a chord in anyone willing to be open enough.

—Lorinda Boyer, author of *Straight Enough*

Taming the Dragon is one man's journey into wholeness, a courageous examination of all that gets in the way of being complete.

—Rev. Dr. Kathianne Lewis, Senior Minister, Center for Spiritual Living

Confronting personal demons can lead to a powder keg of suppressed emotions and dysfunction. How Tubbs survived the explosion and found peace within himself is told in his highly readable *Taming the Dragon* with openness, clarity and deep insight. It's a personal journey at times grueling, at times racy, and one that takes the reader along at pace.

—Robert Campbell, Australian editor and writer

In *Taming the Dragon*, Gary Tubbs gives us an example not only of what it takes to claim one's identity as a gay man in the eighties when such a declaration was seen by many as taboo, but he also shows the reader what courage looks like in the face of rejection by a parent. Tubbs details his struggles and triumphs and shows us that being true to yourself is worth the fight.

—Cami Ostman, author of *Second Wind: One Woman's Midlife Quest to Run Seven Marathons on Seven Continents*

Tubbs lays bare those parts of himself that most of us spend our lifetimes trying to hide. His vivid depiction of the gay experience and his insights into forgiveness invite the reader to connect to their own vulnerabilities and traumas in a healing journey that unfolds on the page. A courageously honest memoir about discovering the inner soul that lives inside all of us.

—Jeanne Rawdin, author and editor

With incredible honesty, Gary Tubbs crafts his memoir in a way that grips you from the first page and powerfully brings you into his lifelong journey to love his true self. *Taming the Dragon* is a must read for men (and women) who struggle with their own sexual identity and for educators, parents, grandparents, and other adults who nurture and support them.

—John Morefield, retired Seattle principal

This memoir is moving, insightful, and compassionate: an education for me, and one, I imagine, for many other readers as well—how appropriate, given the author's beginnings as a teacher. May this book find its "classroom" of readers.

—Dana Tye Rally, writing coach, editor, and author

TAMING THE DRAGON

MY MEMOIR OF COMING OUT, ADDICTION, AND AWAKENING

GARY TUBBS

Catherine —
Together we Awaken!

Gary

TAMING THE DRAGON

MY MEMOIR OF COMING OUT, ADDICTION, AND AWAKENING

GARY TUBBS

Sidekick Press
Bellingham, Washington

This memoir represents the author's recollection of his past. These true stories are faithfully composed based on memory, photographs, diary entries, and other supporting documents. Some names, places, and other identifying details have been changed to protect the privacy of those represented. Conversations between individuals are meant to reflect the essence, meaning, and spirit of the events described.

Published 2022
Printed in the United States of America
ISBN: 978-1-7369351-7-0
LCCN: 2022906465

Sidekick Press
2950 Newmarket Street, Suite 101-329
Bellingham, Washington 98226
sidekickpress.com

Gary Tubbs, 1952-
Taming the Dragon: My Memoir of Coming Out, Addiction, and Awakening

Cover design by Andrea Gabriel

DEDICATION

For Adiku

Standing in silence on the black stone porch, Adi and I looked out over our lush tropical gardens of heliconia, orchids, and palms.

"I know what you're thinking," I said in a playful tone, even though I had no idea.

He didn't react to my comment, which was not unusual. I often found it quite impossible to know whether Adi was deep in thought, not hearing me, or simply feeling no need to respond. His Indonesian culture and personality challenged me in the early years, but over our fourteen years together, I'd developed a comfortable place of acceptance and adoration. More importantly, I'd become secure enough in myself and Adi's love to not take his silence personally.

"You're thinking how grateful you are for your beautiful life here in Bali with your amazing husband."

Adi turned to me with his huge smile and sparkly eyes—the same soulful man who'd stolen my heart the first evening I met him. He reached out to tickle my ribs. But, even at seventy, I was too quick, and I jumped away laughing, off to do my daily gardening on a warm morning caressed by a soft breeze with only a few cottony clouds in the crystal blue sky.

How did we get to this place of satisfaction and contentment? How did I, an emotionally challenged man, after decades of dysfunctional relationships, end up happily married, enjoying a life of abundant beauty and inner peace?

Well, the journey was sometimes messy and often dramatic but, miraculously, love found a way.

2

Love and family filled my earliest years. Life in our safe, humble neighborhood was probably quite typical for a small-town American boy in the 1950s. I felt seen and supported as a valued member of a family who liked to laugh, hug, and tease. By the age of four, I already believed myself to be smart, clever, and creative, with Jesus as my friend and Sunday school a great joy.

Dad was a jack-of-all-trades and an excellent provider. Mom stayed home to handle all chores domestic with two in diapers for half-a-dozen years. She raised us pretty much single-handedly given Dad's travel schedule with the government. For most of our childhood years, we kissed him goodbye twice a month, then got excited when he returned home a week or two later.

Like many children from the semi-arid town of Richland in southeastern Washington state, I never knew much about my dad's job no matter how many times I asked. Security restrictions prevented employees from discussing their work on the expansive Hanford Nuclear Reservation north of town. It wasn't until my adult years that I understood Dad worked as an armed courier, guarding classified shipments for the U.S. Atomic Energy Commission.

Mom, although a confident and exceptionally competent woman, seemed less so when Dad was home. He wore the pants and made the big decisions, especially those costing money. Mom sometimes complained about feeling overworked and underappreciated by a husband who enjoyed sports and drinking beer with his buddies more than spending time with his wife and kids.

Growing up with an often absent father seemed normal to me. Fortunately, Mom encouraged the exploration of my creative nature, with my greatest joys being performing and movement. I often danced and put on dramatic performances in our living room with my family as a captive audience. Even my outside play with friends included movement with a jump rope, cartwheels, and acrobatics. I idolized the talented Mouseketeers, with *The Mickey Mouse Club* on TV providing an imaginary doorway into the wonderful world of entertainment.

In the summer after my first-grade year, Mom announced an opportunity that got my full attention.

"Sandy Freeman is going to start teaching ballet in September. Do you kids want to take lessons?"

Debi and I shouted, "Yes!" without hesitation. Nancy, although less enthusiastic, agreed to give it a try. Davy was only three and too young for Sandy's classes.

We all liked Sandy, a pretty, vivacious brunette who recently graduated high school and had occasionally been our babysitter.

I loved shopping for my ballet tights and slippers. I loved going to class. I loved the space with its varnished, hardwood floors, ballet bars, and mirrors. And I loved the classical music, along with Sandy's encouragement to move freely while also remaining disciplined.

During each of my three years' dancing, I observed myself becoming more confident and proficient, strong and flexible. I believed in the importance of dancing correctly and wanted my positions and movements to be precise. Although I never achieved a high level of proficiency, I did hope to enjoy ballet for many years.

Very quickly, I discovered how alive I felt on stage during recitals. Connecting with the audience was natural and soaking up the applause became addictive. My spirit knew what brought it joy and the creative expression of dance and performance made my soul sing. I imagined myself a rising star, willing to work as hard as necessary to make my dreams come true.

3

"Mom! I forgot to tell you!" I exclaimed with desperation. "I need a cowboy or Indian costume for our powwow at school today!"

As a conscientious boy who loved to wear costumes, my forgetfulness was completely out of character. But I awoke that morning with startling clarity and charged into the kitchen to give Mom the bad news about the costume.

"What? There's no time for that! You have to leave in a few minutes."

"Mom, please! It's important!" I begged.

Fortunately, Mom came up with an idea. She sent my brother and sisters off to school, then pulled out some brown fabric and threaded her sewing machine. After hemming and adding a drawstring, she cut fringe and used crayons and pens to draw a zigzag design around the "native breechcloth."

"That's the best I can do on such short notice," Mom huffed.

"Thanks, Mom. Sorry I forgot to tell you."

And off I went to school with a note to excuse my tardiness.

When it was time to put on our costumes for the powwow, Mrs. Leathers, our third-grade teacher, excused my friend, Pete, and me to change in the boys' bathroom.

"I look stupid!" Pete laughed as he modeled in the mirror wearing a silly cowboy getup. "And you look like a girl in a skirt!"

Although kids had teased me for being so small and dancing ballet, I hadn't felt too deterred. But Pete's teasing unsettled me. When I looked in the mirror, I was devastated to see he was right.

I did look like a girl. I took off my breechcloth and walked back to the classroom.

"Mrs. Leathers, I don't want to wear my costume."

"Why not, Gary?"

"Pete said I look like a girl."

"I'm sorry he said that. Let me look at it. Oh, I like it! Did your mom sew this for you? She did a good job. I think you should wear it and have fun with your classmates. Don't worry about what Peter said."

When Pete saw me later in my costume, he said, "Sorry." Evidently, Mrs. Leathers had spoken with him. Then as he walked away I heard him add, "I didn't know you were such a sissy."

In truth, I didn't know what "sissy" meant. I only had a vague idea from the first time I'd heard the word at Grandma Susie's house the prior Easter.

We had just finished dinner when Grandma told everyone to quiet down. Someone named Liberace was about to play the piano.

"Oh, he's so talented!" Grandma said when Liberace made his grand entrance wearing a full-length, white fur coat. He greeted his audience with a huge smile and breathy voice that gave me the creeps. His poofy brown hair was brushed straight back, every hair sprayed into place.

"Seems a little light in the slippers if you ask me," said Grandpa with a chuckle. The other men smirked and nodded in agreement.

"Well, no one's asking you," Grandma snarked. "His piano playing is beautiful, so just be quiet so I can hear."

"Queer as a three-dollar bill," mumbled my dad in a low voice, knowing his mom was hard of hearing.

A cute, young, blond man entered the stage. He was dressed in a white tuxedo adorned with an elaborate pattern of rhinestones. Gracefully, he removed Liberace's fur coat, revealing a similar but even more dazzling and extravagant white tuxedo. It all seemed very elegant and glamorous, but also made me uncomfortable in a way I didn't understand at the time.

Liberace walked to the center of the stage, his hands seeming to float about, then seated himself at a white grand piano, a huge candelabra set atop its lid. The camera zoomed in on his smile, then panned to his hands resting on the keys, adorned with heavy, bejeweled rings. The concert began and I became enthralled by the music and his flamboyant performance.

My loving Aunt Vera, her smiling eyes directed at me, said with a wink, "He's such a sweet, sissy man." Her comment confused me. I quickly turned away, terrified she saw something in me that reminded her of Liberace.

But Pete using the word "sissy" to describe my sensitive reaction to his teasing felt much more direct and embarrassing than Aunt Vera's comment. It flashed a glaring spotlight on me, making me want to hide in the shadows.

Issues of gender and sexuality were still beyond my conscious understanding, when, during a fourth-grade writing lesson, I heard my teacher, Miss Morn, ask from across the room, "May I help you?"

I looked up to see her approaching the classroom door where my dad stood waiting. "I'm sorry to interrupt," he said. "I need to take Gary out of school early."

I cleared my desk, wondering if something was wrong, while Miss Morn and Dad chatted in the hall.

When I joined them, Miss Morn said, "Have a nice weekend in Spokane with your cousins, Gary."

"Thank you," I replied, now understanding that we were simply departing earlier than planned.

"Is your teacher married?" Dad asked as we walked down the long halls of the school to round up my siblings.

"No, she's *Miss* Morn."

"Hmm . . . must be something wrong with her," Dad said.

"What do you mean something's wrong with her?"

"Well, she's a nice-looking woman. Lots of guys would like to be with a woman like that. But at her age and still not married . . . must be something wrong."

I still didn't understand, so I took a side glance at him and waited for something more.

"Some women don't like men," he said. End of discussion.

Even though that conversation would remain as clear as mud, it jogged my memory of another time Dad had used the expression, "must be something wrong." We were sitting in the stands of the high school gymnasium for the first game of the new basketball season. When the cheerleaders ran out onto the floor, my eyes sprung open like my grandpa's pocket watch.

"Dad! They have boy cheerleaders this year!" I couldn't believe it. I'd always been fascinated by the cheerleaders and often got permission to sit in the bottom bleachers for a better view.

At home, with the bathroom door locked, I sometimes stood in front of the mirror to choreograph simple cheers. But never had I considered a boy could actually be a cheerleader.

I looked to see if Dad shared my excitement. He did not.

"That tall boy is Simmons' son. You know the ref everyone yells at? He must be thrilled his son's a cheerleader," Dad said with bitter sarcasm.

"But did you see him do those flips? I bet Simmons is proud his son can do that!" I said, still overwhelmed with excitement.

"I don't think any father would be proud of his son for being a cheerleader. Must be something wrong with those boys."

After giving myself a minute for his words to sink in, I felt my new dream of cheerleading die before it could even take a breath.

While Dad's comments frequently put me on edge, causing a fair amount of disequilibrium, my interactions with Mom were generally more pleasant and relaxed. I especially liked helping her in the kitchen, and before I turned ten, I knew how to boil and mash potatoes, fry chicken, and even make gravy. So it was only natural I enjoyed accompanying Mom when she went grocery shopping. She let me push the cart when I was tall enough and old enough to avoid clipping her heels. Once I learned the market rules, we enjoyed our time together. She liked to glance in other people's shopping baskets to get ideas. I hunted the shelves, practicing my reading and suggesting new items.

"Have you ever tried cow tongue, Mom?"

"Ewww . . . no," she replied as if gagging.

"I ate it at Pete's house. His family loves it! It was chewy but the flavor's good."

"Well, we're not buying cow tongue, so get that idea out of your head. But we haven't had liver and onions for a while. Let's get some liver."

That's how Mom and I shopped—like two friends.

"Wow! These must be some fancy napkins!" I exclaimed, reading a multisyllabic word on one of the products on the store shelf.

"What are you talking about?" she asked, eyebrows furrowed.

"San-i-tar-y," I read. "Why would anyone need sanitary napkins?"

Mom choked in her attempt not to laugh, but finally let it out with tears streaming down her face. When she explained, I laughed, too—certain not to make that mistake again.

After shopping with Mom on a delightful day in May, I leaned out the side window of the car, relishing the warm wind blowing on my face and catching a subtle whiff of lilacs.

"I need to talk to you about something," Mom suddenly said.

I sat up straight, instantly alert. She had never begun a conversation like that before.

"Okay. What?"

She drew a breath, then said, "Dad wants you to quit ballet."

"What? Why?" They knew I loved ballet. I never missed a class.

"Well, Dad's worried that when boys are around girls too much, they can begin to act too much like a girl."

My face flushed, but I managed a quick comeback. "Sandy says I'm good enough to dance with the older boys next season."

Sandy's compliment the month prior had motivated me to work even harder in anticipation of taking classes with the teenage boys, whom I so admired. I even had a crush on one handsome, dark-haired boy with muscles. One day, when I arrived early for class, I pulled open the dressing room curtain and discovered him behind it.

"Oh! Sorry!" I blurted out and closed the curtain.

"That's okay," he said in a relaxed voice. "You can come in. There's room enough for both of us."

My heart raced. I felt shy but also excited to undress with a high school boy in a small, private space. I entered to find him in his tighty-whities and his bulge practically in my face. My breath caught. I turned my back as I got undressed to hide my rising excitement. The thought of dancing with the older boys in the coming season was so thrilling, I desperately wanted to change the course of my conversation with Mom.

But instead, I heard, "Your dad's concerned about you dancing with the older boys, too."

Dad's words echoed in my head. *Must be something wrong with those boys.*

All was quiet in the car for the remainder of our trip home. But my mind screamed: *Too much like a girl. Something's wrong with boy ballet dancers. Something's wrong with boy cheerleaders. Sissy . . . sissy!*

The world I thought I knew had died while the reality of my new world slapped me in the face. Something was wrong with me. I held my chin high and directed my eyes forward. No one would ever know I was emotionally scattered like spilled sugar on the floor.

As we pulled into the driveway, I managed to say, "Okay, well, I've been thinking about acting anyway. Maybe there'll be a school play for my grade next year."

Mom had the concession she needed for her report to Dad, but highly potent, toxic seeds were planted deep in my psyche that afternoon—pain, shame, anger, and resentment. The Gary I believed myself to be was no longer acceptable.

4

Believing my father's love was conditioned on becoming more acceptable, I started to examine every aspect of myself. Michelangelo sculpted David from a single slab of marble by chipping away at whatever was not David until the spectacular man revealed himself. My task was almost the opposite. I looked at every potentially unacceptable thing about myself and hid it, modified it, or protected it with armor. Of course, it never occurred to me as a child how such patchwork re-sculpting might play out in later years.

The most obvious change I believed I needed to make as a ten-year-old boy was to behave less "like a girl." Did that mean less expressive and creative? I wasn't sure. But I began to take whatever steps I felt necessary, because for my dad to think there was something wrong with me was far more terrifying than dimming my own light.

In hindsight, it's clear my father's disapproval was rooted in his own fears. Raised in conservative, rural Montana by a strong Christian woman and a salt-of-the-earth stepfather, he did his best to provide for and protect his family. Having a "sissy son" would reflect poorly on him.

The shame of not being the son my dad wanted weighed heavily on my troubled mind. I began to model myself after boys he seemed to admire, paying attention to every detail. I changed my walk, my laugh, how I crossed my legs, and monitored my hands so they didn't flail about. The color pink never came near me—no pink clothes, of course, and not a bit of pink on my book covers or in my artwork. My sissy-antenna was tuned-up to be hypersensitive so that I could avoid anything and everything I thought others, particularly my dad, would consider girly. All had to appear "normal."

At school, I started to play more kickball and less two-square, more flag football and less jump rope. Because I was small, team captains often chose me last until I studied how the games worked and figured out how to contribute in my own way. What I lacked in natural talent I made up for in quickness and cleverness.

I avoided the effeminate boys and steered clear of loud bullies who were likely to pick on me. Constantly on guard and aware of my surroundings, I never fully relaxed, believing I needed to be perfect in order to win approval.

Even at home when Dad was away, I sometimes got caught off guard.

"I didn't know men examined their nails like that," Mom said as I gave myself a manicure.

"What do you mean?"

She demonstrated how men bent their fingers, then turned their nails inward for examination. Women held their fingers straight up.

"And I've seen men clip their nails, but I've never seen your dad file them," Mom added.

Although I generally saw Mom as being in my camp, I sometimes wondered if she might be helping Dad change me by executing some kind of master plan.

Many of my friends were active in Cub Scouts, and with Dad's encouragement, I joined the troop in the fourth grade. I didn't enjoy it much. The whole pledge, pack, and badge routine didn't motivate me, and carving little cars for the Pinewood Derby seemed like a waste of time. In the spring, my troop encouraged me to join their softball team. I had no confidence or interest, but they needed another player, and pressured me until I agreed.

My fear of playing softball was rooted in experiences with Dad teaching me to catch, throw, and hit a ball at a very young age. I enjoyed his attention, but didn't enjoy embarrassing him—or myself. I was a terrible thrower, primarily because he insisted I learn to throw with my right hand, even though I was left-handed. He saw me as a quick infielder. Being left-handed made it problematic to throw to first base in time in order to get the runner out. Dad held big dreams for his young son, who showed no interest in anything outside of dancing and performing.

At first I didn't tell him about playing softball. I didn't want him to come to a game and be embarrassed or critical of me. But after some confidence-building practices and a few victorious games, I decided to let the cat out of the bag one evening during dinner.

"My softball team is doing pretty good so far," I said.

"What softball team?" he asked.

"Cub Scouts."

"Is that right? What position are you playing?"

"I'm just in the outfield. Not many balls come out there," I admitted.

Dad wanted to know the schedule so he could attend a game, which he did the following weekend. Fortunately, I played okay and even drove in a run to help us win.

"Well, that turned out pretty good," Dad commented as we walked back to the car.

"Yeah, we won. Did you see my hit?" I asked, fishing for a compliment.

"I did . . . and I also saw you misjudge that pop fly," he commented with a side-glance and a grin.

"Yeah, the sun got in my eyes."

"Next time, hold your glove up to block the sun until you have a line on the ball."

I wasn't sure what he meant, but I nodded, hoping he'd change the subject.

"I wish I had time to help coach your team," Dad said.

I didn't understand why he didn't have time, since he found time to bowl, hunt, fish, and play softball with his buddies. But I kept quiet and stared out the window as we drove home.

"How about some ice cream?" Dad asked. "I remember it was always a treat to get ice cream after a ball game."

"That'd be good. I'll take a chocolate cone," I said, suddenly relaxing into our father-son outing. I enjoyed him taking an interest in something I was doing. Of course, it wasn't something I loved doing, but still, it was pleasant.

"Welcome to Tastee Freez, what can I get you?" asked the pretty high school girl with her hair pulled back in a ponytail.

"One vanilla cone and one chocolate, please," replied my dad.

"Would you like hard or soft ice cream?"

"Well, since we get a choice, we'll take hard," Dad said with a smile. When he looked at me for confirmation, I grinned and nodded, even though I wanted soft. He answered the girl so quickly I assumed he knew better than me, and my desire to win his approval had silenced my voice.

The following school year I had an experience that changed the trajectory of my life.

"Hey, Mom! Look at this!" I shouted as I brought the newspaper into the kitchen. "The Richland Players are holding open auditions for *The Miracle Worker*."

The announcement went on to give details about the Helen Keller story, plus the dates and times for auditions the coming weekend. One part was for a boy, ten-to-twelve years old.

"I want to audition," I said. "Can I? Please!"

Since I'd been forced to quit ballet, I knew Mom wouldn't refuse me.

"I suppose I could drive you down, but I can't stay too long. You can call when you need a ride home."

When Saturday arrived, Mom drove me to tryouts for the minor role. The next evening, I got a call from the assistant director, Trish. I had landed the part.

The cast quickly became my theatre family and the entire *Miracle Worker* experience was life-enhancing—going to rehearsals and getting excited for opening night. The director, Stan, asked me if I was willing to also be the recorded voice of Annie Sullivan's dying little brother.

"Of course!" I said, complimented to be asked.

But when it came time for the evening recording session, I found it intimidating to be in a small room with adults and expected to act afraid because I was dying and my sister might be leaving me alone. After a few takes and being coached to show more and more terror, I practically screamed my lines with a quivering voice.

"That's it! We got it. Good job, Gary," Stan said.

I noticed Trish smiling at me. "Looks like we have a little actor in our midst," she said.

Tears welled. Maybe they saw something special in me. Right then and there, a new dream was born.

I started ordering photographs of movie stars from teen magazines using my weekly allowance—money I earned for taking out the trash, feeding and watering the dog, and shoveling dog shit. Two years later, by the end of seventh grade, I'd collected hundreds of pictures, which I'd taped onto my bedroom wall. When I couldn't find any more tape in the house, I used glue. I spent hours admiring them, fantasizing how, one day, the stars and I would perform together.

My two favorites, based on charm and good looks, were Annette Funicello and Richard Chamberlain. Both were featured in framed photos sitting atop my dresser. I treasured my movie-star pictures. Many nights, lying in bed and staring at the dark ceiling, I brought myself to tears pondering my desire to become a famous actor—loved, admired, and adored.

At the end of that summer, my parents drove us kids home from our Uncle Sonny and Aunt Lori's farm in eastern Oregon where we had spent an adventurous week with our cousins, hiking the hills, milking cows, and collecting eggs. As we approached Richland on the desolate, two-lane highway, Mom broke the tired silence of the crowded car. "We have a surprise for you when we get home."

We took wild stabs at the surprise but Mom was determined to keep it a secret.

Upon arrival, we discovered our bedrooms had been updated with fresh paint, new window treatments, and matching bedspreads. The room I shared with my little brother was painted a soft gray, the drapes and bedspreads a primary red corduroy.

"Mom, where are my movie-star pictures?" I asked when I found her in the kitchen.

"Well, many of them ripped when we took them down. It was really quite a mess. You'd used so much tape and some of them were glued! Why did you use glue? Don't you think your room looks nice now? We went to a lot of work and—"

"Yes, it looks nice," I said, interrupting her, "but what did you do with my pictures?".

Mom looked perturbed. I waited for an answer.

"Well, I'm not sure," she replied, looking away from me. "Maybe your dad threw them out."

"What?! Why would he do that?" I rushed outside to dig through the trash can. It didn't take long to know they weren't there. I tried to puzzle it out and my conclusion smacked me in the face like a hard-thrown snowball. I stomped back into the house.

"Mom, did Dad go to the dump this week?"

"Hmm . . . you know, he might have. I'm not sure."

Sadly, I knew it was all bullshit. Dad had judged the photos unacceptable for a thirteen-year-old boy. There had been no attempt to preserve them.

But what about my framed photos of Annette Funicello and Richard Chamberlain? Panic ensued. I ran to my bedroom, pulled open the top drawer of my dresser and there they were—the survivors of the massacre. I held them to my heart as I grieved the loss of so many others.

Our family dinner was unusually quiet that night. Everyone knew I was upset. We said our nightly grace together, "For health and food, for love and friends, for everything Thy goodness sends, Father in heaven, we thank Thee. Amen." Then, after passing the food around, I took a breath and in my most acceptable voice, calmly asked, "Dad, what did you do with my movie-star pictures?"

He chewed, then swallowed before replying. "I'm not sure what happened to them. Most of them tore when we took them off the wall."

"Okay, but where did they go? They're not in the garbage can. Did you take them to the dump?"

"Well, I did take a load to the dump—paint cans and yard waste, so maybe they were in there, too."

To both my parents, I risked saying, "Well, I don't think it was very nice of you to throw them away. They were important to me."

Predictably, my dad fell silent and Mom turned red, but Nancy, who hated conflict of any kind, charged in for the rescue. "You should just appreciate your nice room and not make such a big deal about your movie-star pictures."

I cut my eyes at her and allowed my anger to show. "I do appreciate my room, but I don't think it's fair my pictures were thrown out and nobody will even tell me where they are!"

"Okay, okay, that's enough!" Mom said, now at the end of her guilty, defensive rope. "We don't know where the pictures are and we're sorry you're upset. We didn't know they were so important to you," she said, lying again.

But I was done. It was a lost cause. I would now do what I had always done: repress my resentment and swallow my anger. Evidently, I had more to learn about being an acceptable son.

Two weeks later, on a family trip to visit our relatives in Spokane, Mom's sister, Pat, called Dad to the phone. The tension in her voice froze the room. How strange for Dad to get a call at Aunt Pat's house.

"Hello? Oh, no . . . no . . . NO!" he wailed in such agony I couldn't breathe.

We had recently seen Dad shed a few tears when he was laid off from his job after more than twenty years, but we had never seen him sob. He was a puddle on the red linoleum floor of Aunt Pat's tiny kitchen.

Aunt Vera had tracked him down. There had been a flash flood at our cousins' farm where we had just visited. The power of the flood had gathered tremendous momentum from a rainstorm emanating some ten miles away in the Blue Mountains. Small, overflow streams joined together to create a ferocious river where none had previously existed. The floodwater barreled down the low points between the hills, destroying everything in its path. A hundred yards before it reached the Grande Ronde River, it smashed into my cousin's house, tearing off the roof and sweeping away the entire family. When the floodwater collided with the river, it reversed the current momentarily, stifling the power of the flash flood and giving Uncle Sonny time to miraculously rescue the children.

Tragically, however, Aunt Lori was lost, her body discovered three days later. It became my dad's responsibility to identify the body when Uncle Sonny confessed he couldn't do it. Dad returned home from the morgue looking ashen. He sat in our living room with Mom, Aunt Vera, and a few close friends, then broke down as he recalled how bad his deceased sister looked—like a wrinkled old woman with only a few stringy strands of hair. He wasn't sure he could identify her, but then he saw her delicate hands and wedding ring.

Overwhelmed with horror, I bound off the sofa and headed for my bedroom. Lying face down on my bed, trying to comfort myself, I soon felt Dad's strong arms cradle me in a way I had so craved but had never before experienced, at least not that I could recall. We cried together for several minutes, father and son—my skinny, thirteen-year-old arms wrapped around his muscular chest.

I wanted that moment to never end, and in some ways, I suppose it never did. Even if I wasn't the son my dad had dreamed of having, I knew he loved me in his own way. A man broken in his grief over the tragic death of his lovely, sweet sister had become raw and vulnerable, a creature of love and only love.

5

Tender moments with my dad were rare and father-son talks non-existent. So, how was I to learn about sex in the early 1960s with absolutely no information coming from my parents? Catechism classes at church certainly didn't go near the subject and my school's sex ed unit didn't occur until eighth-grade science. I could only glean so much from the *World Book Encyclopedia* and our family's thick medical guide. Sex was never discussed—only joked about in coded language or alluded to in judgmental ways. My dad's comments gave me the impression he thought girls who wore too much makeup were easy, but boys who chased after girls were studs. It was almost as if the grown men in my young life were vicariously aroused by the sexual prowess of horny boys.

As a five-year-old, I'd had questions, of course, but never felt encouraged or comfortable asking them, with the exception of "Mom, where do babies come from?"

She paused, then said, "They come from a secret hole in the mother's 'weeje.'"

"What's a weeje?" I asked.

Her face turned red.

"It's a private place between a woman's legs. A man has a penis and a woman has a weeje. But this is a conversation you should have with your dad."

Since I didn't have another pressing question in mind, I let the subject drop.

About that same time, I got busted having an experience of "show me yours, I'll show you mine" with the two sisters who lived next door. My dad put me in his big tan recliner and told me to "think about it." That's all he said. "I want you to sit here and think about it while I go next door and talk with their dad. He might be very upset about this."

"Shame on you, Gary Claude," still rings in my ears when I recall my mom's reaction.

What's a boy supposed to learn sitting alone, his siblings directed not to speak to him? The conversation Mom said I should have with Dad never happened, and after my chair-of-shame experience, I chose silence and secrecy over questions. Of course, I also became more careful not to get caught with my pants down.

One September day with Dad at work, Nancy at school, and my younger siblings napping, I experienced a sexual hit I would never forget. It took place in the little toy room of my first childhood home. The room was too small to be a bedroom, so it had become a delightful, junk-filled playroom with Lincoln Logs, Tinker Toys, and Old Maid cards.

My mom was hosting a pinochle party with three of her lady friends. As the women sat around the green, Formica-topped kitchen table drinking iced tea and smoking cigarettes, their sons, all of us morning-only kindergarteners, entertained themselves in the toy room with the door closed. One activity led to another until someone suggested we show each other our underwear. That led to quick peeks at penises, followed by some touching and little erections. I loved it! I wanted more, but it became apparent the experience for me was different than it was for them. They were over it, laughing and already finding other things to do, while I couldn't get it out of my mind.

In my later childhood years, most of what I learned about bodies and touching was through summer sleep-outs under the starry sky with clandestine games of strip poker and Truth or Dare. And what I learned about sex and adolescent sexual experimentation was from other boys about my age.

My fifteen-year-old cousin taught me about semen and ejaculation when I was twelve. He didn't actually demonstrate, just showed me by rubbing his finger. But before my "jack-off instructions," I had played with the vibrator Mom purchased for sore muscles and enjoyed holding the machine near my crotch. When the feelings grew too intense, I quickly shut it off in my fear and confusion. After learning the facts from my cousin, I pleasured myself routinely and sometimes in creative ways. Who knew what a clever boy could do with cardboard tubing, satin fabric, and salad oil in a plastic bag?

When the jocks in junior high talked about circle jerks and watching each other shoot their wads, I assumed it was normal teenage behavior. And when my friends laughed at stories of some neighborhood boys sucking each other and fucking assholes—pretending they were fucking girls—I found the idea of penetration disturbing but the idea of sex with boys exciting. Was that what adults meant when they said, "Boys will be boys?" That seemed unlikely. But what did I know?

I was never invited to a circle jerk, and would have been terrified to join. The idea certainly fascinated me and sometimes found its way into my fantasies. But my overall sexual ignorance and anxiety remained conflicted and confused for an adolescent boy who had already been given multiple messages, from subtle to overt, that there was something wrong with him. If I were to risk sexual adventures with other boys, it had to be discreet and executed with extreme caution.

The locker room talk continued and even increased as more boys moved into puberty. The loud, popular boys liked to talk about dicks and who had a big one, who had a chubby in the shower, or who didn't have any hair "down there." I smiled without saying anything, always worried I'd say the wrong thing and draw uncomfortable attention to myself. But that didn't stop me from checking out as many dicks as I could. Jock straps were required under our gym shorts and showers enforced after class, two rules I actually welcomed.

Hanging out at Pete's house one Saturday, he talked openly about how big Kerry's dick was. Kerry was a seventh-grader like us and a neighborhood friend.

"You should see it, Gary. It's huge!"

I chuckled but said nothing. As it turned out, Kerry was on his way over to Pete's house at that very moment.

"When Kerry gets here, I'll tell him you want to see it."

"No, don't do that!"

"But you really need to see this thing and Kerry likes to show it off," Pete said, laughing.

Sure enough, Kerry soon showed up at the otherwise empty house. "Hey, Kerry, I told Gary about your dick. He wants to see it."

"No, I don't!" I lied.

"Show it to him, Kerry. Gary, you really need to see it!" Pete said again.

Kerry just smiled and said, "I'll show it to you. Let's go in the bathroom." With my heart pumping wildly, I followed him. "You have to show me yours, too," Kerry added.

That sounded funny to me, but I agreed. Kerry dropped his pants and pulled down his underwear, evidently excited to be exposing himself. It truly was a massively thick and long specimen. He waited for me to pull down my pants, so I did.

"You can touch it," he said, getting harder. I really wanted to, but I was getting overly excited, feeling exposed and vulnerable. I didn't know the rules for this open, adolescent-male sex play. Pete and Kerry were jocks, tough guys. What would they think if I joined in and they got the wrong idea?

"Naw, that's okay. It really is big, though." I pulled up my pants and headed for the bathroom door.

"Wow!" I said to Pete as soon as I got back to the living room. "That is one big dick!"

"That was fast," Pete said. "Did you see it hard?"

"Not really," Kerry chimed in. "He didn't want to touch it."

Pete laughed again and shook his head. I shrugged it off and pretended I wasn't deliriously buzzed, dizzy with erotic energy.

Fortunately, Pete and Kerry were off to the backyard basketball court. For them, the play was fun but unimportant. For me, it was equal parts exhilarating, confusing, and unsettling.

Even though I didn't participate in sex play with Pete or Kerry, my desire persisted and progressed during my seventh-grade year. In the spring, a boy who lived across the street invited me to sneak under the protective tarp covering his parent's cabin cruiser parked on the side of their house. Scott was a year younger than me, but his older brother had shown him something exciting to do and he wanted to try it with me.

"First, we get naked," Scott said, once we were safe inside the boat. "Then, I lay on top of you and you can do the same to me."

He had me at "naked." There was no hesitation. But once he laid on me and started grinding against me, I immediately thought I was coming. The thrill was beyond anything I could ever have imagined.

"Get off!" I said, grabbing my dick in a panic.

"What's wrong?"

"I gotta go home," I said, embarrassed.

I pulled on my clothes, believing I was holding back my orgasm, then ran across the street, into the front door and directly into the bathroom. No one saw me. I locked the bathroom door, took off my clothes and laid down, ready to release.

"Pee!" I exclaimed, as I squeezed my dick again. I kept squeezing until I could stand up and aim my boner toward the toilet bowl.

I cleaned up the mess I'd made, feeling even more embarrassed than before. Not only had I spoiled a fun time with Scott, I now had a secret, humiliating experience I could never share with anyone.

My adolescent sex play escalated when a new friend, John, called late in the summer just before eighth grade. John had the kind of outgoing personality a boy needed when he moved to a new town. It didn't hurt that he was also nice-looking.

"I'm bored and just wondering if you wanted to do something. Got any ideas?" John asked.

"Well, why don't you come to my house and we can think of something."

While waiting for John to walk the two blocks to my house, I thought of things we could do, and just as he showed up, I had a typical teenage suggestion.

"Have you ever been on the roof of Jason Lee?" I asked.

"Jason Lee? You mean that elementary school right over there?" asked John, pointing in the correct direction.

"Yeah, there's a pretty easy way to climb onto the roof. It's cool up there."

John smiled and laughed in a mischievous way. "Let's do it!"

We walked over to the school, then climbed onto the six-foot privacy wall outside the exit doors of the locker rooms. From there, we climbed onto the overhang, then onto the lowest roof level where there were ladders to the gym roof and access to the five wings running perpendicular to the long main hall.

We had fun exploring and running around, capturing views from different locations and retrieving balls that had been kicked up and trapped in rain gutters. On our adventures, we discovered a ladder that led to the top of the auditorium where the sun was hitting the angled roof.

"Hey, we can work on our tans," John suggested as he took off his shirt, laid it on the angled roof and leaned back against it. His idea sounded good to me, so I joined him.

"God, I'm horny!" he laughed. "And this sunshine's giving me a hard-on!"

I laughed with him as my heart pounded, wondering how this nice boy could be so open and comfortable with his private thoughts.

"Nobody can see us up here. We could even suntan in our underwear," I said, tossing out bait to see if he nibbled.

"You're right! Even naked," John replied. "Okay, first down to our underwear." He removed his summer shorts and I could see he was pretty swollen already.

I followed suit and checked to see if he was looking at my own engorged crotch. He was. *Oh, God! What's happening?* I felt both excited and nervous as hell but played it cool, waiting to see if John would take the lead.

"I feel like jerkin' off," he sighed, with his face tilted to the sun and his hand gently rubbing his underwear.

"Go ahead if you want."

"You have to do it, too," he insisted.

No arm-twisting necessary. I said, "Okay."

We each pulled down our underwear and watched each other rub his dick until . . .

"Who's up here?" a man's voice shouted from another location on the roof. "You kids need to get down!"

"Oh, shit!" John laughed in a whisper. We looked in the direction of the man's voice but couldn't see him, which meant he couldn't see us either. We got dressed as quickly and quietly as possible, then started to make our way back to where we got on the auditorium roof, first peeking around the corner to see if we could catch a glimpse of the shouting man, probably the custodian. He must have heard us running around on other parts of the roof and decided to investigate.

"There he is!" I whispered as he walked away from us on the far side of the gym roof. "Hurry, let's go!" I led the way as quietly as I could, the adrenaline working alongside fear to create an exciting ninja experience and a successful escape.

John and I ran from the school laughing like fools, still hyped-up from the sexual play, plus a close encounter of the embarrassing kind.

"Hey, want to come to my house? No one's home, but my dad will be home soon, so we can't jerk off or anything."

"Sure," I agreed.

"Do you know what a rubber is?" John asked as we walked along. He could tell I didn't by the confused look on my face. "Well, it's something a man puts on his cock so he doesn't squirt in the woman when he's fucking her and she doesn't get pregnant. I found something in my dad's dresser and wondered if it's a rubber."

"I wouldn't know. What's it look like?"

"Well, it's . . ." John started to make a shape with his hands but then stopped and said, "I'll show it to you when we get to my house, but we have to be quick."

I couldn't believe he secretly rummaged through his father's dresser. At my house, we didn't go near my dad's dresser without expressed permission.

When we got to John's house, we rushed to his parents' bedroom where John pulled out a thick, latex, tube-like casing wrapped in a clean handkerchief. It definitely had a phallic shape, but the opening was too small for a man's erect penis. We just looked at it and laughed, totally clueless.

To this day, I'm not sure what we saw. It wasn't a condom. Perhaps it was a sex toy of some kind. I guess I'll never know.

Once John and I were safely out of the master bedroom and tucked away in his room, he started talking about sex again.

"I've been thinking about fucking," John said. I stayed quiet. The boy was amazing! He said whatever he was thinking. I couldn't imagine such courage and freedom. "I think we're too young to fuck girls and I don't know any girls that well, anyway, but I've heard of boys fucking other boys. Have you ever heard of that?"

"I did hear someone talking about it once, but I don't get it."

"Well, one guy puts Vaseline on his dick. The other guy lays on his stomach so the first guy can slide his dick up the other guy's butthole." John explained like an expert. "I heard the feeling is incredible, like fucking a girl."

"So do you want to fuck or get fucked?" I asked. The idea of sticking my dick in some guy's butt had no appeal to me then. Actually, getting fucked had no appeal either, but I was considering it since John displayed such enthusiasm.

"I want to fuck. Really bad," he admitted, his big smile returning.

"Well, I'm not sure, but maybe we can try it sometime if you want."

"Really?" John exclaimed. "That'd be great!"

"But how? Where?" I asked, more to myself than to John. My brain searched for answers, not wanting to miss out on a new sexual experience. It was almost like a small hungry beast or baby dragon had come to life inside my mind and was whispering to me: *Get naked with John. Have fun!*

"I guess we could sleep out somewhere, maybe take a tent to the desert and try it there," I said. "I know! There's going to be a concert tonight at the airplane hangar out by my dad's work. It's just a fifteen-minute walk from here. We could pitch a tent, go to the concert, then try it afterwards."

"Excellent!" John practically shouted. "I'll bring some Vaseline."

We put the details on our plan and I headed home to inform my parents I'd be tenting in the desert with John. I got our little pup tent, my sleeping bag, some snacks, water in a canteen, and a flashlight. After dinner, I headed back to John's house where he met me at the front door, eager and ready to go.

We walked across the highway and down the railroad tracks until we found a remote, sandy spot with enough space among the sagebrush to set up the tent. After storing our things inside, we walked toward the airplane hangar, hearing the loud, echoing rock 'n' roll music long before we arrived. The small crowd in attendance was high school age or older. John and I quickly lost interest.

Besides, we had other things on our minds.

"God, I'm so excited to do this!" John said as we walked back to the tent. "I already have a boner! See?" He pressed his hands next to his erection so I could see the outline through his pants.

My heart raced, no longer shy to say, "Well, let's get back to the tent and try it. We don't have to wait until dark. There's nobody out here anyway."

"Really? Okay!" John's enthusiasm was contagious and his interest in getting naked with me real—so natural and comfortable. I'd never met anyone like him.

We got back to the tent, rolled out our sleeping bags, and put the snacks and other stuff out of the way. John took out a square of tin foil.

"What's that?" I asked, hoping it wasn't LSD or some other drug I had no interest in trying.

"Vaseline," he replied, opening the foil to show me a blob of the jelly inside.

"So, how do we do this?" I asked. I enjoyed John leading so I didn't risk rejection or embarrassment from saying or doing the wrong thing.

He told me to get naked and he undressed at the same time. It was still daylight so we could see we were both already rock hard. He rubbed Vaseline all over the head of his dick and told me to lie on my stomach and spread my legs. Then he mounted onto my backside and searched around for my asshole. Again and again he missed the target, so I reached back to direct him.

"Okay". . . and that's all I had time to say before the searing pain from his abrupt entry forced me to scream, "TAKE IT OUT! TAKE IT OUT!" while I pulled back on his cock. Once it was out, all I could do was curl up my legs and moan until the pain subsided.

John sat stone-cold silent, waiting to see if I was okay. After a few minutes, I was able to catch my breath. "I can't believe how much that hurt."

"I'm so sorry. I didn't even know it was going in." John tried to wear his smile, but could only grimace in concern.

My ass hurt, my stomach hurt, I felt sick. Shame swallowed me up even as confusion strangled me like a noose. I just wanted to go home and forget it ever happened. In short order we did, in fact, pack up everything and silently walk to John's house where we parted ways. Whatever I felt on my solo walk from John's house to mine, I suppressed as best I could. I refused to feel disappointed that my fun day of adventures with John had ended so badly. I refused to feel embarrassed for my inability to do for him what he wanted to experience. I refused to acknowledge my shame for doing nasty things I believed other boys were doing. I simply refused to feel anything—even as I promised myself I would never get fucked again.

"Why are you home so early?" Dad asked when he noticed me sneaking in the house with the camping supplies.

"I don't feel so good, I just wanted to come home."

"Did something happen?" He seemed concerned, maybe even suspicious.

"No, I just don't feel good," I said, walking away to put an end to the conversation.

He probably didn't believe me and I didn't care. I sure as hell wasn't going to tell him I just got butt-fucked in the desert.

John and I never talked about our time in the tent, even though we remained friends until going our separate ways after graduation, some six years later.

The experience did, however, convince me I would no longer be interested in sex with boys. I would prefer girls from that day forward and prove it by making sure I always had a short, cute girl in my head and heart.

6

I wanted nothing more than to win my dad's approval and make him proud of me. Since he was an athlete and sports played a big role in my junior high school, I assumed he'd be delighted if I joined a team. I considered my options. Wrestling intrigued me. The thought of grabbing another boy through his legs sounded fun, but after a week of practice, I realized pain and sweaty armpits in my face were involved. No thanks.

When gymnastics was offered, I'd found my niche. In many ways, gymnastics was similar to ballet but without the social stigma. Unfortunately, Dad showed no interest, and after my two years of training in junior high, the program didn't continue into high school.

I also found success in ninth grade track. My dad came to one meet when I got off the blocks for an excellent start in the low hurdles. I found myself in first place rather than my usual position of second. It unsettled me being a stride ahead of my eighth-grade buddy, Alan, a handsome and kindhearted boy. Still in the lead as we approached the final hurdle, I heard Dad's loud voice shout "Go!" My toe nicked the top edge of the hurdle's wooden crossbar, causing me to lose momentum and stumble across the finish line. Second place, again.

Nevertheless, I knew my dad approved of my performance when I later overheard him mention to Uncle Sonny, "Yeah, the track program has Gary running pretty good these days." He didn't praise me directly, but even an overheard compliment was better than none.

Sports weren't the highlight of my junior high years, however. That would be Mr. St. John's drama program. I auditioned and landed a role each year. In ninth grade, I was selected for the lead role with more than two hundred lines and didn't drop a single line in any of the performances. Although a mediocre play, the challenge and experience satisfied my love of the theatre. As an unexpected accolade, the school's journalism class voted me Most Talented for the yearbook. Acting seemed so natural to me, I hadn't previously even considered it a talent.

Mom insisted the family, including Dad, attend my final performance. After the play, Mom gave an encouraging word but Dad struggled.

"Aren't you going to say something to your son?" Mom asked.

Dad laughed, "How many hours long was that play anyway?"

The sad moment hurt my feelings, but I recovered enough to say, "It wasn't a very good play, I know. But memorizing two hundred lines was a big challenge."

"Yeah, I'm sure it was," Dad said softly, examining the pavement as we walked to the car in silence.

I tried not to care about his inability to express pride in me. Instead, fifteen years old and on my way to high school, I started to distance myself from my father and focus almost exclusively on school and friends—gaining approval and attention by working hard to always appear smart, popular and, of course, perfect.

Just before ninth grade ended, some kids I knew from the junior high across town said they had a girl for me. Her name was Debbie, and I should bring a few friends to meet up with them in the parking lot of Mayfair market, midway between our schools.

Debbie was sweet and quiet. She had straight, blond hair that curved nicely around her jaw, framing her pleasant smile. Her eyes were expressive, and even though she had a little bump on the bridge of her nose, it didn't detract from her lovely face. Her shyness charmed me and we managed a relatively easy conversation as I walked her home.

We became boyfriend and girlfriend that summer. For the next two years, Debbie and I developed a genuine friendship, enjoying many adventures—movies, rafting, dances, and making out. For me it was safe and comfortable, more about fun and doing the socially acceptable thing than it was a serious romance.

Debbie let me feel her up. She had great breasts and looked hot in a bikini. Eventually, she let me feel her down. We rubbed each other until we both came. Well, I thought she came. Truth be told, I was so ignorant I didn't know a clitoris from a hemorrhoid. I was focused on getting off and very grateful for her willingness to help. We repeated our petting routine many times, often on warm nights, lying on the soft lawn of a school near her home.

When I got my driver's license, things progressed. We almost had sex in the back seat of my car. When I tried to enter her—no condom—she said, "It hurts." I pulled back, relieved, knowing I wasn't ready. I never tried again.

Enjoying sexual adventures with Debbie helped me believe I was an all-American, heterosexual boy. However, the excitement primarily stemmed from the novelty of touching and being touched by someone I liked. I would later learn the difference between a pleasant experience and a thrilling one. I wasn't at that point yet.

In the summer after our junior year, I realized Debbie's feelings for me had become serious, while mine had diminished. I knew I had to break it off with her, but was ill-equipped to have that conversation. Instead, when she and a group of her friends left for a girls' camp in the mountains, I did the classless, chickenshit act of mailing her a breakup letter. Eventually, we talked and I forced myself to verbalize that I didn't love her. She stomped her foot in anger and gave me a look of pure hatred, which was what I had been trying to avoid. But, of course, avoidance never provides a true escape. In fact, my avoidant behavior with Debbie exposed deeper intimacy issues that would challenge me throughout my adult years.

After our breakup, I played around with a few other girls, because that's what boys were expected to do. One drunk friend wanted me to fuck her, but I was scared and talked my way out of it. I asked her about her cycle, then counted the days forward until her next ovulation. When I informed her of the risk of pregnancy, she sobered up and I escaped with dignity. Another friend went down on me and wanted me to return the favor. I sucked her nipples and kissed her down to her pelvic bone but then stopped short. I just couldn't go any further.

During my senior year, I felt compelled to shift my priorities in order to more authentically reflect who I wanted to be. I no longer cared so much about being popular or approved of by the in-crowd. Instead, I began protesting the Vietnam War and filed as a conscientious objector with the draft board. I joined a progressive and spiritually minded youth group that engaged in social activism and studied the works of Ralph Waldo Emerson, Paul Tillich, and other existentialist philosophers. The group met before school at a Protestant church under the guidance of the youth minister. Our achievements included an anti-war demonstration in the school's courtyard and the successful election of a slate of associated student body officers.

I dressed more hippy-like, and my hair also reflected my admiration for the peace movement. Dad did not approve. Half-drunk one evening, he grabbed the back pocket of my faded, worn-out jeans and ripped them off my ass.

"I pay for your clothes and you wear that crap?" he slurred.

"Goddamn you!" I screamed. "Leave me alone!"

He staggered away grumbling while I stormed into my bedroom and slammed the door. It had become clear I would never feel free to be myself until I moved away.

Being ahead in credits for graduation enabled me to reduce my senior class-load to only four morning classes. In the afternoons, I worked at the school district's production laboratory creating instructional materials for teachers. I kept my focus on honor-roll-level grades and making money for clothes, beer, and gas.

I enjoyed regular weekend adventures with my best friends, Dave, Ken, and Paul. When we added a new friend, Stephen, to the mix, I discovered we also added a bit of wildness. Stephen, a gangly blond known for his quirky personality, was irreverent, fearless, and hilarious. He constantly pushed society's boundaries and demonstrated very few of his own.

Not surprisingly, it was the free-spirited Stephen who would, just after our graduation, seduce me into boy-on-boy play. I was driving the two of us over the Yakima River bridge connecting Richland to Kennewick. The weather had turned hot that weekend and we wanted to swim, but the Columbia River remained too cold. Stephen suggested we park on the shoulder of the highway to swim in the much warmer Yakima. Warmer, yes, but also dirty and rumored to have dead cattle floating in it from time to time.

Stephen had an unusual look on his face that I couldn't read. His reputation as a prankster made me wonder if he was up to something. But after some convincing, I pulled the car over and we walked down the embankment to the water's edge, hanging our shirts on a bush and removing our shoes and socks.

"Hey," Stephen said, "no one can see us. Let's swim in our underwear. Then we'll have dry shorts to put on later."

I looked around for other people, then looked up to the cars traveling on the highway above us.

"Come on!" he insisted. "No one's looking down here. Besides, we'll be in the water."

Convinced, I stripped down to my underwear. The well-endowed and obviously excited Stephen did the same. Admittedly, the hot sun, warm water, underwear, and Stephen's chubby created a sexy environment, arousing me, too. I walked in, waist-high, without delay. The marshy areas of the river never got very deep as we waded and swam around the little brush islands that dotted the shore. Stephen led us where it was more remote and private—no way for passing cars to see us.

"Let's skinny-dip!" Stephen more than suggested as he stripped off his undies to wear them around his neck, freeing his hands for swimming.

"You're crazy!" I said, even though I wanted to join—if I could just relax. "What if other people show up?"

"So what? Just get down in the water."

Stephen was right. It was a terrific opportunity to enjoy skinny-dipping, even though I worried he might see my hard-on. But as we paddled around and the water got shallow, Stephen unashamedly stood up to display his own erection. We stared at each other. He smiled with eyebrows raised. Something unusual was in the air. Erotic, mysterious, and unnerving.

Stephen had only talked about his lust for girls, but he sure seemed to be trying to seduce me. This new behavior was confusing. He chuckled mischievously and continued to play the exhibitionist while I got paranoid—conflicted between fear and desire. I walked into deeper water, then feigning a lack of interest, told him we should get going.

"Why?" he shouted. "This is fun!"

Having become unwilling to expose my intense intrigue and temptations, I put my underwear back on.

"This muddy water is giving me the creeps and there are too many mosquitoes, I complained. "Come on! Let's go!"

Clearly disappointed, he nevertheless agreed. When we walked back to shore, we stripped off our wet underwear before putting on our dry shorts. Not a word was uttered, the erections gone. We had pushed the envelope as far as we dared.

Just two weeks later, however, on a sultry, summer night in late June, Stephen and I found ourselves alone again. Our friends were either on family vacations or working at Zip's as fry-cooks where Stephen and I were headed in his family's Rambler. Nothing tasted better on a summer night than a cheeseburger with fries and a Cherry 7Up. Heading home after our meal, I noticed Stephen adjusting himself as he drove. His hand was on his crotch, moving his junk around.

"You okay?" I joked. "Need some help with that?"

"Sure, you can help me!" he laughed as he took his hand away, spreading his knees, and looking at me with his eyebrows raised like before. I reached over and rubbed him for a moment, then laughed and moved my hand away.

"Don't stop!" he said. "That felt good!"

I looked at him to be sure he was serious, then reached over for more touching. Quite breathless, I said, "Let's go somewhere."

"Where?" he said with genuine anticipation. I thought for a moment, then directed him out Swift Boulevard and across the bypass highway onto a dirt road where I had hidden a few beers in the desert. They were leftovers from the previous weekend. When the dirt road curved and forked with another, I said, "Stop here and keep your headlights on for a minute so I can find the paper bag."

Stephen turned off the ignition but kept the headlights on and helped me search under the sage brush until we found the brown bag with four beers inside. They were, of course, incredibly warm, but after parking the car we drank them under a blanket of stars. With the beers gone and feeling tipsy enough to be bold, we looked at each other and nodded.

"I gotta pee first," I said and without bothering to turn away, pulled out my swollen cock and peed with Stephen standing next to me. He did the same. The party was about to begin.

I climbed back into the passenger side of the car, reclined the seat, and adjusted my erection in my tight 501s. Stephen got in on the driver's side and reclined his seat to match mine. The energy became intoxicating and all inhibitions broke down as we moved closer together, fondling one another, removing shirts, and unbuttoning jeans. We took turns lying on each other, rubbing, kicking off our shoes, squirming out of our pants and underpants. Not since I was a boy had I experienced my naked erection against another boy's. The erotic delight held overwhelming sensations as we experimented with sucking and dry humping. I took his big dick and stuck it between my thighs to feel it rubbing behind me.

"What are you doing?" he gasped.

I panicked. Had I done something wrong? Did he think I liked this . . . this near-fucking? Does it make me queer and now he was shocked? All of these fearful thoughts flashed through my head.

"I'm just feeling you against me" was my weak explanation.

The interruption made me lose most of my uninhibited wildness. I became passive and only followed his lead, not daring to do anything that might cause another shocked reaction.

Stephen suggested we get out of the car to jack off on the ground.

"Jiz stains might be hard to explain to Mom and Dad," he said, laughing.

We stood naked in the moonlight and did our business separately but next to each other. With all the built-up erotic energy, it didn't take long to come.

Before I could even get my clothes back on, feelings of fear and guilt invaded me. I didn't want to be a homosexual. Now, here I was trying to wrap my head around having my first gay experience as a young man.

We got dressed in silence, then Stephen drove me directly to my house just five minutes away. It was an uncomfortable five minutes of feeling dirty. I couldn't wait to take a hot shower and wash away the smells, the tastes, the shame.

As Stephen pulled his car up to the curb at my house, I asked, "Does this mean we're queer?"

"No! We still like girls. We were just playing around."

"Yeah, okay. That's what I think, too," I said. "Could it mean we're bisexual?"

"I don't know. Maybe," Stephen confessed. "But I think if I'm having sex with a woman, I won't want to have sex with a man."

That made sense to me—sort of. But it also made me more confused and disconcerted because, even though I was disgusted by what we had done, I also knew I had never felt such breathtaking excitement in all my life. It was a high—like a drug of erotic pleasure. But I didn't want more. I wanted it to go away.

7

July almost always meant gorgeous weather in Richland and the morning I pulled into the parking lot at work and saw her was no exception. She appeared as lovely as her photo. She held back her long, ash brown hair as she descended with feminine grace the three steps from the production lab porch. Then, with a smooth, floating stride, she made her way up the sidewalk to enter the back door of the administration building where her mom, Dolores, worked. She didn't notice me sitting behind the wheel of my car, but I certainly noticed everything about her. She wore boldly striped, orange, yellow, and beige bell-bottoms with a knit top to match. The outfit was hip, snugly fitting her slender yet shapely body.

I knew I was expected to meet her. Nancy Allen, my production lab coworker, had made that crystal clear.

"Gary, you must meet Dolores' daughter, Colleen. She's really neat! She just graduated, too, but from Kennewick High."

"Oh, really?" I replied with a grin.

"I think she'll be visiting her mom tomorrow."

"Okay, Nancy, I'll meet Colleen when I see her," I said, laughing.

Nancy was a generation older than me and close friends with Dolores Clark who operated the printshop for the school district. I liked and admired both of these women and the three of us got along famously. Nancy was a bit of a busybody and, in this case, attempting to be a matchmaker. Dolores seemed more like a trusted older friend who took an interest in my life. She had already shown me a graduation photo of her striking daughter.

I was looking forward to a lazy summer before attending college in September and not terribly interested in meeting Dolores' daughter or getting involved with anyone at that point.

After seeing her, however, I was intrigued and compelled to meet her—and not just because I told Nancy I would. I took a deep breath and climbed out of my car into the discomfort of meeting a girl who appeared a bit taller than me. Once I entered the back door to the printshop, I heard the whir and rhythmic *stomp, stomp, stomp* of Dolores' offset press, which meant she would be standing near, making sure the product was coming off the line with perfection. Yep, there she was with the girl in the striped outfit standing next to her. I drew on my courage and walked over.

"Hi, I'm Gary and under strict orders from Nancy Allen to meet you today," I said with a sunny summer smile as I held out my hand.

Colleen giggled and shook my hand. "Hi, I'm Colleen."

She appeared shy and uncomfortable but kept her wide green eyes on me. Her warm smile made me feel at ease.

Dolores shut down the machine and helped facilitate a short conversation about our separate graduations and college plans.

"Well, I need to get to work," I said, feeling relaxed in Colleen's company. "It was nice meeting you."

"Nice meeting you, too," she replied, with a sweet grin.

"If you wanna help me with the kids this morning, just come over to the school. I'm in the last room to the right as you enter the double doors," I said.

The week prior, Mr. Carlson, an elementary principal I'd met through Dolores, asked me if I'd be interested in a teacher's assistant position at a three-week summer school for gifted kids. Since my production lab job was wrapping up, I had jumped at the opportunity.

When I started my new job, however, I discovered I wasn't assisting teachers. I had my own classroom and a different group of eight students every hour for the morning program. I was shown the art supply closet and told to have fun.

After meeting Colleen and walking from the printshop to the nearby elementary school, I wondered why I'd invited her to help. It wasn't typical of me. Was I just being friendly? Did I hope she would join? Regardless of my motive, I didn't worry about it. If she showed up, I was confident the kids would love having her in the room.

About an hour later, as my students were working on their creations, I heard one precocious child say, "Gary, there's a girl at the door. Is that your girlfriend?"

I looked up to see Colleen.

"No," I said, laughing. "We just met this morning. This is Colleen. Is it okay if she joins us?"

The kids smiled and nodded.

"Welcome to our room," I said.

"Thanks. How can I help?" she asked, looking at me, then the children.

"Well, who would like some help?" I asked.

One of the girls threw up her hand. "Me! Can you help me?"

"Sure!" Colleen replied. "Oh, this is cool! I like those colors. What can I help you with?"

Colleen was soon in demand as she flowed about the room giving positive attention to each student. The shy girl I'd met in the printshop seemed comfortable and natural with the children. She helped get materials and even tossed out a few motivational ideas. I was impressed.

We hit an easy stride working together, laughing with the kids as we caught eyes and grinned. I'd flirted with girls before but this felt different, more mature and grounded perhaps.

"That was fun," Colleen said as the last class was dismissed.

"It was," I agreed. "If you want to help again, I can check to make sure it's okay with Mr. Carlson."

"I'd like that! I'll give you my number. You can let me know what he says."

I smiled as she wrote down her number and handed it to me. *I don't think a girl has ever offered me her phone number before*, I thought to myself. I rather liked being pursued, if that's what was happening.

With the principal's permission, Colleen Clark became my teaching partner for the next two weeks. Each day together was more fun and more comfortable than the day before. She was lighthearted and laughed frequently—even at my quirky sense of humor. I liked to tease and fortunately she could take it—and dish it out in return. A genuine friendship was budding.

In the final days of the summer school, the kids painted little rockets they had built in another class. All attention was on getting the rockets completed for the Friday launch, which would serve as the culminating event of the summer session.

Teachers aren't supposed to have favorites, but Colleen and I both fell in love with the darling, brilliant Ero. When he struggled to get his rocket completed, we worked together like he was our own child so he could finish and catch the field trip bus with the other kids.

"He's so excited," Colleen said as we tidied up the room. "I wish we could watch him launch his rocket."

"Let's do it!" I suggested. "The launch field is over by my old elementary school, just five minutes from here."

"Really? Okay!" Colleen and I were all smiles as we hustled over to the printshop to inform her mom.

"Well, how late will you be? I'm leaving at five," Dolores said.

"I'm not sure," I admitted, "but I can drive Colleen home. No problem."

And just like that, Colleen and I were off together in my car to witness the delight of the students launching their rockets. When Ero's rocket blasted cockeyed and the parachute ejected without fully opening, he was heartbroken. I took off in a sprint into the sagebrush to retrieve the capsule for him. His big smile was all the thanks I needed.

Back in my car and on the road, Colleen seemed happy.

"Did you enjoy that?" I asked.

"I did, but I can't believe you chased after Ero's rocket," she teased.

"I know," I chuckled. "But he was so sad, I couldn't stand it."

I glanced at her as I drove. She was grinning at me.

"What?" I asked.

"So you're a good guy, huh?"

"I have my moments."

In the next glance, our eyes caught. Something special was happening.

Even though we'd become friends, I was rather surprised when Colleen called a few days later to invite me to join her family on a two-week Priest Lake vacation in northern Idaho. I wasn't sure I wanted to use two weeks of my summer to be on vacation with a family I hardly knew. But I liked Colleen. She was fun to be around. And since I had absolutely no summer plans until August, I accepted the generous invitation.

A couple of days later, a pickup/camper towing a small ski boat pulled up to the curb outside my house. Quick introductions were made. I had never met Colleen's dad, Bill, or her cute little brother, Tom, a rising junior, who had brought along his friend, Allan.

The four of us loaded into the back of the camper to get acquainted, leaving the driving to the parents. Tom was as chatty as Colleen was quiet, asking me question after question: "Can you water ski?" "How old were you when you first skied?" "What about trick skis?" "No? It's easy. I can teach you." "Are the girls in Richland hot? Because the Kennewick girls are dogs!"

"Tom! Geez!" Colleen said, rolling her eyes. "Let's play cards or something. Does everyone know how to play Hearts?"

Hours of playing cards in the back of a camper was a good way to get to know someone better, especially when midway, Colleen's kid brother and his buddy crammed into the cab with the parents.

"Cribbage?" Colleen asked, pulling out the cribbage board.

"Sure, I'd be happy to whoop you at cribbage."

She laughed, then repeatedly spanked me at the game, making sure to rub it in.

"Ooooh . . . I smell something. Is that a skunk? Yep, I think it is cuz you are about to get skunked!"

I liked this girl with the quiet but sassy personality. After cards, snacks, and hours of being jostled about in the back of the camper, I started to yawn.

"You can take a nap on the overhead bunk if you want," Colleen suggested.

"What about you? Are you tired?"

"I could nap. It's a big bed, there's room for both of us."

"Your parents won't mind?" I asked, not wanting to cause trouble.

She laughed. "No, it's a nap! They won't care."

Since my experience with Stephen had been so electrifying, albeit guilt-ridden, feeling aroused lying next to Colleen helped remind and reassure me of my desire for girls. Who knew the soft touching of bare arms could be so sensual? Maybe my occasional attraction to male bodies was typical for horny boys my age.

The two weeks at Priest Lake were flawless: delightful weather, fun times with the Clark family, and getting to know Colleen better. Even the frustrated bear that clawed my tent one dawn provided a story worth telling later. Fortunately, he sauntered away, leaving me to shake in my sleeping bag.

Colleen and I grew progressively more comfortable with each other. We shared our favorite season by waterskiing, canoeing, and baking our bodies. We held hands as we lay on a blanket listening to the Carpenters sing "Close to You" on the radio. We took daily walks down Indian Creek, which ran adjacent to the campground. In the evenings, we snuck away to kiss under the stars near the beach. The first time I tried to feel under her top she jerked so hard I pulled my hand away, not wanting to try for second base if it was too soon.

"Sorry, I'm ticklish," she said, giggling.

"Oh! I thought I was moving too fast or something."

"No, it's okay, it's just my ribs . . ."

"Oh, like here? Or here?" I teased, as I gently touched her ribs. She giggled and squirmed. I held her tight and kissed her as I moved my hand up her bare back to unfasten her bra, then made my way around her arm. She kissed me back and the giggling stopped. I had found a new route to second base.

Colleen and I were definitely falling for each other, but there were things we needed to discuss before I could let it go any further. At my request, we had a serious talk, sitting on a fallen log in a wooded area away from everyone else.

"I just wanted to talk about some things," I said, not really knowing how to proceed.

"Okay, like what?"

"Well, I'm really enjoying getting to know you. This has been great, but you know I'm heading off to college soon, and before that I'm taking that bicycle trip with my friends."

"Yeah, I know. So what are you saying?"

"Well, I just don't know how much time we can spend together this summer and once I'm at school, I'll need to focus on my studies. So I just think we need to be careful."

"I agree. But maybe we can talk on the phone sometimes and then see each other around Thanksgiving," Colleen suggested.

"Yeah, that'll work," I said, then paused and looked down.

"And?" she asked, sensing there was something else on my mind.

"Well, I was just thinking we should talk about other people we've dated and maybe the experiences we've had."

Although uncomfortable at first, we began to share on a more intimate level. A mutual trust grew and I cautiously entered the territory of my dark secret.

"And there's one more thing I need to tell you, but it's not easy. I've really never told anyone," I said, finding it hard to breathe.

Colleen took my hand. "You can tell me."

"Well, sometimes I feel really confused and frightened because even though I like girls, and I like you and making out with you and everything, but sometimes . . ." I couldn't go on. Colleen waited.

"Sometimes . . ." I tried again, taking a deep breath and pushing through my shame, "sometimes I feel attracted to boys and I don't know what to think about that."

I did not give specifics and she didn't ask. It was the best I could do at the time. Nevertheless, I felt guilty for not telling her about Stephen, since it had happened so recently. Showing such vulnerability terrified me. I believed it exposed weakness and imperfection, which might result in disapproval or rejection.

"Are you attracted to me?" Colleen asked.

"Yes."

"Then I don't think it's anything to worry about. In fact, I read in *Cosmopolitan* magazine that everyone is sometimes attracted to the same sex. I'm sure it's just a phase."

I was relieved by our conversation and Colleen's acceptance of my secret. Our remaining days at Priest Lake were filled with laughter and sweet, young love. Colleen became my new, most trusted friend.

8

Upon returning home from Priest Lake, I had only a week of preparations before leaving with my friends for our bicycle trip down the Oregon Coast. After that, Colleen and I found time for a few dates and then I was off to Central Washington University in the small rodeo town of Ellensburg, a two-hour drive from Richland. The school was not my preferred university, but it was the best choice of the three state colleges Dad would support.

By mid-October, I was into the rhythm of my classes but not into the rhythm of dorm life. I hated it. Most of the guys were nice enough and I made a few friends, but the all-White, predominantly conservative dorm dynamic became unbearable with the arguing, posturing, and racist comments. It had not occurred to me that so many narrow-minded people from the surrounding rural areas would be interested in attending university. I got so fed up with the racism, I told everyone my dad was Black then posted a magazine photo of a militant Angela Davis on my dorm room door with the headline, "Stop pretending you understand the Black experience."

About that same time, I received a card from Colleen. On the outside of the card was a cartoon of a little girl saying, "Thinking about you is like eating potato chips." Inside read, "Once I start, I can't stop." The card made me smile and warmed my heart. Folded inside was a newspaper clipping of a photograph showing the newly elected Columbia Basin Community College cheerleaders. Colleen's pretty face and big smile sent a beacon of light into my otherwise humdrum college existence.

I kept looking at the photo, considering what to do. Having someone special to write to would ease my loneliness of living where I didn't fit in. Plus, Colleen was a lovely girl who accepted me and apparently liked me. I had mixed feelings about starting a relationship but wrote back a few days later. Soon I was receiving a letter almost every day, and I replied when I was caught up with my assignments. Colleen's letters became more personal with sweet sentiments mixed in. At first she went for a silly approach by heading her letter, "Hey, Babycakes!" That made me cringe, but I didn't say anything. Then she wrote about a romantic dream with me in it. No details were forthcoming. I kept my letters light and noncommittal but also shared about my challenges with dorm life.

In mid-November, she wrote, "Do you want to go to Bainbridge Island with us for Thanksgiving? My mom's sister and family live there. We can pick you up on our way." I had no strong pull to join my family for Thanksgiving, and being with Colleen for a few days sounded pleasant. So I accepted the invitation and informed my mom I would not be home for the holiday.

Two weeks later, I was once again traveling with Colleen but this time in the family car. Our two-hour drive over the Cascade Mountains and through the city of Seattle was followed by a short ferry ride to Bainbridge Island. Ten minutes later, we pulled into the gravel driveway of a wooden beachfront house. Colleen's Aunt Carol rushed out a side door with a big smile and her husband, Bob, a Seattle attorney, followed right behind.

"Hey! Welcome!" Bob boomed in a magnificent baritone voice. "So glad you could join us!"

I didn't know if Bob was a trial lawyer, but he had a great voice for it. He talked practically the entire weekend, telling story after story, with Carol laughing and saying, "Oh, Bob!" I found him fascinating, even if somewhat autocratic. Tired of turkey for Thanksgiving, he announced he was preparing a standing rib roast. It sounded great to me, but Bob and I were definitely in the minority.

"What?" Colleen's dad blurted with a chuckle. "No turkey dinner?"

"I knew you wouldn't be thrilled, Bill," said Carol, smiling and shaking her head.

Nevertheless, Bob had decided and there would be no rebuttal.

The weekend was a whirlwind of laughing, eating, and swimming in their indoor pool. At one point I saw two men sashaying up the driveway together. Their appearance and mannerisms made me curious and a little uncomfortable. The gentlemen guests were Bob's buddies, although they were friendly with Carol as well. Later that night, while the rest of the house residents were in bed, Bob and his friends stayed up drinking scotch and discussing politics, sometimes with dramatic flamboyance. I found myself being drawn in, fascinated, as I lay on a nearby sofa.

The next morning, while Bob busily prepared our breakfast in his well-appointed kitchen, I risked asking, "Bob, your friends who visited last night, are they homosexual?"

Looking surprised, Bob said, "I'm not one to put much energy into worrying about what other people do in their private lives."

I nodded, ready to move away from the awkward conversation. Then, he added, "But I would surmise they are. Why do you ask?"

"No reason. Just curious, I guess."

"Never met any gay people before, Gary?" Bob asked with a grin and a twinkle in his eye.

"Actually, I don't think so."

When I returned to Ellensburg and my college life, I again engaged in regular communication with Colleen. My feelings for her had grown. I took a crowded train on a snowy Christmas Eve to spend time with my family but mostly with Colleen. Then, as winter turned to spring, I hitchhiked almost every weekend to see her. We became the best of friends and more physically affectionate when we found privacy, generally in her parents' basement pretending to watch TV.

In early May, my teacher prep program planned a chartered bus trip to Kennewick to visit a new open-concept high school near Colleen's house. As the other students and I boarded the bus to return to campus, I snuck Colleen on with me. Of course, her parents thought she would be sleeping in the girls' dorm next to mine, but she and I had other plans. We had agreed it was time to go "all the way."

"We need to do some shopping," I said to Colleen with a smile after safely sneaking her into my dorm room.

"For what?"

"Well, I still have these," I said, taking two condoms from a little tote I'd received at freshman orientation. Colleen's eyebrows flew up as she pulled her mouth tight to make a funny face. I laughed, knowing she was acting goofy in anticipation of our big evening.

"But we still need something more," I continued, showing her an information sheet suggesting a double-protection method. "And I am not going in the drugstore to buy vaginal foam! You have to do that."

"What? By myself? I can't do it!" she gasped.

"Well, if you want all of this," I joked, running my hands down my body, "You'll need to buy some of that!"

A concerned look came over her face. "You'll go in the store with me, right?"

"No way! I'll give you the money and wait outside. It doesn't take two people to buy it and walking in together seems silly."

The experience turned out to be excruciating for Colleen. Red-faced and flustered, she exited the store and started walking as fast as she could to get away from the scene of her humiliation. I had to practically jog in my attempt to keep up with her.

Laughing, I teased, "Now that wasn't so bad, was it?"

"Jeezzzz! That was horrible!"

"Slow down!" I said, laughing harder. "I'm so proud of you, and tonight I'll give you your reward."

She could no longer keep from laughing and sassed back, "You'll be lucky to get anything after that!"

A few blocks later she slowed down enough to tell me the story.

"I couldn't find it right away, but when the saleslady asked if I needed help, I told her no. A minute later, she walked over and stood right next to me, so I finally whispered to her and she showed me the right shelf. I didn't know what kind to buy so I just grabbed one and fumbled in my wallet to pay for it so I could get out of there! I have never been so embarrassed in my whole life!"

That evening, Colleen visited the guest bathroom in the lobby of the dorm to wash up and insert the foam according to the instructions we had carefully read together. After stealthily returning to my room, she unpacked an Emeraude candle and matches from a small bag she had smuggled onto the bus with her.

"That's against dorm rules, actually," I informed her.

"Oh, I didn't know," she said, looking disappointed.

"But we can break the rules for a few minutes. Go ahead and light it."

Colleen bit her bottom lip and opened her eyes wide like a child trying to be sneaky as she lit the forbidden candle. She then applied Emeraude perfume to her body, matching the candle's sensual scent of citrus with touches of jasmine and vanilla. But she insisted I turn around as she slipped on a slinky baby doll nightgown. Switching off the overhead light, she quickly slid under the top sheet of the single bed, then pulled the sheet up to her chin.

I was all smiles as I stripped and climbed in next to her, making sure the lube and condom were nearby and the condom package already torn open. As Colleen cuddled up, my bare skin rubbed against her warm, perfumed body and the satin material of the nightgown, heightening my state of arousal. As much as I loved the erotic sensations of the satin, I had the nightgown up and over her head in less than a minute.

I took my time entering her, sensitive to her discomfort. But soon she gave me a soft, "okay," and we melted into the throes of passion and enjoyed being young, first-time lovers.

On Sunday afternoon, Colleen caught a Greyhound bus back home, but over the next months, my weekend hitchhiking continued so we could be together as often as possible. I knew I wanted Colleen in my life. We started closing our letters more affectionately: "With Love, Gary." "All My Love, Colleen." Soon, "I love you" felt perfectly comfortable even when said aloud.

Then, one warm weekend in mid-June, as we sat outside at a picnic table enjoying burgers, fries, and chocolate milkshakes, I fumbled around saying something as unromantic as, "Colleen, if things keep going as good as they are right now, would you maybe be interested in talking about marriage?" I didn't intend it as an actual proposal. I just wanted to discuss the idea generally, but once the word "marriage" was spoken, it quickly took on a life of its own.

She looked at me with those big green eyes and silently nodded her head as tears welled up. I held her and we shed a few tears of happiness together. I loved Colleen. And because my attraction to boys had become minimal, I hoped I was "out of the woods" when it came to the queer phase I had worried so much about.

"I think we're too young to get married right away," I continued. "Would it be okay if we just lived together first?"

"I'm okay with that. I think it's a good idea, actually. I just don't know how my parents will feel about it," she admitted.

"I know," I said. "I have to talk to mine, too."

"Well, do you love her?" my dad asked when I told him Colleen and I were engaged but wanted to live together before getting married. It was 1971, and living together was still considered a sinful, hippy thing to do in the eyes of many, including my dad.

"Yes, I love her," I said.

"Well, then just marry her. Forget about this living together idea," he pushed.

I felt cornered. I wanted to be strong and say, "Not yet. It's too soon and we're too young." But instead, I just nodded.

Soon, Colleen was wearing a plastic ring with a fake gem I'd saved in my junk drawer for the past decade. I had gotten it from a gumball machine for a quarter. *The best prize among the lot*, I'd thought as a boy. *It almost looks real.* I'd imagined giving it to an elementary school girlfriend who never materialized. But Colleen and I also picked out simple rings at JCPenney that we put on layaway.

Colleen and her mom started pressuring me to decide on a wedding date. I weighed my options. If we didn't get married within the next few months, I'd have no choice but to live in a dorm again and be separated from Colleen. But if there was to be a wedding, the preparations had to begin immediately.

Standing in the mall during the Fourth of July weekend, Colleen and Dolores stared at me, waiting for an answer. They were eager to purchase fabric for dresses, on sale for the holiday. Again, I felt cornered. I wanted to insist on more time. But again, I took the path of least resistance.

So, on September 11, 1971, Colleen and I married at Redeemer Lutheran Church in Richland. Moments before walking out to join my best man and groomsmen, doubts surfaced. I nearly panicked—worried I was making a mistake, worried we were too young, worried I might hurt Colleen because deep down in a place too terrifying to face, I worried I might be queer. I prayed with all my heart and asked God for strength and guidance.

"I love her," I reminded myself. "We'll make it work."

9

Colleen and I set up house about a mile north of campus. I stayed busy as a student with a heavy class schedule and part-time employment at the library's production lab, again creating instructional materials, similar to what I did as a high school senior. Colleen got bored and started taking in other people's ironing, happy to contribute to our meager resources. Once in a while we could actually splurge on pizza rather than hot dogs with macaroni and powdered cheese. We scrimped by, yet absolutely enjoyed being married.

The cherry blossoms and yellow-green leaves of spring made the snot-freezing winds of an Ellensburg winter seem like a bad dream. My classes were appropriately challenging and engaging, with my only frustration being a tall, smiley junior—the Hollywood-handsome man with the curly, light-brown hair in my phonics class.

I never spoke to him except to say, "Hi, how ya doin'?" He didn't give me the time of day and I assumed he was straight since one or two pretty girls always accompanied him, laughing and carrying on like close friends.

Yet my intrigue with Mr. Phonics grew into an obsession and a sharp point of distraction. I strategically sat where I could gawk without him noticing. If I saw him in the student union building, I walked by, attempting to make a connection. At night, I fantasized and made up elaborate, sexy stories that were never going to happen.

By the second month of that insanity, I became agitated. I couldn't keep him out of my thoughts. Colleen asked me about my mood swings and as uncomfortable as that conversation made me, I forced myself to share the fears of being attracted to a boy—someone I didn't even know. It was similar to our conversation at Priest Lake. Once again, I downplayed the intensity of my desires and once again, she brushed it off as just a normal crush.

In fact, after bringing the fantasy to light, it did pass. I still noticed him and considered him spectacular but the obsessive feelings dissipated as did the nighttime fantasies. Well, most of the time my feelings were under control—at least the situation became manageable and not threatening to my marriage. Great relief set in, and I fell back into relative contentment, still in love with Colleen.

That summer, Colleen's brother, Tom, who temporarily worked on the back of a garbage truck, showed me a porn magazine he'd discovered in someone's trash. In the magazine were photos of men with women, women with women, and men with men. The male photos triggered me sexually and I sought opportunities to sneak yet another peak at the masculine men fucking. Tom said he didn't want the magazine anymore and offered it to me. Colleen knew I had it, but she didn't know I had tucked it away so I could privately fantasize when there was no risk of getting caught.

I masturbated while viewing the photos, sometimes using them with mirrors in an attempt to put myself in the scene, even going so far as to lay a full length mirror nearly on top of me, creating the illusion of being with another living man. It wasn't a narcissistic act—rather, an increased pull toward gay sexuality.

I started using fantasy as a means for lulling myself to sleep. The images in my head numbed my mind from reality. Sometimes I fantasized about being with someone in particular, like the man who sat at the front desk of the campus library. Other times a celebrity joined me in my mind—the young actors, Kurt Russell or Erik Estrada, to name two. I created exciting romantic and erotic stories.

Occasionally, when I felt safe, I masturbated while in a state of fantasy. But at night, with Colleen beside me, I only needed to disappear into my secret, sexy world for a few minutes to achieve a soothing mental vibration, slowing my brain and helping me drift off to sleep. The routine seemed harmless. I believed it kept me faithful to my wife. Little did I know I would one day become powerless over this habitual fantasizing. And like the spiritual author Iyanla Vanzant wrote, "Where the mind goes, the behind follows."

Shame began to accumulate for being less than fully honest with Colleen about my feelings and fantasies. I tried to bury it. But buried shame doesn't evaporate or magically disappear. It hides in one's cells, becoming self-induced poisoning—difficult to detect at first, eventually debilitating, and sometimes fatal. At some point in one's lifetime, accumulated shame must come to the surface in one painful way or another.

Staying busy seemed to help. I loaded up my class schedules and enrolled in summer sessions to complete the required course work in three years. But every time I walked through campus, had downtime at work, or did research in the library, I imagined a chance meeting with an enticing man. I took no risks, however—always too afraid of exposure.

Over time, those repressed feelings intensified, making me emotionally unbalanced and mentally unhealthy. I decided I needed to have a gay sexual encounter to satisfy my cravings and better understand my curiosity. I then waited for a stealth opportunity to materialize, one that came with no chance of Colleen finding out.

For my final quarter before graduation, I was given a student teaching assignment at an elementary school in Kennewick, back in the Tri-Cities. Colleen left Ellensburg with her parents two days before me, most of our belongings loaded in the back of their pickup truck. I needed to wrap up my part-time job, then load our car with clothes before joining her at our new apartment.

That left me with a free afternoon and evening alone with nothing to do. The opportunity I had been waiting for had arrived. The little dragon within me, the seductive voice of lust and temptation, had gained power in recent years, and was now itching for action. I felt a mixture of excitement and trepidation, plus a shitload of guilt.

The town of Ellensburg was small and the campus practically deserted at the end of summer session. I knew my odds of anything happening were poor. Still, there was the thrill of the hunt and I was determined to give it my best shot.

As dusk approached at the end of the sizzling summer day, I wandered around campus, sniffing out any possible targets. No luck. I walked through the library. The handsome man who usually worked at the checkout counter wasn't there. Then, I made my way to the student union building to saunter about. But there was not one boy like me to be found. A lonely feeling came over me.

I decided to make my way downtown, just a ten-minute walk from campus, and have a cocktail at a lounge popular with students. I sat at a dark table in the very back corner. It seemed the safest place to hide out, drink, and calm my nerves.

I was on my second bourbon and starting to feel a buzz, when a man about forty with a Liberace hairdo walked in alone and sat at the bar. I watched his mannerisms and became suspicious. He wasn't the slightest bit attractive to me. In fact, a man who styled himself in that manner, with the gold jewelry and slinky shirt opened an extra button, rather disgusted me.

Years later, I would come to understand my judgmental thinking was, in fact, internalized homophobia. I projected onto other gay men, or those I assumed to be gay, my own discomfort and self-loathing. I hated anything about them that seemed queer to me—how they dressed or talked or moved. My repulsion emanated from a deep fear, keeping me closeted and what I believed to be safe.

But that evening in the bar, on my last day on campus, horny desperation took control and I pursued the man regardless of his appearance.

I watched him finish his drink and find his way to the bathroom, located in the opposite back corner from where I was sitting. I finished my own drink and followed after him. He stood at the urinal, so I took my time at the mirror combing my hair until he finished. Then, as he approached the sink to wash his hands, I put my comb away, caught his eye and gave him a little smile.

"How ya doin'?" I asked with a nod, then exited the bathroom without using the urinal or toilet.

It seemed enough to me. A conversation in a public restroom didn't feel appropriate. His face was fine. His body was okay, but nothing about him turned me on, except that he was a man with whom I might have a sexual adventure.

I went back to my table and waited for him to exit the bathroom. When he did, he walked back to the bar and ordered another drink. I made sure I did, too. With a third drink, I would lose all inhibitions and have the courage to follow through with anything that might yet happen.

I watched him take his time turning on his barstool, scanning the room. The entire lounge had perhaps twenty tables and less than a dozen customers. He spotted me and our eyes locked. My heart thumped, knowing he was looking at me looking at him. The reality of what was happening in that moment was an exciting jolt of unfamiliar energy.

He finished his drink and prepared to leave, first taking a quick glance in my direction. I followed suit, paying my server, then casually walking out of the bar. He wasn't on the sidewalk. I walked around the nearest corner. Nothing. Disappointed but also relieved, I told myself it was time to walk home and jack off.

However, as I crossed the street I heard a parked car start up behind me. I turned around to see its brake lights flash a few times but no headlights. It was a big, flamboyant-looking, turquoise-blue Mercury sedan. Half-drunk from my three drinks and feeling bold as hell, I reversed my direction and walked in front of the idling car to look at the driver. He stared directly into my eyes. I walked to the passenger door. He unlocked it. I got in.

We chatted, small talk, the car's air conditioning too cold, his cologne too strong, his cigarette too stinky. However, he was soft-spoken and seemed kind. He lived on campus, working on his master's thesis and staying in a dorm.

"Would you like to come to my place for a little while?" he asked in his soft voice.

"Okay," I said. My heart beat wildly as I wondered what the fuck I was doing.

It was a short drive to the east side of campus, not more than five minutes. He parked the car and we made our way in the dark from the parking lot to the dorm, an older, single-level, barrack-style structure. He explained there weren't many occupants in the building, but that we needed to be as quiet as possible. I followed him to his room and entered into the yellowish light that filtered through the thin window curtains from the streetlamp outside. He didn't turn on any interior lights, for which I was grateful. I didn't want to see anything that was going to happen.

He was very gentle with me, clearly sensitive to my inexperience and nervousness. There was no fucking and I rejected his attempt to kiss me. But I let him undress me and put his hands and mouth all over my body, helping me come. I did my best to reciprocate, but I was selfish. There was no desire to touch him in any way. I wanted to be consumed but not consume. Simple as that. He managed his own orgasm with only minimal assistance from me.

I cleaned myself up with tissue, not bothering to go down the hall to the shared bathroom. I wanted out. So I told him, "It was nice to meet you," and made my escape. With my head down, I walked home as quickly as I could, chastising myself the entire way.

I couldn't shut off my scolding thoughts. *I will never have sex with a man again! If that's all it is then I want nothing to do with it. This was an experiment. Yes, I had sex . . . sort of. Yes, I was unfaithful to my wife, but at least I now know I'm not gay. Any future temptations will simply be my cross to bear!*

My successful student teaching in the fall led me directly into my first special education position at Jefferson Elementary in Richland with an annual salary of $7,865. I was soon encouraged by the superintendent, Dr. Iller, and Jefferson's principal, Mr. Lane, to pursue my master's degree and administrative credentials. They saw my leadership potential. That meant local night classes and two summer terms back on campus in Ellensburg.

Midway during the school year, Colleen and I conceived our first baby. Then, on the afternoon of October 2, 1975, she went into labor. Instead of attending a high school football game between our alma maters, we spent the night at the hospital working as a team, implementing everything we had learned during our Lamaze classes. Our son Eric was born, perfect and beautiful, shortly after midnight. I had never known such joy. Each day, week, and month with our bright little guy was a gift. Eric was nine months old and just learning to walk as I prepared to pack up and head to Ellensburg alone for summer school. In so doing, I again struggled in fear and confusion.

My fantasies had been returning. I had not acted on them, but found myself obsessed with tempting thoughts and terrified something would happen during summer school. I became detached and fell into depression, causing Colleen to become concerned enough to ask me to talk to her. For the third time, I reiterated my fears regarding my sexuality.

This time, she cried. "But do you love me?" she asked through her tears.

"I can't even love myself," I responded as honestly as I could, my own tears now falling. It broke my heart to see her heart breaking, so I managed to say, "Yes, Colleen, I love you. I'm just afraid. That's all."

"As long as we love each other, we can work through it," she concluded and promptly ended the discussion. There were no further questions or admissions. I knew I should say more and she knew I would answer her questions. But neither of us wanted to give voice to the deep truth that lay beneath the surface. Once spoken, it would have become real.

I did my best to stay faithful during summer school, even arranging to share an apartment with my teaching colleague and her husband, thinking that would help me feel less lonely, less tempted to sexually act out. But the attractive young man still working at the library checkout desk became a distraction. There was something intriguing in his smile and the attention he gave me. Over the course of the summer, we started to chat, then flirt. Eventually, he asked me to a movie and I accepted. We ended up in his dorm room where I experienced my first kiss with a man. It was clammy, the sex awkward, unmemorable. Still, it happened and I decided to accept I was perhaps thirty percent gay, seventy percent straight. Probably bisexual.

I gave myself permission to have one experience with a man per year. I would just have to be okay with that and cope with the shame of living a double life.

10

After three years of teaching special education, I sought a regular education position to make me more marketable for administrative positions. Mr. Lane supported my plan and gave me the choice between grade one and grade five. I chose the younger kids, since my current students were older, again expanding the breadth of my experiences.

Teaching first grade was delightful and challenging. I loved the exhausting reality of being on "center stage" from 9 a.m. to 3 p.m., keeping twenty-six six-year-olds engaged in learning. My students were delightful, joy-filled little sponges. They laughed at my jokes and never criticized my mediocre guitar-playing as we sang songs together with our whole hearts. I started to connect how my perceived lack of acceptance as a young boy had led me to be a relentless advocate for my students, celebrating each child's creative uniqueness and brilliance.

Colleen got pregnant again and our darling, entertaining Ben was born in early November 1978, during my second year teaching first grade. I had completed my master's degree and administrative credentials that summer, putting me in position for potential principalships.

Two openings were announced. I prepared my application and spent many hours writing and rewriting answers to possible questions in all areas of education.

The March date for my interview arrived—two weeks before my twenty-sixth birthday. Arriving early for my appointment, I sat in my car and centered myself, turning to God for peace.

Finally, I straightened my tie, checked my teeth, and took a deep breath as I found my way to the waiting area outside the school board's conference room. Even though a thick fog of nervousness clouded my brain, I felt focused and confident.

The interview lasted nearly an hour, and after the first few shaky moments, it flowed beautifully. I made them smile, had them nodding to my responses, and even heard some chuckles when I answered the question, "Mr. Tubbs, how can you be an effective disciplinarian when some of the sixth grade boys are as tall as you?"

Although I was put off by the short joke, I smiled and started with a textbook answer: "Research has informed us that by creating a positive school climate, children feel a sense of belonging and are less inclined to act inappropriately."

Then, mysteriously, I was guided in a different direction.

"My elementary principal was Lilly Peterson. She was petite, unhealthy, and old. But without raising her voice she could command respect and good behavior from even the most challenging students because she meant what she said and she followed through. Now, if a little old lady can be an effective disciplinarian, I don't see why a short, healthy, young man with a master's degree in special education and experience working with behaviorally disabled children should have any trouble doing the same."

Feeling like I had nailed the interview, I gave myself a quiet but exuberant "Yes!" as I walked back to my car. Two evenings later, I received a call informing me I had been selected as the new principal of Jason Lee Elementary where I had been a student fourteen years earlier. The next week, I attended the evening school board meeting with my wife, my sister, and my father. We sat together and held our breath as my name was formally recommended and approved, making the assignment official. As we exited the meeting and walked to our cars, I heard the words I had waited twenty-six years to hear: "I'm proud of you, son." Dad shook my hand, we hugged, and everything felt in place.

The next morning, as I drove to work listening to the local news on the radio, I heard my name announced as Jason Lee's new principal. Then, later, while preparing lessons for the school day, colleague after colleague entered my classroom to congratulate me with hugs and high fives.

After my teaching responsibilities ended in June, I spent my entire summer working more than full time, preparing for the opening of school. And, with my new salary, Colleen and I spent our weekends shopping for a bigger house. We found a beautiful, four-bedroom, new-construction rambler in west Kennewick that fit our needs and budget. It was an incredibly busy summer, diminishing any temptations I might have had to fantasize, hunt, or act out. When such thoughts came, I just worked harder and longer hours.

Each evening, when I got home, I hugged the boys, set the egg timer for thirty minutes, then crashed on the bed for a power nap, asleep in seconds. When the timer buzzed, the boys charged into the bedroom to jump on me. We had dinner as a family, then Eric, Ben, and I played games until it was time for bed. Once under the covers, they practiced their ABC cards with me, followed by a storybook. To help them relax, I rubbed their backs and patted their bottoms until they were quiet and calm. I loved my sons so much I could hardly breathe.

On the rare occasion I had down time, or when the warm spring weather brought those old sexy feelings back, there were moments I thought I would go crazy in my lust for a man's body. Fortunately, each phase abated. Then, for months, without struggle, I was content.

Sex with Colleen was always pleasant and loving. My ability to perform was not a problem, and even though I didn't initiate sex as frequently as she might have liked, I never refused her when she gave me "the look" or brought herself to me wrapped naked in a blanket. I don't recall feeling dissatisfied, although perhaps never fully satisfied.

My life appeared perfect on the surface while, in truth, I often felt alone, even in the company of friends or loved ones. I didn't personally know one gay or bisexual man in the entire world— not one person with whom I could relate or talk. Was I the only one like me? Assuming other men questioning or hiding their sexuality existed, where might they be? Lying in bed and unable to sleep, I sometimes imagined possible locations where men were safely meeting up.

Then, one lovely day in late spring, I decided to exit the freeway early on my way home from work and take the leisurely five-mile scenic drive through Columbia Park that stretched along the river. I was horny as hell, noticing men without shirts throwing Frisbees and nearly naked young men jogging along the trail. I also noticed a few stray cars parked on the dirt roads that meandered through the trees in several places throughout the park. My imagination ran wild.

I wondered who else might be driving through the park. Were they men? Were they alone? If I was cruising slowly with fantasies invading my thoughts, maybe I wasn't the only one. Sure enough, as I looked more intently at the drivers going the other direction, there was occasionally a man alone, looking out his side window at me. When I looked in my rearview mirror after he had passed, taillights sometimes flashed once or twice, reminding me of the turquoise-blue Mercury back on campus. Was it a signal? Did these men driving through the park want to talk with me?

I had no desire to meet these particular men. All were old or unattractive, making me feel dirty and, ironically, even more alone. But perhaps younger men were also somewhere in the park. The dragon within became alert and impatient. Time to go hunting again.

I began to carve out an hour or two on the weekends to jog along the river, getting much-needed exercise while also continuing my search. One day, I noticed a bright yellow VW beetle parked far off the main road near the grandstands for the hydroplane races. A young man stood facing the river. From a distance, he seemed about my size and age. My hopes were up as I jogged in his direction. *Should I stop and chat or just jog by and check him out?* As I got nearer, my questions were answered. He looked directly at me with an invitational nod and grin. He was adorable.

"Hey, how ya doin'?" I asked, as I stopped jogging and walked up near him. He had round brown eyes, full lips, a button nose, and curly, dark hair. He was Caucasian—or perhaps biracial. In any case, his facial features were the opposite of mine with my small blue eyes, thin lips, and long nose. He wore shorts and a sleeveless T-shirt exposing tanned, olive-brown skin. A tingle of excitement that seemed both familiar and new ran through my body.

I never understood my attraction to brown skin—where or when it started—but there had always been an undeniable draw to what I considered exotic. And that attraction was crossing into sexual desire.

His name was Glen. We talked about the beautiful day. Then, although neither one of us seemed ready to end our conversation, we found ourselves without anything to say. Little looks back-and-forth kept me intrigued enough to hang out in the silence.

"You come down here often?" he eventually asked.

"I just recently started coming here to jog," I answered.

He smirked and responded cynically: "Jog? Yeah, right."

I felt exposed and defensive.

"Yeah, it's a great place to jog," I said, smiling and trying to lighten up what seemed like negative energy. It was then he looked at me with such openness and vulnerability, it helped me to be more honest. I knew his pain, his loneliness.

"Of course," I added, "it's always fun to look around while jogging. You never know when you might see someone nice to look at."

There was only a moment's pause until Glen locked his eyes on mine and asked, "So, have you seen someone nice to look at today?"

I blushed but tried not to look away. "I have, actually, yes."

He smiled. There was a new sense of calm in the air as we began to talk more freely.

I admitted I was married and confused. He shared his desire to move away from the Tri-Cities, totally disillusioned with the gay men in the area. They were either married, addicts, old, or bitchy.

"I'm so fucking tired of men who only want sex but can't even be in a true relationship with me," he said. That explained his earlier cynicism and also threw cold water on my prurient pursuit. Since I represented one kind of man Glen wanted to avoid, I gave up any sexual intention.

Glen was twenty-seven years old and lived in Pasco, just on the other side of the river from Columbia Park. He worked as a sous chef in a hotel restaurant with dreams of moving to a major city as soon as he could afford it. Soon, the pull to get home to my family and away from the guilt building up inside me for even having the encounter moved me to draw our brief interaction to a close. "Maybe I'll see you down here again," I offered.

"Maybe," he said, without much conviction or enthusiasm.

I left feeling sorry for Glen, yet encouraged by the prospect of other attractive men in the Tri-Cities for me to meet.

Spring became summer and one evening, Colleen, the boys, and I went to dinner at a restaurant near the shopping mall. Our waiter, with a name tag "Clint" pinned onto his shirt, greeted us with a smile and menus as he filled our water glasses. I felt the air being sucked from my lungs when I looked at his stunning face. Of course, I tried not to stare, but I certainly did return his smile, as did Colleen. In fact, Colleen remarked, "He's sure a cutie," when Clint walked away.

"He is," I agreed, then buried my eyes into the menu I hid behind. There was nothing on the menu I wanted more than Clint.

I avoided looking at him as he walked by our booth or waited on other tables. What if Colleen saw me eyeballing him and asked questions? Instead, I entertained the boys and engaged in comfortable family chatter until Clint returned. After I ordered, and while Colleén ordered for herself and the boys, I again diverted my attention away from him and onto the scuffed, unpolished brown shoes he wore. I hoped his fashion faux pas would temper my lustful thoughts. It didn't work. Later, as we exited the restaurant, I was already planning a return trip and a different kind of interaction with Clint, in spite of his ugly shoes.

Then, one evening after jogging and beginning my drive home, I passed a car near the park's traffic circle going in the opposite direction. The young driver looked remarkably like Clint, the waiter. I caught his eye and he held the look just long enough to send a signal of interest. When I saw his taillights flash in my rearview mirror, I tapped my brakes in return. I held my breath. His brake lights flashed again and he pulled his car over. My heart beat out of my chest. *Now what?* I thought to myself as my car seemed to drive itself around the traffic circle and back to where the man was parked. I pulled up behind him.

He got out and walked toward me. It was him—gorgeous Clint. After a brief exchange of introductory remarks at my window, he asked if he could sit in the car with me.

"Sure," I responded, now getting nervous. We carried on our conversation with him asking lots of questions. I told him the truth: I was married. I had very little gay experience. I thought I was bisexual. My job and marriage would be in jeopardy if I were discovered.

It was getting dark and even though Clint made it quite clear he wanted to fool around, I couldn't imagine doing anything in my car. I needed to get home.

"May I kiss you goodbye?" I surprised myself by asking. I don't know why I asked that question except that he was so damn attractive, the thought of kissing him topped my list of desires at that moment.

"Gary, you can do whatever blows your skirt up," Clint responded with a smile.

Although repulsed by the girly expression and the flashback of Pete teasing me in third grade, I ignored my disgust and leaned in, letting my hands run over his lean, almost skinny body. It was a delicious kiss—warm, soft, and sensual. He melted in my arms and leaned back, pulling me to lay more fully on him. But I drew away, "Sorry, I can't," I said in a panic. "I have to go."

"No problem," he said with an attitude that made me not believe him. His tone was "pissy," as if insulted and irritated.

"Thanks for the talk and the kiss," I offered.

"Yeah, sure," he mumbled as he climbed out of the car. I pulled away and found my way home to my wife and kids.

11

A new principal's first year is a steep learning curve. Mine was no exception. I experienced a few staffing challenges related to substandard teaching, but otherwise enjoyed strong support from the staff and parents. Along with my outstanding midyear review from the assistant superintendent, I also received encouragement to attend the annual convention of the National Association of Elementary School Principals to be held in Washington, D.C., in April. I jumped at the chance for the all-expenses-paid trip, and soon met with the school district's travel agent to set up the itinerary, including a White House tour and a ticket to see a production of *The Wiz*. I couldn't believe it. It would be my first flight, my first East Coast experience, my first major theatre production . . . so many firsts!

I spent hours planning, reading articles, talking to others, and learning as much as I could about what to do and see. The 1979 signing of the Egypt-Israel Peace Treaty would give me an opportunity to witness, from a distance, the historic event on the White House grounds with President Jimmy Carter, Israeli Prime Minister Menachem Begin, and Egyptian President Anwar Sadat. I definitely wanted to spend time on the National Mall and see as many of the D.C. memorials as possible.

The thought of experiencing my first gay bar also weighed on my mind. Not knowing anyone to ask and unfamiliar with resources to guide me, I visited the public library to search through the Washington, D.C., metro-area telephone book. There I found listings for a Gay Resource Center and Gay Community Center.

Jotting down the addresses, I tucked them in my folder of convention materials.

After a smooth flight, I caught a shuttle to the Washington Hilton, then a taxi to my hotel, the Shoreham Americana, where the valet and bellhop greeted me and the doorman politely held open the door. I felt like one of the rich and famous.

The hotel lobby was opulent from the perspective of a small-town boy who had never been anywhere. Three archways gracefully divided the expansive marble-floored reception area, which featured elegant crystal chandeliers and gigantic fresh flower arrangements.

After checking in and purchasing a city map from the gift shop, the bellhop led me to a charming room on the sixth floor. It was splendid—at the end of the hall, very private, very elegant, very quiet.

I immediately fantasized about having a man in my room as I mapped out the gay-related addresses I had packed away and discovered both were located in an area called Dupont Circle. Along with my excitement to explore and learn more about the gay lifestyle, I also experienced a dark, dull ache in my stomach, knowing I was again crossing into dishonesty and infidelity.

As a dedicated professional just completing his first year as a principal, I attended the opening session of the convention, listened to speakers, went to workshops, and visited the booths of the various vendors, getting ideas to bring back to my school and district. However, the convention schedule also allowed time to tour the White House and visit several monuments and museums.

On the third day of the convention, I found my way to Dupont Circle using the "Metro" subway system. I don't know what I expected, but Dupont Circle was a typical city neighborhood. I walked and walked, afraid to ask questions, and since I didn't yet have active "gaydar," I never could be sure if any of the men I passed on the street were gay or not.

Finally, I saw posters of attractive men posing together in a bookstore window. I knew I was getting warm. I entered and looked around. Nothing was happening. No secret back room. No sexy men in the aisles waiting to meet me. But I did find a section featuring books and magazines with obvious gay themes. As I made my way out of the store, I noticed a postcard display near the cashier advertising Mr. P's bar and featuring a photo of guys dancing together.

"Are these free?" I asked the clerk.

"Yeah, help yourself."

Once outside, I studied the postcard for an address. I didn't want to open my map on the street for fear someone might ask, "Hey, do you need some help?" That would be like a spotlight and a loudspeaker revealing my nasty little secret to the world: "Married young man looking for his annual, anonymous gay encounter!"

I found a seat in a small cafe, ordered a soda and took out my map. Mr. P's was very close to my current location, which only added to my excitement to enter my first gay bar. I got my bearings and soon found the bar. "Closed." Huh? Why would a bar be closed at three in the afternoon? The sign on the door read, "Bar opens at 9 p.m." Weird.

And what about the restaurant? I wandered around until I found a different door that opened to the upstairs restaurant. I wasn't hungry and the restaurant was virtually empty, so I came up with a new plan. I'd go back to the hotel, change for an early dinner at Mr. P's restaurant, go to *The Wiz*, then return to the bar after the show.

Already tired from the day's activities, I returned to my room with time to rest and shower before dressing for my big evening. But what about my wedding ring? After a long pause, I slipped it off and put it in the bureau drawer. What was a little more toxic shame to repress? If I was going to do this, I decided to go all the way, even though I instantly felt horribly wrong and exposed. It wasn't that I wanted to be out of my marriage. I didn't. But I wanted to be a single gay man for the evening, anonymous and free.

After double-checking to make sure I had everything I needed—wallet, money, play ticket, map, addresses, jacket, and room key—I walked out of the hotel room, hearing the door click behind me and feeling the powerful pumping of my heart.

Dinner at Mr. P's was boring and uneventful. The restaurant was still practically empty and the food was nothing special. No one flirted with me, not even my waiter.

So, off to *The Wiz* to see my first big show. I made sure to buy the souvenir program to bring home with me. Once I was seated in the last row of the second balcony, I heard the crowd's buzz of disappointment when it was announced the star playing Dorothy would instead be played by her understudy. I didn't care, because I didn't know beans about the star actress. I just knew the musical would be amazing and memorable. And it was. I loved it all, mesmerized by the entire experience and wanting more when it was over. Then I remembered I was headed to a gay bar.

Sitting on the Metro to Dupont Circle, my body informed me in no uncertain terms: *It's almost eleven o'clock! I want sleep!* But I ignored it and forged ahead, determined to have a new experience and, hopefully, an exciting adventure.

After paying the cover charge at the door, I walked into Mr. P's with my *Wiz* souvenir in hand and no pocket in my jacket big enough to hold it. My body was tense and my eyes darted all over the place, not knowing where to stand or what to do. It was a world I'd never seen before. Men everywhere! Men drinking, chatting, and laughing. Men in tight T-shirts—and even tighter Levi's—dancing with other sexy men in a large, darkened room, strobe lights flashing, and a huge disco ball suspended from a chain in the center of the dance floor. Unbelievable.

We're definitely not in Kansas anymore, Toto!

"Hi! How're you doing?"

I don't know where he came from but a very nice-looking man was talking to me. He was taller than me (who isn't?) but not by much. He was about my age, well-groomed, and masculine with an athletic body . . . and he was talking to *me*.

"I'm okay. How are you?"

"I'm good. My name's Mark."

"Hi, I'm Gary." To shake hands, I had to transfer my *Wiz* program from my right hand to my left.

"What's that?"

I showed him the souvenir and we chatted about the show since he'd seen it, too.

"Can I get you a drink?" Mark asked. What a gentleman.

"Sure. Bourbon cola, please."

After sipping our drinks and chatting for a while he asked me to dance. But what to do with my jacket and the program? I started to lay them down on a chair until Mark advised against it. Instead, he led me to the coat check around the corner from the entrance.

We danced and flirted, a definite connection building, with him getting more handsome each minute—like from hot to fuckin' hot. As my tiredness crept in, I knew I had to move fast or forever be disappointed.

I whispered in his ear, "Would you like to come to my hotel?"

"Wow, that was fast," he laughed with a cute smile.

"Well, I've had a busy day and I'm really tired."

"Maybe you want to get some rest and we can meet up again tomorrow," Mark offered.

I was impressed. However . . .

"I'm here on business and have to fly back to Seattle tomorrow night."

"In that case," he said, smiling again, "Sure. Let's go."

While Mark drove us to my hotel in his sporty Peugeot, he talked pretty much nonstop, calling D.C. a "comatose town." He was very articulate, with an impressive vocabulary, as he spoke passionately about politics and his job as a lobbyist. I sat, ignorant, since I didn't even know what a lobbyist did. I just listened politely, trying not to yawn. He started to annoy me with all his talking and rather arrogant, cynical attitude, but I let it slide, knowing I get grumpy when I'm tired. Besides, I just wanted to get naked and have gay sex before I fell asleep. It was all about me without any consideration for Mark. Shallow.

He knew my hotel and drove directly to the visitor parking area. Entering the brightly lit lobby, we finally saw each other clearly. I felt like a lucky guy and hoped his grin meant he approved of me as well. After entering my room, I got us a drink from the minibar and we chatted a few minutes before getting romantic.

Mark took the lead and I so appreciated it. He was knowledgeable and beautifully put together.

"You're a hunk!" I exclaimed when I saw him without his shirt, his gym body flawless.

"Naw," he said, brushing off the compliment as if I'd made him shy. "But thanks."

Sexually, Mark took me to new heights as he devoured me in all ways. He wasn't an inexperienced thirteen-year-old boy ramming himself into me. No, he was a sexy, gentle, and patient man who knew all the tricks to help me relax and receive him without pain. I experienced sensations I never knew were possible as he expertly delayed our orgasms until I thought I would burst.

For my first experience of true gay sex, I had been blessed with a hot, skilled lover who made me feel everything I had only fantasized about and more.

Mark was in no hurry to leave and asked if he could spend the night.

"Sorry, but I need to get up for meetings in the morning and I'll probably have trouble sleeping if you're in the bed."

"Okay, I get it, but can I see you again? I mean, I feel like we hit it off and I travel to Seattle a couple times a year. I'll call you if you give me your number."

"Sorry, I can't."

"Why not?" He looked so disappointed and I felt like the big fraud I was.

"Actually, I'm married."

"To a woman?"

"Yeah."

"Where's your ring?"

"In the drawer."

"So basically, you used me like a piece of meat."

"No, I like you, but I can't see you again."

His anger grew and he shook his head in disgust. Without another word, he dressed and headed for the door.

That's when I said the most pitiful thing ever: "Thanks for talking to me." As if he hadn't heard me, Mark continued his march out the door and down the hall.

I closed and locked the door behind him, ashamed of myself, jumbled with conflicting feelings and wanting nothing more than to shower, put my wedding ring back on, and commit to another year without gay sex.

12

Two months after my trip to Washington, D.C., summer approached and I decided Colleen and I deserved a real vacation. We had never enjoyed a honeymoon or traveled anywhere exotic. Hawaii became our desired destination and we invited our parents to join us. Colleen's cousin, Darlene, agreed to watch the boys while we were away. A week on Oahu would be followed by a few quiet days on the garden island of Kauai.

Upon arrival, our aloha lei and the warm, tropical air made us giddy with joy. A bus awaited to transport us to the Waikiki strip where our travel agent had reserved three upper-level, oceanfront rooms at the Outrigger Hotel.

A whisper of sensual sea breeze washed over us as we entered the hotel lobby to be greeted by the charming staff. When Colleen slid open the glass door to our private lanai, we heard the ocean gently breaking on the shore and breathed in the warm, salty air hinting of a floral fragrance. Ukulele music floated up, announcing the evening festivities around the swimming pool. This was truly paradise for us. Stripping down to don our bathing suits, we headed to the beach to splash in the warm Pacific Ocean, symbolically toasting our arrival with a saltwater nightcap at the end of a long day of travel.

The next day, Colleen and I took a surfing lesson and each had success standing on the board. At least we stood up long enough for a photo to be taken which, of course, we had to purchase as proof of our accomplishment. The photo also gave witness to the absolute tininess of the wave.

Surfing was hard work: the paddling, the falling, remounting the board, and paddling out again. Exhausted, we took naps on the beach, luxuriating in the lovely tropical sun. We then made our way back to our room to shower and meet up with our parents for cocktails and an early dinner. I knew I was pink from the sun, but after my shower, the mirror screamed, "Lobster!"

Colleen sunned the same amount of time but her olive skin tones resulted in a beautiful tan rather than my painful sunburn. By bedtime, I felt miserable and had to find a drugstore to purchase ointment to keep the itching and burning away as much as possible.

The next day, I avoided the sun and instead walked around with Colleen. We explored the blocks adjacent to our hotel, stopping for ice cream and hunting for souvenirs in the small sidewalk shops. An hour or so later, we circled back to find our hotel and took a few steps inside the open bamboo door of an interesting-looking club called Hula's. The simple, native decor resembled an expanded grass hut open to the sky. A huge Banyan tree adorned the center of the restaurant area with lights and lanterns strung about. Very charming.

"Maybe we can come back here tonight to dance," I said.

"Maybe," Colleen replied. "We'll have to see what the others want to do."

I exited the venue behind her and noticed a bulletin board with posters advertising the nightly entertainment. The photos caught my eye: drag queens, men dancing together, and nearly nude, male strippers. I looked away and kept walking, not wanting to call attention to what Colleen apparently hadn't noticed. I would not be reminding her of my suggestion to return to the club later that evening!

Here we were in one of the most sensual places on the planet with nearly naked people everywhere. My young hormones raged. Although making love to my wife upon our arrival had been steamy with passion, the idea of visiting a gay bar in this exotic location bombarded my body with fever—and not because of the sunburn.

I kept my mind on Colleen while we walked, talked, and explored, but once we found the hotel and I had time to be alone with my thoughts, I started looking for an escape plan. I couldn't find one. Frustration set in and I became moody and irritable. Blaming it on the sunburn, I said I was going to take a cool shower and rest.

Colleen made plans to meet up with our moms to enjoy time by the pool and then shop in the hotel boutiques. Alone, I fantasized and masturbated with the intention of relieving myself of my obsessive thinking. The relief was short-lived.

At home in the Tri-Cities, this lustful urge challenged but rarely overwhelmed me. In Hawaii, relaxed and on vacation, anonymous except for my family, I became powerless given the climate, the ambiance, and all the beautiful brown skin.

As dusk approached, the six of us went to dinner in the hotel restaurant. The shadows of the evening and cooler temperatures only added to my insanity. I pretended to be present but failed to control the prowling eyes of the wild dragon within.

Night fell with no mention of going out dancing, everyone expressing a tired satisfaction for the delightful day. We made our way back to our rooms to watch TV and settle into bed. My mind raced. I couldn't sleep. I tried reading, then tossed and turned, absolutely beside myself with agitation.

"What's the matter with you?" Colleen snapped, after being repeatedly disturbed by my restlessness.

"I can't sleep!" I blurted out. "I feel like I'm going crazy!"

Now concerned, she wanted to know what was going on. Even though we'd had three prior, very uncomfortable conversations about my temptations, I was no longer willing to have that same conversation. My inclinations and actions had gone too far. What I needed to do was "white-knuckle it" and not burden her. I needed to control myself and make sure I limited my acting-out to no more than once a year. Just a few months earlier, I'd had sex with Mark in Washington, D.C. On vacation with my wife and parents was definitely not a time to fuck up.

"I'm going for a walk," I told her.

"Where are you going?"

"Just walking around until I feel sleepy. I won't be gone long."
I knew she didn't for one second approve of me leaving her alone,
but I also had no intention of inviting her to join me. I knew
where I was going. I slipped on my clothes, made sure I had my
wallet and room key, then left before she had time to protest or
question me further.

With a quick step, I walked back to Hula's. The bar was moderately crowded but far from packed. I bought a beer and walked
around. Clearly, I looked like a tourist with my glaring sunburn
and much too coordinated summer outfit. But I didn't care. My
focus was on hunting. But for what? I wasn't sure. I just knew I
wanted to feel the vibe and freedom I'd experienced at Mr. P's,
even if for only a few minutes.

One beer down, I ordered another and allowed the rhythm of
the music to seep in, relaxing me. People started dancing so I
made my way over to the floor, finding a place to stand in hopes
someone would show an interest in me. Nobody did. Everyone
was engaged with their friends and the whole pickup scene I'd
experienced in D.C. wasn't happening here.

It was 10:00 p.m., still early by club standards, but I didn't
know that then. It already seemed late to me and I couldn't be
gone long. Then, I noticed an Asian man standing by himself on
the opposite side of the dance floor. About my age, nicely
groomed, and handsome, he didn't give off a particularly friendly
vibe, but since he was just standing there, I figured he might like
to dance. With my second beer gone, I asked and he accepted but
with minimal enthusiasm. I then tried to catch his eye to flirt while
we danced. He gave me nothing.

What did I plan on doing even if he showed an interest? What
did I think could possibly happen? I didn't realize it at the time
but I craved a "fix"—some kind of thrill in the form of positive
attention and validation from an attractive man.

Finally, he looked at me and smiled. But it was more of a cour-
tesy grin than anything flirtatious. Still, it was enough for me to
ask if I could buy him a drink.

"No, thank you," he said kindly, "but thanks for the dance," and walked away.

Disillusioned and disappointed, I left the bar in frustration, knowing Colleen would already be worried. But as I approached the first corner on my walk back to the hotel, a very sexy young man dressed in super tight-fitting jeans smiled at me. Returning his smile, I heard my ego announce: *Well, that's more like it!*

After a very brief exchange of pleasantries, he told me he lived in the building next door and would I like to play? I knew I should get back to the hotel, but the dragon within lied, informing me a few minutes of playtime wouldn't make any difference. I foolishly listened to the bad advice and followed Mr. Sexy into his building.

A bad feeling came over me as I followed him down a maze of narrow halls. My gut started to ache and my mind flashed, *prostitute!*

I slowed my pace and as soon as he turned the next corner, I spun around and briskly found my way out of the building. God's grace saved me from a terrible mistake.

Colleen was sitting up in bed watching TV.

"Where did you go?" she asked, her voice shaking.

"Just walking, don't worry, everything's fine." I tried to reassure her, but I saw the tears begin to fall. I went to her and held her with all the love I felt in my heart, which was full and sincere.

"It's okay," I said more gently. "I'm sorry I left, but please don't be upset. Nothing happened. Don't worry." She buried her tear-streaked face into my chest for a few minutes, then returned to her pillow and faced away from me.

In that moment, I prayed I would have the strength to never hurt this wonderful woman. She had done nothing wrong and didn't deserve the kind of pain my sexual struggles would bring should they be discovered. For the remainder of our Hawaii vacation, I made sure I stayed near her almost every minute and gave her nothing more to worry about.

13

Over the next few years, my obsession with sexual fantasy progressed and the annual gay escapade became every six months. A sense of desperation built up as my mounting natural desires required deeper repression, becoming a sickness of the soul. On the surface, my marriage seemed solid, even as the foundations crumbled. I still loved Colleen and adored my young sons, just six and three years old, but what kind of love was I demonstrating by my lies and infidelity?

In August, I drove to Seattle for a principals' conference. Once there, I called Colleen's Uncle Bob, who had returned to the gay lifestyle he had lived before meeting Carol, marrying, and raising a family together. After Bob and Carol divorced, Bob moved back into the city. Since I was in Seattle for my conference, I hoped to find a way to broach the subject of sexuality with him and, if it seemed appropriate, confide in him about my internal struggles.

"Hey, Gary, it's great to hear from you! How long will you be in town? Well, in that case, come on over this evening. I'm hosting a small dinner party and there's room for one more. No, don't bring anything. Just show up around seven, okay? You like lamb, don't you? Great! Let me give you the address . . ."

A private conversation with Bob seemed unlikely at that point, but maybe I would learn something about gay life if the other dinner guests were gay and I listened carefully to their conversation. I was eager for any information that would bring me a step closer to a world I knew existed but didn't know how to enter.

In my drive to Bob's condo, my imagination ran wild, drumming up a vivid fantasy. *Maybe one of the men will be especially attractive. I'll flirt then secretly signal to leave the party together.* But like most of my fantasies, I didn't take that one too seriously. Meeting a man while in Seattle had definitely been on my mind, but it seemed unlikely to happen at Bob's.

I found the condo building and took the elevator to the penthouse where the door was already half open.

"Hello? Bob?"

"In here!" I recognized his splendid voice.

Happy chatter and the mouthwatering smell of roast lamb directed me down the hall to the living/dining room, which featured a wall of large windows overlooking Lake Union. Bob introduced me to his friends, all male and seated around a lovely teak table. He then poured me a scotch that burned my throat and calmed my nerves.

The evening consisted of more scotch, wine with the delicious dinner, and brandy with dessert. Even though I didn't find the men in attendance attractive, I enjoyed the nonstop energy of intellectual conversation laced with gossipy banter. The evening seemed to be drawing to a close when Bob shared a story about meeting an interesting man at "Tugs." I tucked the name Tugs away, wondering if it might be a gay bar. In that moment, I decided to go hunting. I sipped my brandy for a polite amount of time, then swallowed the rest and excused myself, claiming I had an early session in the morning.

Back on the road, buzzed by the booze and horny as hell, I went into action with razor-sharp focus. I located a pair of phone booths with the second one not smelling too much like piss and still having a mostly readable phone book. To my delight, Tugs was listed along with the address on First Avenue. Prepared with my map, I got my bearings and made the easy drive.

Tugs was narrow and dark, small in comparison to Mr. P's. I walked through the bar filled with smoke and men—chatting, drinking, dancing. Based on my D.C. experience, I expected some hot hunk to walk right up and introduce himself. That didn't happen. No one approached the adorable new man, ripe for the picking.

I bought a beer and found a dark corner at the far end of the dance floor where I felt safe. My polo shirt was definitely not the uniform of the tight T-shirt and tank top crowd. My hairstyle and sideburns brutally labeled me, "hick!" I had no muscles like many of these men, and being so short in the crowded room I felt insignificant—invisible.

One bottle drained, I bought another and became more intentional in my hunt for a man to notice me, smile at me, want me. My body started to move fluidly with the music and I felt less like a scared bunny and more like an approachable guy. But not one man I found attractive gave me a glance, everyone engaged with their own little clique.

What's wrong with me? I wondered, feeling out of place and unwelcome.

In a last-ditch effort, I positioned myself up on a step to become more visible. I then methodically checked out every single man, every body, every face, and then . . . there! He was looking my way and smiling. He signaled me over.

His name was Mando, thirty-two years old, friendly and attractive with black wavy hair, big puppy-dog eyes, and light brown skin. Mando engaged me in pleasant conversation while subtly touching my arm, sending chills up my spine. He bought me a beer and asked me to dance. The music and movement set my spirit free, leaving me feeling relaxed and alive. Upon his invitation, I followed Mando in my car to his Capitol Hill apartment and spent the night. He took excellent care of me, knowing I was married and unavailable.

In the morning, he proved to be an attentive host, serving dark roast coffee and fresh croissants as I relaxed at his dinette and glanced around the impeccably decorated apartment. He took an interest in my life and I appreciated having a sweet gay man engage me in conversation. Mando asked about my relationships with my sons and my wife. He wanted to know what led me to marry so young and about my current struggles with sexuality. I spent far more time talking than listening, but Mando didn't seem to mind. He listened with compassion and without judgment. As the noon hour approached, I prepared for my trip home and felt a bit sad saying goodbye to my new friend.

"Call or write anytime. I'd like to hear how you're doing," Mando said as he hugged me, then handed me a slip of paper with his address and telephone number.

Something shifted. I had previously only desired men for brief, sexual encounters. It had never occurred to me I might actually like someone gay and want to hang out with them as a friend. My weekend experiences with Bob, his friends, and Mando awakened me to the possibility I might belong in the gay community—and not just every six months. A new reality began to reveal itself.

As I drove the four hours home, I grappled with my conflicting emotions. I loved my family life but was also drawn to know more about the gay world, a world that remained foreign yet mysteriously compelling. Intuitively, I trusted Mando. Maybe writing to him would help me process my confusion.

The next week, I located a little mail station a few miles from my house and rented a PO box. I wrote Mando a long letter at my office desk after work. The reply I soon received was like a breath of fresh air. Mando was a good counselor. He never pushed or admonished. He simply supported me and posed questions for me to consider.

"I so admire your love for your family, Gary. I can't even imagine your fears around hurting or possibly losing your sons. You say your job could be at risk? Tell me more about that. I don't understand how your personal life has any bearing on your profession."

My correspondence with Mando became a lifeline. I read the letters in my car, then hid them in my briefcase until I could find time and privacy to reply. Later, I disposed of them deep in the dumpster at school.

In early November, I fabricated a reason for a weekend return to Seattle. I told Colleen about a December workshop I wanted to attend, but with no real intention of doing so. Having pre-arranged the scheme with Mando, I knew he was free to host me. The weeks dragged by until it was time to say goodbye to Colleen and the boys. I hated lying to Colleen and felt guilty as hell, but once I drove away, excitement overshadowed my guilt. I was ready to experience my first, full gay weekend.

Mando greeted me with a big smile and an even bigger hug. I settled in while he shared his plans for us, making sure each idea was okay with me. He had purchased tickets for the musical, *Best Little Whorehouse in Texas*, playing at the Opera House. He had made dinner reservations at a restaurant on Broadway and also arranged for me to meet his friends at one point over the weekend. I hadn't previously understood I would be going on actual dates with Mando. Sure, I assumed we'd be hanging out and having sex. I was looking forward to that. But I wasn't sure what to make of all the special attention.

We entered the Opera House dressed in pressed shirts and slacks and made our way to our excellent seats, midway back on the main floor. The musical was delightful, and the dinner later in our private booth, romantic. We topped off the night in Mando's comfortable bed. All evening and well into the night, Mando treated me like royalty. I realized I liked this world of new possibilities.

The next day, he drove me down Broadway and around Capitol Hill, Seattle's historic gay ghetto. Two of his friends sat in the back seat playing a game called "Gay or Straight?" When they saw men walking along they said, "gay" or "straight" or "soooo gay!" then laughed, having a load of fun.

"How can you tell?" I asked.

"Look how he's walking. Could be gay but probably straight."

"See those jeans, how tight they are on his ass. Definitely gay."

"That's a gym body stuffed in a small T-shirt. And that haircut!"

Then, at the corner of Broadway and Pine, we passed a sexy Black man with eye-catching muscles. "Oh, he's gay!" they all said at once.

Stunned, I asked, "Wait a minute! How do you know?"

"Because he's out dancing at the clubs every weekend."

That blew my mind! How could a masculine-appearing, muscular Black man be gay? In retrospect, it seemed preposterous that a relatively intelligent man like me who had already been in two gay bars had not yet realized that gay men came in all shapes and colors. But such was the truth of my ignorance in that moment, and my entire frame of reference regarding gay men once again burst wide open.

As I prepared to depart Seattle early Sunday afternoon, I promised Mando I would write on occasion, but didn't give him any hope beyond that. The idea of a boyfriend or secret lover was not on my radar. I remained a married man who had enjoyed a gay weekend and needed to sort things out.

Back at home, I faced the hard questions: *Can I continue living a double life? Am I gay or bisexual? What about my family? Is my job at risk?* The constant stress of feeling trapped in a desperate situation led to depression, which deepened over the winter. Each evening, once my sons were down for the night, I lay on the living room carpet wearing headphones and listening to sad songs by Jane Olivor and Janis Ian. Something in their lyrics moved me. The sorrow. The lonely desperation.

My gay desires grew so powerful that even an erotic dream came to life. Never before had I experienced such an overwhelming surge of lust. My heart hammered and I struggled for breath as I lay next to a naked man. The breathtaking freedom was beyond my wildest imaginings.

Slowly, I moved my hand onto his stomach.

He didn't move. He didn't say no.

Down a bit more.

Would I feel his erection next? Was he hard like me?

Down more.

Oh my God! He's breathing heavier.

I can't believe I'm going to devour the sexy man beside me.

Here I go. Deep breath. Exhale and . . .

What? No dick? What the fuck?!

Wake up! Wake up!!!

My eyes sprung open and I lay motionless, my heart still pounding as I stared at the ceiling. I was disappointed the man had vanished, then ashamed for feeling disappointed when I realized my hand still rested on my wife's abdomen. I turned my head just enough to study Colleen's sleeping face. When her eyes didn't open, I slowly retracted my hand and regained my breath.

My mind searched for a solution, a way to make everything okay for Colleen, Eric, Ben, and me. But the only way forward pointed to great loss for all of us.

In my desperation, I called Pastor Joe from my office phone the next morning and set up an appointment. Colleen and I had taken membership classes from Pastor Joe and found him to be a progressive thinker and a personable guy. I wanted him to give me hope in a situation that seemed hopeless and possibly some compassionate guidance to help me find my way.

Pastor Joe listened but didn't look me in the eyes once it became clear why I sought his counsel. The meeting was brief and disheartening, with him simply reciting the church's position on homosexuality. I left feeling even more depressed.

From the church parking lot, I could see the entrance to Richland's Mental Health Center. I walked in and asked to speak with someone, then waited a few minutes until a middle-aged gentleman sporting a trim goatee greeted me and escorted me into his nearby office. The counselor was kind and compassionate, very gentle in my fragile state.

"We cannot compartmentalize our lives, Gary, no matter how hard we try," he said. "My recommendation is for you to be true to yourself and consider your mental well-being as you make decisions."

I wasn't entirely sure what he meant, but it seemed as if he had confirmed what I had already decided: living a dishonest, double life had to stop—one way or another.

A week later, as spring and my thirtieth birthday approached, I felt tempted to drive through the park on my way home from work. I resisted, yet perhaps for the first time, I honestly accepted my haunting hunger for a man. Stopped at a red light, I stared in the mirror. Truth demanded to be heard.

"Gary, you're gay," I said out loud in surrender.

Once the words were catapulted into the universe, they became real. My heart broke, knowing the pain I would cause others. But denial had died. I had been living a lie and couldn't continue the charade. Colleen deserved so much better than what I was giving her—better than what I was even capable of giving her.

Unable to make myself drive directly home, I found a bar and drank until dusk. Colleen would be worried.

I parked in front of our house, then forced one heavy foot in front of the other. My wife of ten years stood in the living room, visibly pissed off, holding her purse in one hand, keys in the other. The boys wore their jackets.

"We were just leaving to get hamburgers. Where were you?" she demanded.

"Boys, can you go outside so I can talk with your mom?"

When they were out of earshot, I found my way to the sofa. I needed to sit down and breathe.

"Colleen, I've been needing to talk to you."

"Where were you?" she asked again, still standing, body rigid, face tight.

"Finding the courage to tell you something."

"Are you sick?"

"No."

"Then what?"

After a long pause, I took a deep breath and stepped into the unknown.

"I'm gay."

Her look of disgust stabbed my heart. She threw down her purse and keys.

"I'm so sorry," I managed to say through my tears.

Wading through her own tears, she picked up her purse and keys, then left the house without a word. I was alone. So alone and so frightened, yet somewhere above the fear existed a sense of solace that came with deep honesty. I felt raw but real. Alone but alive.

Little did I know the journey, my new reality, was just the beginning of a long, rocky road to hell and back.

14

After I came out to Colleen, we talked each evening in honest, open conversation, going deeper than we ever had before. Tears flowed in abundance. There was no pretending our marriage would ever be the same. I was a gay man married to a straight woman—willing to stay in the house as long as my wife wanted me there. In the meantime, we agreed to tell no one, not even our parents or best friends.

The following week, I packed my bags and flew to Anaheim, California, for the annual principals' convention, a trip that had been planned for months. The time apart would give Colleen and me an opportunity to reflect and begin to process our thoughts.

I checked into my hotel, then attended just enough of the convention to know I couldn't do it. Given the stress of my life circumstances, I wasn't equipped to sit through presentations and take notes. Instead, I escaped Anaheim to sample life as an "out" gay man. The freedom was exhilarating. The weight of living a double life had been lifted.

Following travel tips I'd received from Mando, I headed to West Hollywood in my rental car to go barhopping and adventure-seeking. It didn't take long to locate a moderately busy gay bar and meet Alfredo and Oscar, best friends who offered refreshing entertainment. We danced, talked, drank beer, and had a delightful time laughing. I felt cute, sassy, and full of life, soaking up the men's attention, which fed my ego and fueled my confidence.

"Hey, let's take Gary to Campers," Alfredo suggested to Oscar. "We'll need to leave soon to get there on time."

"What's Campers?" I asked.

"You'll love it!" Oscar said. "It's a floor show. Come with us!"

"It'll be too late for you to drive back to Anaheim after the show," Alfredo said. "But I'll make sure you have a comfortable place to sleep." An impish smile appeared as he added, "With me."

After only a slight hesitation, I agreed. "Okay! Let's go!" I left my car parked in Hollywood and the three of us hopped into Alfredo's tiny car. I intended to get drunk and appreciated having a designated driver.

When we entered the packed bar, I was amazed by the huge dance floor and adjoining performance stage. Oscar and Alfredo insisted we dance our way to the middle of the floor, drinks in hand. Just before the show, the music would stop, and everyone would sit where they were dancing to get the best view of the stage.

Sure enough, it happened just as they said. The music soon stopped, and the lights blared.

"We're mehhhllltiiing!" men squealed as they sank to the floor, concealing their eyes from the bright lights.

Campers was the comic relief I needed—hilarious, flamboyant, and irreverent. I doubled over with laughter, wiping away healing tears as Oscar and Alfredo looked at me in amusement. The troupe delighted me with their creative expressions of the gay experience. I was right where I belonged, at home with my people, my tribe.

After the show, we went to an all-night diner in West Hollywood full of drag queens and drunk men getting a bite to eat. Our glowering waiter, in character as an over-the-top "pissy queen," stared down at me, eyebrows raised and tapping his pencil on the order pad.

"Are the mashed potatoes real?" I asked.

The tapping stopped. "Honey, this is Hollywood. Nothing's real."

I laughed like an intoxicated country bumpkin who had never heard the old gag, and caught a split-second grin telling me the waiter was pleased. I ordered the hot turkey sandwich, complete with instant potatoes and fake gravy.

After our late-night meal, we drove a short distance to the modest studio apartment the men shared. Oscar's single bed was on one side of the room, while Alfredo and I slept in a single bed against the opposite wall—a cozy situation.

I found myself with a very affectionate and gentle lover, but as usual, after the sex, anxiety set in—wondering about my life, worrying about my family, and feeling very lost in West Hollywood.

The next day, I slept off my hangover in my Anaheim hotel room. Then, still following Mando's travel advice, planned an evening at another gay bar, Forced Heat, in nearby Long Beach. Although I'd been told fairy tales weren't real, there'd be no convincing me of that after my experiences that night.

By early evening, the bar had the R&B music pumping while a diverse, friendly crowd of men socialized. Given my attraction to men of color, my heart beat a little faster when I noticed two sexy guys dancing together but clearly checking me out. Their warm eyes triggered my desire.

I bought a drink and let the music have its way with me. Standing near the dance floor, I watched bodies sensually slither and grind, blending so erotically it became hypnotic.

The lighting was low with a small disco ball and strobes enhancing the scene. Even though I was alone, I didn't feel alone. Instead, I felt loose and happy, my energy harmonious with the room. A man asked me to dance, and I let myself go, relishing the natural flow of my body and shedding years of stress and worry.

After thanking my partner, I used the restroom and smiled at myself in the mirror.

"You're gay, Gary, and you're having fun!"

Maybe it was a tipsy smile, but it was real—an expression of authentic freedom never before experienced. I didn't let myself feel guilty or worry about Colleen and the boys. Instead, I decided to simply relax into the moment.

The dancing continued with one man after another. I tried to reflect their moves, dancing close if they came up to me, enjoying their maleness and muscles. Tired and sweaty, I sat down to rest when a strobe shined its light on a most attractive man just entering the bar. He was medium height and build, with nicely groomed, soft-curly hair and milk-chocolate skin. He wore a pastel blue, mock turtleneck sweater, jeans, and tennis shoes. I was drawn.

I watched him cross the room and noticed how he smiled at people, then presented himself in a pleasant manner to the bartender. Everything about him seemed perfect. I was enchanted, as if Prince Charming had appeared at the ball.

Since I sat in a dark area of the club, he hadn't noticed my lasers on him. But feeling confident from all the attention I'd been receiving, I walked up as he lit a cigarette.

"How can you dance with me if you're going to smoke that cigarette?" I sassed.

He looked up. Our eyes caught.

"I could always put it out," he said, flashing a mouth full of big, white, straight teeth.

"Good idea," I flirted.

We danced well together.

Leaning in, I smelled his delicious cologne. "My name's Gary."

"I'm Phil," he said with a sweet smile and seductive eyes.

We danced several songs, progressively moving more sensually, bodies close enough for soft touching. My hand found his shoulder while his hand rested gently on my hip. Something magical was happening. I became powerless in his presence, already enthralled by romantic feelings straight out of a Disney movie.

We took a break and enjoyed a drink together while he captivated me with effortless conversation and humor. Had we known each other for twenty minutes or twenty years? We talked, laughed, caressed, and kissed.

We left the bar holding hands, which felt like the most wonderful and natural thing in the world.

"Oh, isn't that sweet?" wisecracked a dude hanging with his buddies outside the straight bar next door. "Men holding hands."

I heard his comment and considered it, but it held little power until I suddenly wondered if we were unsafe.

"I don't think they like us holding hands," I said to Phil.

"Don't pay those fools any mind," he calmly replied, squeezing my hand a little tighter.

It was a liberating experience, helping me begin to change how I viewed myself and my sexual orientation. What once felt shameful suddenly felt absolutely right.

Phil lived close, so I followed him in my car to his apartment.

"Sorry for the mess. I just went out for a drink. I had no intention of bringing anyone home tonight," he said as he quickly picked up socks and slippers, then cleared the sofa of newspapers, giving me a place to sit.

I learned he was thirty-four and a mail carrier in Long Beach. Originally from Chicago, he grew up poor, raised by his beloved mother, who'd split from his father when Phil was six.

Phil had been a married Jehovah's Witness minister before gay rumors led to his excommunication. He ran away from the drama in Chicago and found refuge in southern California to begin life anew. He shared openly, then listened as I told my own story. Having both been married and restricted in our abilities to live freely, there was an immediate camaraderie, a connection that ran deep.

When we were too tired to talk anymore, we went to his bed and made love. It wasn't just sex. We made tender love. I had never been kissed or caressed in such an intimate way. I realized God's presence as I fell asleep in Phil's arms and wondered if I'd met my soul mate.

The next morning, it took me a few seconds to remember where I was, but then I saw the man sleeping next to me and smiled. I examined his full lips, the cleft in his chin, and the little freckle on the side of his nose. There was such a gentleness about him. Maybe he was a gift to keep me safe and help me become more sane. For some reason, it didn't concern me that he lived in southern California and I lived a thousand miles to the north. I simply believed a charming Black knight had rescued me.

A kiss on his cheek led to a sleepy "good morning," a big hug, and morning sex—overwhelming, uninhibited, and passionate. I felt like I was already falling in love with a man I didn't really know. The thrill was so great, the feelings so intense, I didn't care about anything except that moment with him.

It was Sunday and I had to fly out in a few hours. Saying goodbye to Phil was difficult, but we promised to call regularly, write every day if we could, and make plans to see each other again as soon as possible.

I had a lot to think about on my flight from LAX to Pasco's little airport. When I disembarked and walked across the tarmac, I was surprised to see Colleen, Eric, and Ben waiting for me. It was heartwarming to hug them hello, yet Colleen later told me it was then she knew she had lost me. The transition would be painful for everyone involved.

15

I fell in love, long-distance, and became absolutely obsessed with Phil. Throughout the day, he came to mind constantly. In the evenings, I wrote him long letters, then drove to the mail station to retrieve his letters to me. Once a week, I called him from a phone booth, a stack of quarters standing nearby.

Phil was smart, funny, and sensitive. Most importantly, he supported me emotionally, so I didn't feel alone during a very painful time. He encouraged me to move to Long Beach, but I couldn't walk away from my sons and a much-needed salary. If he wanted us to be together, he would have to move to the Tri-Cities.

I started to feel relatively content in my new, unusual lifestyle. I enjoyed the security of living with my family while doing my best to focus on work. Colleen and I continued to talk at length, now less often through tears.

When she asked about my letter-writing, I told her about Phil while reassuring her I had no plans to move away. I unrealistically began to think we could manage our living situation indefinitely. But one morning two weeks later, while I was dressing for work, she walked into the bedroom crying.

"Will you please leave? I can't do this."

She fell into my arms, and I held her while we cried together. Our marriage had gasped its final breath, flipping our lives upside down. We were still so young, just thirty years old. I told her we would talk more when I got home, and I'd figure out how to honor her request.

That day I struggled. I had to make immediate personal decisions while remaining functional at work. Somehow, I kept myself together and became too busy to dwell on life outside the school.

As I drove home after work, I decided to pack a few things and head to my parents' house until I could make other arrangements. What I dreaded most was leaving Eric and Ben. Ben was only three, but six-year-old Eric knew enough about separated and divorced parents for this to be a traumatic event. Colleen agreed to be present when I talked to the boys. She understood the importance of them seeing their parents as reasonably okay and not angry with them or each other. Sad and sorry, yes, but not angry.

The boys were playing together in Eric's bedroom, building structures with wooden blocks.

"Hey, boys, come sit up here on the bed with me," I said as Colleen stood nearby. "I need to talk with you about something important."

When they were settled, I continued.

"First of all, you know how much your mom and I love you. We always will. Nothing could ever change that. And your mom and I still love each other, too, but not in a way that makes it okay for us to live in the same house. This is not your fault. We're sorry this is happening, but I'll be moving out."

A single teardrop, the biggest I'd ever seen, fell from Eric's eye. My heart shattered.

"I'll come see you every day and tuck you into bed at night," I said, wiping his tear away and pulling both boys close. No words could make saying goodbye easier. I was crushed and felt dead inside. Leaving my sons, whom I adored and loved unconditionally, was the most painful experience of my entire life.

I don't know how I managed not to fall on the floor in pain. But for their sake, I stayed strong and encouraging. Finally, I pulled away and kissed them, then grabbed my suitcase and said, "I'll see you tomorrow."

I hugged Colleen as we shared our hundredth cry, then I fought through more tears on my drive, recalling our years of joy as a family. No regrets resided in my heart outside of the pain I had caused, which, of course, was considerable. My sons were joyous miracles—loving, healthy, and fun. Smart, cute kids who told stories, appropriately challenged boundaries, and made me laugh on a regular basis. But by moving out, how neglected might they feel? How many of Eric's questions would I never get to answer? How many of Ben's silly antics would I never get to enjoy?

When I walked into my parents' house with my suitcase, I discovered Mom was in Spokane visiting family. But Dad was home, already half-drunk with his bottle of bourbon sitting in front of him on the kitchen table. I grabbed a glass with ice, sat down across from him, and poured myself a good pull.

"We need to talk," I said.

Stalling for time, I held up my glass. "You like this stuff, don't you?" I said gently.

He looked me straight in the eye and said, "I love it," as if it were the love of his life.

I nodded, acknowledging his truth, then took a deep breath and said, "Colleen and I are separating. Is it okay if I move back in for a while?"

He looked at me with such concern and bewilderment it made me ache inside. My family adored Colleen. They had no reason to think we were anything but happy.

Dad wanted to know what was going on. Was it just an argument? Could we work it out? I explained I had discovered something about myself, making it impossible for us to stay married.

"You know, Dad, how growing up I loved to dance, and you worried I acted too much like a girl?"

He seemed to be thinking hard. "Well, I remember you being creative, but I never thought about you acting like a girl."

"Dad, you made me quit ballet because you were worried about that. At least that's what Mom said." He still looked confused, and clearly quite intoxicated.

"Anyway, did you ever worry I might grow up to be queer?"

"Actually, I worried about that for all you kids, not just you," he said, suddenly wide-eyed.

After a moment to let his admission sink in, I said, "Well, Dad, I'm sorry to tell you this but your fear has become a reality."

He sat in silence with his head tilted and his eyebrows furrowed.

"Dad, I'm a fucking queer," I said as I started to cry.

He looked down and nodded his head. It seemed clear he didn't know what to say and I wasn't in the mood to sit there and watch him suffer.

"Well, I'm going to my room," I said calmly. "I need to get my head together before I go crazy."

Soon, I heard him on the telephone talking to Mom. "Gary and Colleen have split up. He's moving in and you should probably come home."

"Dad told you what's going on?" I asked Mom the next morning as we sipped our coffee at the kitchen table.

"Well, he said you and Colleen separated, but he seemed confused about the details."

I shared a summary of my internal struggles and my relatively recent revelations. She started to cry but made no sound.

"Why are you crying?" I asked, taking her tiny hand.

"I'm thinking how alone you must have felt, going through this for such a long time."

What an amazing display of compassion. My mom wasn't upset about me being gay. Her tears were for my personal suffering. I asked her if she or Dad had concerns about my sexuality while I was growing up.

"Well, I remember when you were very young, maybe three. You came running into the kitchen with your dad right behind you. You grabbed my leg for dear life, sobbing, and your dad said something about 'making a man out of you.' I told him to leave you alone. I wouldn't let him drag you back outside where he and his friends were cleaning trout and drinking beer."

At that moment, something rose from deep in my psyche, like a fuzzy memory coming into focus. I put my head on the table and cried. I'd always believed my dad wanted to change me but hadn't realized how young I was when it had started. It hurt like hell to hear Mom's little story, but helped clarify Dad's lack of full acceptance during my childhood. I hadn't been overly sensitive. I had been intuitive, perceptive, and accurate.

16

As promised, I spent time with my sons every day. I played with them, read stories at bedtime, kissed them goodnight, and told them I loved them, always saying, "I'll see you tomorrow"—a promise that did as much good for me as it did for them. I created a simple children's book to delicately explain that while most men grow up to love women, some men grow up to discover they love men. It was a book I read with them over the years to help them better understand.

Colleen started to relax a bit more, and after two months of tears and talk, we became friends again.

"How are things going with Phil?" she asked, as we lounged on lawn chairs in my parents' front yard. The weather had cooperated for the family's Memorial Day barbecue and the smell of freshly mowed lawn still lingered in the air.

"Good. He's working with his supervisor to transfer from the Long Beach post office to the Tri-Cities. It looks like he can move up next month."

"That was fast."

"I know, but he's a good guy. It'll be fine, I hope."

In truth, Phil and I hadn't had enough time to fully know each other, but I knew I wanted him in my life and in my bed. Our communications had been primarily through letter-writing and telephone conversations, although I did manage a romantic weekend trip to Long Beach in early May.

"I went on a date," Colleen admitted with a little smile.

"You did? Great! How was it and where'd you meet him?"

"Well, Darlene insisted on taking me out for a girls' night. We went to the Red Lion and ended up dancing and having a great time. I met him there. Plus, she set me up with a blind date next week. I'm actually having some fun."

Although I was happy for Colleen, I imagined for the first time—and with significant discomfort—one of these strangers becoming a stepfather to my sons. My mind raced, searching for images of available men I knew and trusted. I came up empty. Everyone was already married or had moved away. Then, an unexpected thought surfaced with surprising weight.

"Have you ever thought about dating Dave?"

Dave, my younger brother by four years, had grown into a very kind and responsible twenty-six-year-old man.

"You wouldn't mind?" Colleen replied, eyes growing big.

Amused by her enthusiasm, I grinned and said, "Wait here. I'll be right back."

I walked around the house to the backyard where the kids played, my mom and sisters prepared the tables, and Dad grilled burgers, beer in hand.

Since my coming out, Dad and I hadn't spoken. I sensed his disapproval and perhaps he sensed my lack of respect for him. In any case, we stayed cordial but left the heavy stuff for a later date.

I saw Dave sitting by himself in the backyard and pulled up a chair.

"Hey, Dave, are you dating anyone?"

He looked surprised by my sudden interest in his love life. "Nope, nothing happening right now."

"Have you ever thought about dating Colleen?" I asked.

"You wouldn't mind?" he replied.

His identical response seemed like more than coincidence.

"Come with me," I said with a smile.

Dave followed.

"Have a seat. You two need to talk."

I directed him to the chair next to Colleen and walked away.

They talked, then dated and married fourteen months later. I felt only joy in witnessing their happiness and deep love, which was evident and abundant. I also admit feeling relieved my sons would be well looked after, and I would always feel welcome in their lives, even by their uncle-turned-stepdad. Colleen joked that she'd married Dave to avoid changing the name on the mailbox. While this unconventional arrangement was comfortable to the three of us, we realized other people would have varying reactions. Nevertheless, we learned over time to let those reactions be about them, not us. Everyone who mattered to Dave and Colleen—their families and closest friends—witnessed their happiness and embraced their marriage.

17

As we had hoped, Phil's postal service transfer was approved, freeing him to move to the Tri-Cities in late June. We rented a modern apartment only a five-minute walk from where Colleen and my sons lived. My brother, Dave, soon joined their household, too.

To my surprise, Colleen asked to meet Phil. She showed up on her own and after introductions, the three of us sat around the kitchen table.

"So what do you think of the Tri-Cities so far?" Colleen asked.

"Well, it's small but very friendly. I really didn't know I'd be living in the desert, though. Isn't Washington supposed to be the Evergreen State?" Phil said with a chuckle.

"Well, half of the state anyway," Colleen laughed. "Has Gary shown you around, like down to the river and the mall?"

"Oh, yes, I've had the grand tour," he smiled. "But, Colleen, I want to thank you for coming here to meet me. That means a lot."

"I was curious, I have to admit. I knew you had to be special for Gary to want you to move here."

"He's only said wonderful things about you, Colleen, so I'm glad we had this chance to meet."

My heart swelled with love for them both.

Every day that summer, I walked over to see the boys or Dave walked them to my apartment. The first time I saw Ben holding Dave's hand as they walked to meet me midway, my heart sank. I felt replaced but grateful that Dave had stepped up to help care for Eric and Ben in my absence. It was all working out quite well—that is, until gossip spewed its toxic venom.

In September, the gay rumors were started by a former classmate named Karen—a slim blond who turned many men's heads and worked as a teachers' assistant. After learning of my separation from Colleen, Karen began sidling up to me even more than before, coming into my office to lend what I believed to be a caring ear and inviting me to join her for coffee. I thought I had someone in my corner, someone who truly cared about me.

During one conversation, Karen shared her own marriage struggles. "I'm not the kind of woman to get divorced, but I *am* the kind to have an affair with the right man."

Oh my God, she's coming on to me.

Colleen had been right about Karen, telling me she didn't trust her. Looking back as far as seventh grade, Karen had flirted with me. But she flirted with all the boys, so I never gave it much thought.

To get out of the awkward situation, I gently, and foolishly, explained to Karen why I would not be having an affair with her—I had met someone special and he had moved from California to be with me.

"That's great!" she said. "You seem happy and that makes me happy for you."

"Thanks, but you know this has to remain confidential. It would cause big problems if it got out."

"Oh, I know! I'm very concerned about that. This is such a conservative town." Karen seemed to understand. What she didn't understand, apparently, was the definition of "confidential."

It only took a week for Colleen's dad, Bill, who worked for Westinghouse twenty miles outside of town, to be quizzed by a coworker about me being gay. The coworker was the husband of a close friend of Karen's. Bill, of course, hadn't the vaguest notion what the man was talking about but later asked his wife, Dolores, who didn't know anything, either. Dolores, unsure of what to do, decided to call Darlene, Colleen's cousin and best friend. Darlene was also in the dark but said she would call Colleen.

Later that evening when I visited the boys, Colleen half-laughed and half-snarled, "You would think you could be a little more discreet! How embarrassing!"

The blood drained from my face. The secret had been leaked and I couldn't pull it back.

I immediately called Colleen's parents.

"Hi, Dolores, would it be okay if I came over to talk with you and Bill?"

"Sure, Gary. I think that's a good idea."

I showed up on their doorstep with a box of tissue for our talk at the kitchen table. They were compassionate and understanding, not at all judgmental, but naturally concerned for the welfare of their daughter and grandsons. Our mutual pledge to always support one another for the benefit of the kids made me love them more than I already did.

Over the decades, I remained close to Bill and Dolores. Bill passed away in the nineties, but Dolores, as of this writing, is ninety-five years young and has been like my second mother. We have video chatted weekly to discuss everything from the weather to family to world events, and the aches and pains of aging. Dolores is a treasure and I have been blessed to call her a friend since my youth.

In the weeks after speaking with Colleen's parents, the rumor mill gained momentum. The principal at Karen's daughter's school on the other side of town called to tell me that Karen had confided in him, claiming she wanted to "build support for me."

My sweet PTA president, who happened to be married to a Mormon deacon, came into my office unannounced and closed the door. She warned me to be careful. The Mormon leadership had heard the rumors.

A smiling second-grader reported as he passed me in the hall, "Mr. Tubbs, we prayed for you in church yesterday."

I started smoking cigarettes, feeling constantly on edge.

In mid-October, my beloved secretary, Betty, leaned into my office. "Mr. Tubbs, the superintendent is on line one." Betty had been my trusted confidante since day one as a new principal. She knew something was happening behind the scenes but didn't ask questions.

I sat back in my executive chair, totally forgetting about the teacher evaluation I was writing.

"Okay, Betty. Thanks." We shared a look of concern as she closed the door.

I steadied myself with a deep breath and a silent prayer for courage before pushing the button on the phone.

"Good morning, Dr. Evans."

"Good morning, Gary. Would you be able to meet with me after school today, say 4 p.m.?"

"Yes, I can do that."

"Okay, well, I'll see you then."

Dr. Marv Evans, the new superintendent, was a handsome forty-something. He fit right in with the "good ol' boys" of Richland, and although he seemed friendly as he yucked-it-up with the other administrators, there existed, for me, an uncomfortable edge about him.

I arrived early for the meeting and was asked to wait in the reception area by the thin-lipped, old secretary who always seemed in a bad mood. Today, however, she spoke gently—like a prison warden waiting with an inmate just before announcing, "Dead man walking."

"Mr. Tubbs, Dr. Evans will see you now."

I entered the large office to see him sitting behind his huge desk on the far side of the room. He didn't stand to greet me. I walked the distance and held out my hand, which he shook without eye contact.

"Please have a seat," he said, directing me to an upholstered chair at least six feet away from his desk. Power over intimacy.

"Gary, I need to let you know I'm hearing rumors about you. Do you know anything about this?"

"I've heard a couple things."

"Well, just this morning, several men from the Mormon church visited me. They wanted to know if the rumor about you being gay is true. I called some of the other principals. They know you're going through a divorce and one of them thinks you hold your cigarette a little funny, but other than that, they're as baffled as I am."

Having had a few hours to prepare for my meeting with the superintendent, I fell into my rehearsed script. "Is there something about my job performance at issue here?"

"Not at all. I've heard only positive things about your performance. But what about this gay rumor?"

"Well, I have friends who are gay and I respect their right to privacy. So, can you help me understand why you need to know whether a rumor is true or not?"

"Well, if it's not true, I want to support you through this problem."

Deep breath. "And if it's true?"

He leaned over his desk and finally looked me dead in the eyes. His face morphed into a diabolical lizard as he spat, "I want you out!"

I exhaled the breath I didn't realize I was holding. A weird grin formed on my face and I mentally scrambled to grasp the nightmarish moment. Like a stunned sparrow after crashing into a window, I shook my head, attempting to fend off the blunt force trauma.

"I need to think about this," I heard myself say through a smothering fog.

The superintendent's face softened and his voice sounded almost kind. "Of course. Take some time and let me know what you want to do."

Somehow I managed to walk out of his office, despite legs of putty, to exit the building and find my car.

18

I discussed the situation with Colleen and suggested we call her Uncle Bob in Seattle for legal advice. She panicked.

"If you fight this, the newspaper will run a story. Everyone will be in our business. What if someone says something to the boys at school?"

I agreed to lay low. We could see how painfully unprepared we were to handle the intensity of the unfolding events.

Three days later, on Friday morning, I phoned the superintendent to inform him I would resign for personal reasons in exchange for a fair severance package. I was hoping he also wanted to avoid controversy and media attention. My meetings later that day with the personnel director and business manager resulted in a mutual agreement of full pay and benefits for six months.

In an empty school over the weekend, I cleaned out my office and loaded my pickup truck with personal items, then engaged in the tearful affair of composing farewell letters to the staff and students' families. I left my keys on the desk and walked out the doors of Jason Lee Elementary School, never to return.

I had no idea how to find my way forward. As a man motivated by acceptance and adoration from others, I became plagued by a resurgence of deep-rooted childhood messages of feeling unacceptable, further reinforced by the vicious rejection, "I want you out!" How could I begin to wrap my head around being an outcast and a member of one of the most despised and persecuted minorities in history?

Shrouded in depression, I attempted to feel more alive by masking my pain with cigarettes, alcohol, and sex with my lover.

I clung to Phil as my rescuer, desperate and afraid I would die of aloneness should I lose him, too.

Over the next couple months, Phil and I managed to make a few friends in the small Tri-Cities gay community—heavy drinkers mostly, big partiers. It resembled fun, but I couldn't be fully present. Socializing served little purpose other than to temporarily numb me. Life, as I knew it, had crumbled. Out of my house, out of a job, and at risk of being publicly shamed as an out gay man.

"Let's get out of here," I said to Phil as the holidays approached.

"What do you mean?"

"Let's move to Seattle. The city has a law making it illegal to discriminate against gay people," I said. "We can start over." I was grasping at a fuzzy image of the future.

"Why not Long Beach?" Phil asked. "The county has the same protections. Plus, the weather's better and I can get my old job back while you look for work."

"That makes sense, but it's so far from my kids."

"My friends Mona and Joan can put us up until we get our own place," Phil said. Then he added with a laugh, "and these Washington bourbon prices are killing me!"

The discussion continued over the next week, and like the pressure to get married before I was ready, I agreed to Long Beach from a place of fear and weakness—worried I'd be left alone if I didn't agree with Phil.

Shortly after Christmas, we packed our belongings in a rental truck with Dave and Colleen's help. Seven-year-old Eric and four-year-old Ben pitched in as they could, giving me multiple opportunities to hug them throughout the morning. Mom had warned Dad he would lose his son if he didn't change his attitude, so when I asked him to help me hitch my car behind the truck, he volunteered without hesitation. Colleen's parents and my mom and siblings all dropped by for a pizza lunch, followed by an exchange of hugs in a very sad farewell.

"I miss you already," I told my sons with a final, tearful squeeze.

Phil and I arrived in Huntington Beach to live temporarily with Joan and Mona, a lesbian couple a few years older than me. Although sweet and generous, the school-bus drivers were also loud and foul-mouthed. I soon learned they were Phil's drinking buddies, having met each other years before when Phil also drove a school bus.

Dear Joan was clearly an alcoholic and delightful Mona wasn't far behind. I started drinking more to fit in. They encouraged me to join them on the weekends for canned peaches topped with cheap champagne before breakfast, beer midday around the pool, and cocktails every night before, during, and after dinner. Phil seemed content with the arrangements, which included sleeping on their living room hide-a-bed, but I insisted we find our own place as soon as possible. Within the next week or two, we'd rented a lovely oceanfront apartment in Belmont Shores, Long Beach. The reasonable rent was too good to be true.

I applied for jobs in all the surrounding school districts. Fortunately, Long Beach hired me as an elementary math specialist, working with small groups of students. The inner-city school was located only fifteen minutes from our apartment, and after purchasing a little red motor scooter, I enjoyed my commute in the California sunshine.

Phil returned to his mail carrier position and expressed delight at being back in familiar territory. Five days a week, he kissed me when he got home, then poured himself a drink from the half-gallon of bourbon he kept cold in the refrigerator. He relaxed his tired body on the sofa to read the newspaper while he smoked and drank. When Sundays rolled around, he scoured the ads looking for sales on menthol cigarettes and bourbon.

We created our routines and fell into a relaxed rhythm, nesting and enjoying each other's company. But I began noticing that Phil lacked interest in doing things in public. He didn't want to go out to dinner because he worried about the cleanliness of the food, and going to a movie or shopping was a hard sell. The only thing we could agree on was dancing at the gay bar near us. Phil avoided restaurants, but after a night of drinking he didn't hesitate to order greasy fast food at the drive-up window, reminding me once again how little I knew about this man for whom I'd abandoned my kids. I found things I enjoyed doing on my own, like yoga classes and going to the beach adjacent to our apartment building. One cloudless day while I worked on my tan, three young men laid their blanket relatively near me and stripped down to their Speedos. Until that very moment, I hadn't realized how lonesome I'd become with Phil and his drinking buddies as my only friends. I found one of the men attractive—and he was looking my way. He reminded me of a teen magazine model with his fit, bronzed body, blond hair, and Hollywood-handsome face. I smiled and nodded my hello but then felt suddenly uncomfortable, concerned about being flirtatious. I resisted giving him any more eye contact and instead walked out to play in the gentle surf that rolled up the Long Beach shore.

As I returned to my towel, however, I sensed eyes on me and glanced to see the young man waving me over.

"Hey, come sit with us a minute!" he shouted.

We introduced ourselves followed by small talk. "Do you live in Long Beach?" "Oh! Where did you move from?"

I mentioned my boyfriend in my responses, and although my relationship status seemed to register, it didn't stop my young pursuer from complimenting my blue eyes.

I began to feel guilty when I noticed a fluttering of desire.

"Well, it's been nice meeting you, but I need to get dinner started. My boyfriend will be home soon." Perhaps I sounded like a housewife from a fifties sitcom, but it gave me a clean getaway.

I told Phil about my day and the boys on the beach, but I wasn't fully honest. I skirted around my feelings of attraction and desire.

"Be careful," he warned. "I doubt they were just being friendly, and boys like that could have all sorts of STDs. You never know."

Phil's judgmental comments confused me. Did he want to protect me or admonish me?

"I don't see anything wrong with making new friends," I replied. "Even if they were attracted to me, so what? It takes two to have sex and besides, I told them I have a partner."

He chuckled. "They don't care if you have a partner. You don't know what guys are like around here. You're so innocent. I should take you to some bathhouses and backrooms so you're not so trusting of these characters."

On one level, Phil was correct. I was ignorant about gay culture and gay social dynamics. In an effort to educate me, he arranged for us to visit the seedy side of gay life. We drove to West Hollywood and rented a tiny, terrible room in a shabby, foul-smelling gay hotel. Porn movies played nonstop on the TV monitors in each room. Old, out-of-shape men walked the halls wearing only a towel, sniffing out fresh (or not-so-fresh) meat. I hated the place and had no desire to leave our room. We drank the bourbon we had brought and watched porn. Phil introduced me to "poppers," chemical drugs technically known as alkyl nitrites. When I inhaled the fumes from the solvent in the tiny brown jar, I experienced an instantaneous rush, relaxing my muscles and accentuating all tactile sensations. Poppers stunk and gave me a headache, but there could be no denying the surreal eroticism I experienced during our sexual romp in that disgusting hotel. After a short rest, Phil announced it was time to visit a bathhouse.

We entered a nondescript door off a side street and stood in a small security area where an unpleasant combination of smells struck me: cigarettes, bleach, poppers, and musty carpet. We paid the entrance fee and each received a single white towel.

The man behind the desk pressed a button to unlock the adjacent door and I entered my first bathhouse. Walking down the halls on our way to the locker room, I saw at least a hundred men of every shape, age, and color, all wearing only tiny white towels. Phil and I stripped and stored our clothes, then took a tour of the various rooms where I got an eyeful of men fondling each other in a workout room, playing in the showers, sucking cock in an orgy room, and rubbing bodies in a dark maze.

As we walked down one dimly lit hall, I noticed a small room with the door open and the light on. A naked man lay flat on his stomach with his head away from the door and his feet quite near the entrance, legs slightly apart. His finely toned body struck me—golden-brown, oiled and shiny, moderately long and athletic. I couldn't see his face but the rest of him was gorgeous.

"What's he doing?" I whispered to Phil.

"Advertising. He has the door open to invite people in to fuck him."

My heart pounded in my chest, the dragon within heated up. "You mean we could just walk in there and say, 'Hi, I want to fuck you?'"

"Basically," Phil said.

My feet stuck to the floor, and not just because of the cum-soaked carpet. I couldn't catch my breath and my mouth hung open like an ogling fool. I wanted to touch him. I wanted to run my fingers along the length of his body, down his butt crack, and feel between his sexy thighs as he writhed and lifted himself up, spreading his legs and clearing the way for my adventurous, hungry hands . . .

"What are you doing?" Phil whispered as he stared at me in my lascivious stupor.

Shaking the fantasy from my head, I said, "Nothing. Let's go."

My bathhouse experience was fascinating and disturbing, titillating and dark. But I'd seen enough. My conflicting feelings of love for Phil but lust for others had thrown me off balance. I wanted to retreat to the safety of my own bed with the one man I knew and trusted.

However, the long day and the booze had gotten the best of Phil. He directed me to the movie room at the far end of the bathhouse so he could rest. The large room was packed with dozens of men sitting on built-in benches or lying on the carpeted floor watching an old movie. I didn't get it. How could anyone lay their bare skin on that nasty carpet? What was the attraction here? It all seemed so sad and lonely.

Making sure my towel covered me, I sat on the carpet next to Phil in about the only space available. I pretended to watch the movie so as to appear disinterested in the others around me. Phil lay back and closed his eyes. Within minutes his breathing slowed, followed by a soft snore.

My eyes began to wander, only to be distracted by the activity not three feet away. Two men lay next to each other. One had slid down the other's body to open the towel and perform fellatio. After everything I'd seen in the past hour it was no big deal. However, the blower noticed me watching, gave me a dirty look, and changed the angle of performance to block my view. I chuckled in silence, thinking: *Here you are in a public room with dozens of others, you're sucking off some guy, and you want to get pissy with me because I'm watching you do it? This place is fucking crazy!*

Eventually, I leaned back on my elbows, then forgetting about the carpet, cuddled up to my drunk boyfriend until he woke up and took me out of that hellhole.

"So, what did you think of the bathhouse?" Phil asked the next day when we were comfortable in our own home.

"Well, it was interesting but once was enough for me. How about you?"

"I used to enjoy going but not anymore. I just wanted you to see what's happening out there so you're careful."

"Phil, I don't understand. What do you mean, 'careful'? Do you think I want to have sex with other men or what?"

"Well, you're just coming out. You haven't had a lot of sex so at some point you might get tired of an old fuddy-duddy like me."

Walking over to give him a reassuring hug, I said, smiling, "Well, I'm very happy with my old fuddy-duddy. So can we just enjoy being together and not worry about stuff like that?"

After only four months in our Belmont Shores apartment, we received notice that the building would soon be converted into condominiums. Phil admitted the manager had mentioned that possibility when she'd offered him the unit at such a low rate. He had kept that information to himself, not wanting to worry me.

As fate would have it, however, an affordable apartment became available just four doors down from Mona and Joan. At first, I spoke out against it, not wanting to live so near Phil's drink-ing buddies. But the apartment had a second bedroom for when Eric and Ben would be visiting in July and a swimming pool in the common courtyard. We made the move, and as I suspected, Phil found his way to Joan and Mona's almost every evening.

Instead of worrying about Phil, I kept my attention on teach-ing school and preparing for my sons' visit. With only a teacher's salary and the California cost of living, plus my monthly child support payment, I decided to seek a second job for a few months to build up my savings. But when I looked through the paper's Help Wanted column, I saw nothing promising. Discouraged, I set down the paper only to "hear" a quiet inner-voice: *The job is there. You missed it.*

All my life I'd felt guided by an invisible hand, but never be-fore had I been so certain of an inner message. I grabbed a pen and carefully read down the column again, ad by ad, crossing out each one only after seriously considering it. Finally, there it was! Part-time cashier, Deli/Wine Shop, evenings and weekends, lo-cated less than a mile from our apartment. I applied within the hour, interviewed that same day, and started work a few evenings later. Twenty hours each week helped me save enough money for airline tickets and an eventful summer with my boys.

The time with Eric and Ben that July was a blessing. With the pool only four steps from our front door, the beach a short drive away, and all of Orange and L.A. counties at our disposal, we ex-perienced many adventures together. But the best part for me was reading bedtime stories, kissing them goodnight, and seeing their smiling faces for breakfast each morning.

When the month came to an end, my mom and sister Nancy pulled up in my parents' motorhome. Two days later, my sons loaded into the motorhome to join the women for the long trip back to Washington. Watching them drive away, the pain in my heart became unbearable. I retreated to my bed to cry and sleep, physically and emotionally drained.

19

On the heels of my sons leaving, three party friends from the Tri-Cities arrived in Long Beach to visit Phil and me. Connie, a muscular construction worker, and Mary, her smaller, more feminine partner, were two of the funniest people I'd ever known. The tall, boisterous Larry, who later became one of my very best friends, joined them. I found myself in a much better headspace than the year before, so having them visit was a treat. We swam, grilled food, and simply enjoyed one another's company.

When they asked us to take them out to the clubs in Hollywood an hour away, I agreed to be the designated driver. We loaded up in a van Phil had recently purchased, bringing with us an ice chest of alcoholic beverages and snacks for the road.

Once in Hollywood, we barhopped, danced, and ate late-night food at a greasy-spoon cafe. It was fun except for watching my boyfriend repeatedly stagger to the bar for yet another drink. I'd seen Phil intoxicated before, but never the sloppy drunk I witnessed that night. Flashbacks of my father's drunkenness came to mind, accompanied by feelings of embarrassment and disgust.

The drive back to Long Beach was difficult for me. I was exhausted while the rest of the rowdy group partied in the back of the van. All of a sudden, I heard someone yell, "Stop! Stop the car!"

I quickly pulled over onto the shoulder of the freeway. As soon as the van stopped, Connie slid open the side door. "I gotta pee!" she screamed to the world as she leapt out and dropped her drawers to squat. Having a hearty laugh helped me relax for the remainder of the drive.

When we finally got home, the passengers unloaded and walked up the courtyard sidewalk while I collected the ice chest, empty cups, and other items left in the van. I caught up with the group and noticed Phil had stumbled and fallen into a large bush. Without a word, I kept walking.

"Gary, Phil fell in the bush," Connie said, laughing.

"Yeah, well, just leave him there," I grumbled as I entered the apartment and busied myself with turning on lights and putting things away in the kitchen. The others soon staggered in with Phil, dirty from his fall, twigs and leaves stuck on his clothes and in his hair. Grinning with squinty eyes, he swayed his way to the freezer, removed a carton of vanilla ice cream, and started eating it with his fingers.

"For God's sake, Phil, use a spoon!" I snapped.

Semi-conscious and wearing a Joker-like smile, he slapped me across the face with his messy, ice-cream hand.

Connie and Mary, standing nearby, sucked in their air with audible gasps then stood frozen in shock. Before I could even think, rage rose and I slapped him back. Hard.

"Goddamn you! Don't you slap me!" I yelled.

The women ran for the guest room, dragging a drunk Larry with them. The apartment became deathly silent.

"You sleep on the couch! Do not come in the bedroom," I hissed at Phil as I made my way down the hall to take a shower, trying to breathe through my anger and settle my emotions before a futile attempt at sleep.

That night was the beginning of the end of our relationship. Phil and I tried to patch things up as best we could, but he showed no interest in curbing his drinking. I had awoken to the realization that I loved a man who reflected my father—a charming, handsome alcoholic. I felt trapped with no way out—yet. That would take planning, and time to save money.

Meanwhile, I poured all my energy into my new teaching assignment. The previous spring, the principal had offered me a third-grade classroom and I'd accepted. The ethnic makeup of my

TAMING THE DRAGON · 127

student roster was half Mexican-American, one-fourth Asian-American, and one-fourth Black. Most of the kids came from poverty in gang-riddled central Long Beach. A few had never been to the beach only a mile away. One darling boy, Miguel, stared at me with a serious and fascinated expression. "Mr. Tubbs, you have blue eyes!"

I loved my students and enjoyed the challenging assignment of being their teacher. However, I arrived in a fog, came alive during the day, only to reenter the fog on my thirty-minute commute home: depression.

Phil was a good person. But the disease of alcoholism poisons everyone in its circle, making life unbearable for so many. My relationship with Phil continued to go downhill and I started to fantasize about meeting other men in an effort to numb my pain and soothe my sadness. Yes, I desired sex outside my relationship, but what I really wanted was attention and excitement.

In late September, I informed Phil I wanted to go out dancing on my own. In our two years together, I'd often taken myself to the beach or a movie, but I'd never gone to a bar without him. There was no discussion and, frankly, I didn't care what he thought. I had become passive-aggressive, acting out my hostility by avoiding honest communication.

"Be careful," Phil said.

Based on previous conversations, I interpreted his warning as "Be careful of STDs." In my repressed state of anger toward Phil I gave no response and felt only annoyance that he should make such a comment.

Once I escaped my stressful home life, however, I felt vibrant heading to the Sunday "tea dance" in Long Beach, where the music started in the afternoon for people who worked the next day. There were very few men in the bar when I arrived and that was just fine with me. I greeted the bartender with a smile, bought a beer, and found my way to freedom via the dance floor, dancing only with myself. The bar began to fill up and I soon had fun meeting people, getting tipsy, and being flirtatious.

An attractive man dressed in tight, bubble-butt-fitting jeans and a loose, white cotton shirt worked his fit little body on the dance floor. Feeling sassy, I strutted over and started dancing near him, then with him. His name was Luis and as one dance led to another, the eye contact and sexy dancing heated up the minimal space between us. I not only noticed my horniness but my hungriness as well.

"Have you had dinner?" I asked.

"Not yet," he replied, "I'm starving. Wanna go get some food?"

"Yes!" I exclaimed. I mean, going to a real restaurant with a sexy man? You bet!

Luis offered to drive. Being from Long Beach, he knew a place serving gourmet burgers. He had a boyfriend at home, but they had an agreement, which meant he could have sex outside his relationship once in a while.

"However, I don't have sex the first time I meet someone. I just want you to know that up front," he warned me.

"That's okay," I lied, attempting to hide my disappointment. "I'm wanting friends more than sex." After I said it, I wondered if it might be true.

Luis was even more attractive in the bright lights of the restaurant and a delightful dinner date. I turned on the charm as I became ravenous for a delectable Latin dessert.

"Any chance you're willing to break your no-sex rule?" I asked as he drove me back to my car.

He smiled but shook his head. "Nope. If you want to call me, I'll give you my number, but since you're just pissed off at your boyfriend, I'm not expecting you to call."

Wise man. He dropped me off. I drove home. I never called. Truth was, I didn't want friends in California. Friends anchor you to a place. I didn't want to be anchored. I wanted out.

20

By late December, my relationship remained in tatters. I boarded a flight to Seattle, intent on spending a weekend with Larry, who had relocated to Seattle, before traveling on to the Tri-Cities for Christmas with my family. Phil knew I'd been contemplating a permanent move to Seattle at the end of my teaching contract if our relationship didn't improve. I couldn't see myself living with an alcoholic, a diagnosis he didn't yet acknowledge.

Larry met me at the airport, then drove us directly to the Capitol Hill area where the decorations and holiday music on Broadway created a wonderful, festive atmosphere. The weather, unusually cold for Seattle, made a hot, spiced cider at the Elite Tavern a delightful treat. We then relaxed at Larry's apartment until it was time to head to Neighbors—a large gay dance bar.

We arrived early enough to play pool and drink beer before the crowd arrived. I breathed in the relief of being away from Long Beach and the tensions of my unhealthy relationship. I had forgotten the joy of feeling so alive, especially after Larry and I made our way to the dance floor.

Several hours later, I noticed a short, athletic-looking, young Black man with smooth skin and closely cut hair moving uninhibitedly to the music. He oozed with entertaining energy and I asked him to dance. He tossed me an endearing smile and said, "Sure, I'll dance with you!"

We moved in our own styles, flirted while we danced, and introduced ourselves. I found James pleasant-looking, although not exactly handsome. There was a charm, an exuberance for life that he expressed through his personality. His eyes—bedroom eyes—seemed only half-open, but when he flirted or laughed, they widened and sparkled.

At twenty-two, James was ten years younger than me. He introduced me to his friends and I introduced Larry. It was a friendly group, everyone in the mood to simply have fun. Sure, we were drinking, but we spent far more time on the dance floor—a stark difference from my Long Beach life. I had a blast!

At one point in the evening as James and I faced each other talking, I leaned in and gave him a little peck on the lips. I don't know why; I hadn't planned it. It just happened spontaneously, surprising us both.

"You taste good," I said, enjoying his full, pillow lips.

"Lip balm!" he said with a silly laugh as he pulled out a little, round white jar with a primary yellow lid. "I'm addicted to it."

While I enjoyed James' company and would have liked spending more time with him, my final destination was the Tri-Cities to be with my sons and other family. Five months apart had been five months too long.

Touching down in Pasco, Washington, during icy conditions proved to be unnerving but once reunited with my sons, I felt balanced and whole again. Christmas morning greeted us with incredibly cold weather and blustery winds. Fortunately, the roads remained safe. So, after opening presents, Colleen, Dave, Eric, Ben, and I made a tour around the three towns, visiting grandparents and cousins.

"Merry Christmas!" we shouted as we entered each house to the warmth of loved ones and the tempting smells of ham, turkey, dinner rolls, and pumpkin pies. Of course, the boys ran lickety-split to the Christmas tree knowing other presents awaited them. The grandpas played cheery Santas as they helped Eric and Ben locate their gifts. The day helped remind me how blessed I was to be part of such a remarkable extended family.

Once my holiday time was over, I headed back to Long Beach and to a relationship in bad shape. A gloomy Phil met me at the airport for our quiet drive from LAX to Huntington Beach.

"I think I need to move closer to my family, Phil," I finally said.

He nodded while saying nothing, eyes on the road.

Although sadness occupied our lives, things were calm. Phil remained witty and kind, compassionate and caring. In so many ways, I still loved him while hating the disease of alcoholism.

In early April, Colleen called on a weeknight. Generally, I called the boys on the weekend, always before their bedtimes. But Colleen's call came later, raising immediate concern. She had discovered a lump on her breast. A biopsy had been scheduled. I couldn't breathe and became afraid I might pass out but stayed encouraging while on the phone. It was a short conversation with not much to say except "I love you." She would call back with the test results.

When I hung up the phone, I fell into Phil's arms and cried—afraid for Colleen, sorry for Dave, and concerned about the boys. To be a thousand miles away during a time of crisis was hard. Damn hard.

Colleen called back a few days later.

Malignant.

Cancer.

"Gary, can you fly up and join me and Dave when we meet with the doctor next week? We talked about it and we hope you can."

"Of course I'll fly up," I replied, not thinking about work or money or anything but getting up north as soon as possible. I booked my ticket using my credit card, made arrangements with my principal, and flew to Washington.

In my confused and frightened state of mind, I packed a dark-blue suit as if I'd be attending a funeral instead of a doctor's appointment. In later years, I would experience the realities of cancer diagnoses with other friends and loved ones, but at thirty-two, Colleen's diagnosis was my first. It caught me ignorant and terrified that she could die within days.

Fortunately, I also packed appropriate clothes for our meeting with the doctor, which took place in a typical, small examination room. Dave and Colleen sat in the two available plastic bucket-chairs. I stood.

When the doctor entered, Colleen got right to the point. "How long do I have to live?"

He looked in her eyes and said, "We have every reason to believe you have a good number of years and a good chance to be a long-term survivor. There has been encouraging progress in the treatment of breast cancer." He then went step-by-step through the options and procedures—the same talk almost every cancer patient hears: surgery, chemo, radiation, remission, and the chance of the cancer returning at some mysterious point in the future.

When Dave, Colleen, and I left the doctor's office, we were giddy with relief to the point of making inappropriate death jokes. I admitted I brought my funeral suit and we laughed until we cried. Dave and I promised to raise the boys together and Colleen reminded us she wasn't dead yet. We demonstrated our resilience as a family and our willingness to band together in crisis.

As I made my way back to Long Beach, I had ample time to think. I knew I would be moving to Seattle in June. I didn't hesitate to tell Phil.

"I understand, Gary. Your family must come first."

There was no talk of him joining me.

James, the young man I had met in Seattle over the Christmas holiday, called me out of the blue to see how I was doing. He knew I'd been struggling in my relationship. He also knew I'd been considering a move to Seattle. James proved to be quite a natural conversationalist, asking questions that gave me the impression he cared about me. It was refreshing to have someone take such a personal interest in my life.

"Yeah, I've decided I'm definitely moving to Seattle in June," I informed him.

"Great! When you get here, let's hang out."

"Sounds good. Hey, James? You remember my friend, Larry? Yeah, well, he's moved out of the city and I really don't have a place to stay. I could get a hotel room, but you wouldn't happen to know someone with a sofa I can sleep on for a few days, do ya? Just until I can rent an apartment."

I knew James still lived with family members and putting me up was not an option.

"I can try. Let me talk to my friends and see what I can come up with."

James and I communicated a time or two after that. He did, in fact, arrange for me to stay with his best friend, Lane. I looked forward to meeting Lane and spending more time with James when I arrived in Seattle. I noticed I was developing a little crush on James, given his kindness and attention. Although my relationship with Phil had not yet ended, I was already finding false security in fantasizing about sex with James.

In late June, with my car packed, my motorbike strapped to the front bumper, and a small U-Haul in tow, I drove away from a sad Phil. I cried for a moment but didn't look back. My cigarettes went in the trash and I didn't light up again until I was unhappy in the next relationship.

During my first two years in Seattle, Phil visited me twice. He limited his drinking to only a few beers and expressed subtle interest in reconciliation. I enjoyed spending time with him but knew enough about alcoholism not to trust the "beer only" plan. In fact, when I would travel to southern California several years later, a sober Phil would tell me his story of hitting bottom.

He had become progressively more ill and refused to acknowledge his alcoholism until he drank himself into a stupor, passed out, and missed an entire day. He woke up on his sofa and dragged himself to the kitchen to fix his coffee and smoke a cigarette. When he saw the blinking light on his answering machine, he pushed the button to retrieve the message. His supervisor at the post office wondered why he hadn't reported to work. Phil flipped on the TV to the cable listings and discovered a full twenty-four hours were nowhere in his memory. It scared him shitless. With the support of his supervisor and friends, he checked himself into rehab followed by active participation in the twelve-step program of Alcoholics Anonymous. It saved his life.

21

Thirty-two, unemployed, and single for the first time in my adult life, I used the long drive from California to Washington as an opportunity to shed the stress of past events and focus on a brighter future. However, midway along the I-5 corridor—a long, monotonous stretch of flatlands and sleepy truck-stop towns—an unsettling loneliness crept in to dim my optimism. I called James from a pay phone when I stopped for gas. His upbeat energy relaxed me. I felt less alone, knowing I had a friend waiting for me in Seattle.

I'd saved nearly two thousand dollars, hoping that would be enough to get me settled, but assumed a summer job would also be required. Applying for fall teaching positions had to wait until I could interview in-person, and even then, my first paycheck would be delayed until October first.

Of course, I would have loved a principal's position, but I had to accept that might not happen right away. A part of me also feared I was not yet emotionally ready for that role. The trauma of my forced resignation still prevailed in my psyche.

After unloading my belongings into a storage unit in Seattle, I made a quick trip to Kennewick to hug my family. I returned to Seattle the next day, called James, and arranged to meet him at Lane's Capitol Hill apartment. Lane had not yet returned home from work when I arrived.

"Give me a hug!" James said. "It's so great to see you!"

I accepted his warm hug that lingered long enough to arouse us both.

"Mmm . . . you feel good," James cooed.

"Oh, my!" I said, laughing. "I guess I'm happy to see you, too." James giggled. "Let's sit on the sofa and catch up."

He asked about my trip and how I had been since leaving Phil. I told him I was anxious to get settled and needed to find work as soon as possible. Spending even those few minutes with James helped me feel more comfortable and very welcome in Seattle.

It was a pleasure meeting Lane when he arrived home, an equally kind and funny guy. Lane trusted me with a key to his apartment so I could go hunting for my own apartment the very next morning.

I'd heard it said that there's no place on earth more beautiful than Seattle on a sunny day, and my short walk up to Broadway that morning proved those words to be true. I inhaled the life-renewing air and counted my blessings, reassuring myself every-thing would be fine—a teaching job would be offered and an ideal apartment would be found.

The apartment I imagined would feel warm and cozy and have two bedrooms, a decent kitchen and bathroom, natural light, and be within my budget. Desirables would be a laundry, ground-level entrance, and perhaps a little garden or grassy area where my kids, now eight and five years old, could play.

As I casually made my way through the dense residential neighborhood of tree-lined streets with massive blue-and-pink hydrangeas in bloom, I searched for "Apartment Available" signs. I saw one in the window of a three-story, motel-style building, probably built for the 1962 World's Fair. I loved my memories of the World's Fair but detested that style of apartment building.

The next sign was in the window of a second-floor corner apartment of an old, classic brick building. It probably had great charm but I didn't want to enter into a common lobby and walk upstairs to my apartment. It just didn't feel like me and it wasn't the apartment I envisioned.

Then, walking down Boylston Avenue, I passed a red sign, "2 Bedroom Apartment for Rent," and a phone number. The sign was taped to one of three garage doors, built under the single-story, brick apartment building. Without hesitation, I climbed the eight stone steps welcoming me up to a small, grassy yard surrounded by flower gardens. The connected apartments were turned sideways and ran away from the street, each having its own porch edged with a black, wrought-iron railing.

The drapes of the middle apartment were drawn open, so I pressed my face up to the large picture window. A tingly feeling resonated through me and a loud "yes!" echoed in my head. My whole body rejoiced when I saw the hardwood floors of my ideal apartment. I had learned to trust such strong reactions, as if the right gear of a mechanism had locked into place with a solid clunk—all systems aligned to propel me forward with assurance.

Suddenly, I began worrying someone else was already calling the landlord. I rushed back to the street, memorized the phone number, and kept repeating it for the short walk back to Lane's place. I made the call. No answer. *Shit.* I found a pen and wrote down the number, fretting and trying to think of what else I could do. I called again. Still no answer. Then it dawned on me: *Take the fucking sign off the garage door!*

I negotiated with my conscience. *Okay, here's the plan. I'll try calling one more time. If there's no answer, I'll grab the sign, run back here, and keep calling until I got an answer. Then, I'll replace the sign before the landlord arrives to show me the apartment.*

Convinced it was a good plan, I made the call. Still, no answer. I ran to get the sign, but there was a car in the driveway that wasn't there before. My heart skipped a beat. Someone had arrived before me. I ran up the steps and saw a little, middle-aged woman in a beige business suit and no-nonsense loafers unlocking the door to the vacant apartment.

"Hello!" I blurted out. "Is the apartment still available?"

Lifting her chin and turning my way, she replied with a stony expression. "It is. I'm expecting someone, but they haven't arrived yet. Do you have any kids or dogs?"

"No dogs," I replied. "I have two sons but they'll only visit once in a while. They live with their mom in eastern Washington. May I see the apartment?"

"Okay, come in, as long as you understand I must consider the other people first."

"Yes, I understand."

Everything about the apartment was exactly as I had imagined. Nothing fancy. Small, but perfect.

"How much is the rent?" I asked, praying I could afford it.

"Three-fifty a month, first and last plus deposit up front," she replied tersely.

"Perfect!" I said, giving her my best smile. "This is just perfect for me. I love it! Is there a laundry?"

"Yes, out the back door and down the stairs to the basement. There's a washer and dryer," she replied, still in a clipped, businesslike tone. "Will you live here alone?"

"Yes, except when my sons visit. But if I were to get a roommate later on, would that be a problem?"

"No problem, but they would have to fill out an application form, too."

"Sure, of course," I said, continuing to walk around and take a closer look. Although a tour of the entire apartment took less than two minutes, I extended my visit by opening cabinets, peering out the back door, and simply refusing to leave the premises while thinking of other ways to schmooze this tough old bird.

"I love to garden if you need help with the outside . . ."

"I hire it done. I know how I want it, so I ask tenants not to plant anything without my permission."

"That makes sense. It's very tidy and pleasant. Not many places have an actual yard right out the front door."

Perhaps I was laying it on thick, but I was also being honest. I loved the small front yard and well-kept garden.

She cocked her head and grinned, then invited me to join her outside as we walked around the yard. She told me which flowers bloomed when and how she planned it so there would be color and fragrance almost all year. The more she talked about the garden, the more her demeanor softened.

Looking at her watch, she said with a scowl, "Maybe they're not coming."

My face perked up with hope and opportunity. "Then I think I should write you a check so you can go home and enjoy your evening."

She actually laughed out loud. "Well, first you need to fill out the paperwork and I need to make sure everything is okay. Where do you work?"

Oh, fuck! I hadn't thought about employment as a requirement for renting a place on my own. Her scowl returned as if she was trying to read my startled face.

I quickly recovered. "I'm a schoolteacher and school administrator. I just moved up from California where I was teaching. I'm sure I'll be hired here. There's always a need for special education teachers. Plus, I'll be looking for summer temp work starting tomorrow."

She tilted her head and looked at me through squinty eyes. After a moment's thought, she said, "I'm sure it will work out."

"Great! Thank you!"

As she walked to her car to get the tenant application, I heard her grumbling, "Why are so many Californians moving up here?"

I smiled to myself. I would explain my roots later. But right then I only wanted to breathe deeply and look to the heavens in gratitude. My ideal apartment had manifested.

That evening, my new landlord called to approve my application and gave me permission to move in the very next day. With the sparsest of furnishings, I settled in, satisfied and content. For last-minute essentials, including something to sleep on, I visited a nearby discount store on Broadway. Two blue, cloth-covered, thick foam chairs that sat low to the floor were on sale. When I discovered they unfolded to serve as a sleeping mattress, I happily lugged them home.

James visited or called daily. Our time together remained light-hearted and fun but also became more affectionate. What began as hugging and some kissing soon led to more. We found our-selves compatible both socially and sexually. James turned out to be an entertaining host, introducing me to his many friends and inviting me to join them for movies and nights out at the bars.

The hefty check I wrote to my landlord left my savings lacking the funds to make it through the summer. I needed to hustle up some work. But before I could spend time looking for a summer job, I had to submit applications for teaching and administrative positions for the fall. With careful planning and efficiency, I dropped off the required paperwork at the personnel offices of seven local school districts. I knew it might be weeks before I heard back, giving me time to seek temp work and call Colleen's Uncle Bob.

It had been three years since the lamb dinner at Bob's condo on Lake Union. While still in Long Beach, I had written him a humor-laced but serious coming-out letter and informed him of my upcoming move to Seattle. When I called Bob, he invited me to visit his law office at the close of the workday that Friday.

The dour, poorly groomed receptionist with the name plaque "Charlotte" directed me to the office at the end of the hall where Bob and I had a delightful chat. He then introduced me to his colleagues and staff who were all gay: the cute young attorney, Tarl, the sexy office manager, Tony, and Bob's handsome law partner, Dean. With the five of us crowded in Bob's cluttered of-fice to enjoy a nip of Scotch, they asked me about my coming-out experiences and told me how much they had enjoyed reading my letter to Bob. The fact that Bob had shared my letter surprised me, but I gathered his staff must be like a gay family and sharing juicy news was commonplace.

"But Bob, when Gary came to your condo for dinner, weren't you even the slightest bit curious about him then?" Tony asked.

"No!" Bob laughed. "He's my nephew. I thought he just came for a visit."

"Bob doesn't tune in to things like that," Dean offered. "He's a gay man with absolutely zero gaydar!"

The others laughed and nodded in agreement.

"Oh, Bob," Tony said. "I forgot to tell you. Charlotte will be late on Monday . . . again."

Bob looked disgusted and the others each had something negative to say about the receptionist. I told them about my experience just a few minutes earlier. Suddenly, an idea popped into my head.

"Why don't you fire her and hire me for the summer?" I suggested with a smile, only half-serious.

The room got quiet. They looked at each other. Tony broke the silence.

"Sounds like a plan, Bob. Just give me the word and I'll take care of it," Tony said, winking at me.

Bob chuckled and said, "Let us confer and I'll have Tony call you one way or the other. Make sure he has your phone number."

I said goodbye to everyone, except the receptionist, and left the law offices, feeling like divine intervention may have once again blessed me with a serendipitous opportunity.

Sure enough, later that evening Tony called and invited me to report to work on Monday. I was loving Seattle!

Being the receptionist at the law offices kept me busy but never stressed. I spent my day setting appointments, making copies, welcoming clients, and serving coffee. During my second week, I returned home to see the red light blinking on my answering machine. Kent School District had called, inviting me to interview for a principal's position. I'd heard Kent was a conservative district, raising my concerns. Still, I decided to interview.

A few days later, I sat before an interview panel of six people. A burly man leaned forward in his seat and glared at me with a sneer on his face. His odd and aggressive opening question caught me off guard.

"Mr. Tubbs, how do you handle stress and emotional issues?"

I'd been trained to begin interviews with a friendly question to help candidates relax. "If you want the best interview, you want the candidate to settle in and feel safe," my professor had instructed.

But this man's question, body language, and tone seemed hostile. I froze, feeling exposed. Voices whispered in my head: *He knows! Gay. Unacceptable!* I fumbled through my response. The rest of the interview went much better, but I knew I wouldn't be offered the job.

The next week I interviewed for a third-grade teaching position in the Highline District south of Seattle. The principal—a hip-looking, middle-aged man with his shirt collar open and a gold chain around his neck—welcomed me with a long, warm handshake and a big smile. His constant eye contact made me uneasy.

A few minutes later, two teachers joined us for the interview—which I found delightful. The four of us soon fell into a comfortable conversation about kids, curriculum, and instruction. With the interview wrapped up, the teachers departed and the principal toured me through his school.

"I'm very impressed!" the principal effused. "Let's talk more at lunch if you're free to join me?"

"Sure, I can do that. Thank you," I replied, even though somewhat uncomfortable with the invitation.

He drove us to a pleasant Mexican restaurant about ten minutes from the school where he surprised me by ordering a beer and encouraging me to do the same. I agreed. Our business lunch soon became something else. I began to suspect the married principal with the jewelry, open shirt, and carefully coiffed hair was hitting on me.

"Did you spend any time at the Seafair festivities last week?" he asked.

"I did. My friends and I went to a house party for the Blue Angels' show."

"Well, it sure was a sensational weekend. I have to admit all the bare skin can make a man horny," he said with a laugh.

I looked at the food on my plate with a tight smile and a quiet chuckle.

"And I'm sure a handsome guy like you has no trouble finding some fun," he continued.

I avoided engaging in the unprofessional dialogue and felt relieved when lunch was over and he dropped me at my car. I didn't want to work for this man, but I needed a contract.

The next morning at the law offices, I answered the phone to be greeted by the perky voice of the principal. "Good morning, Gary. How are you doing today?"

"Fine, thank you," I responded, fully expecting to be offered the teaching position.

"Hey, are you free tonight? My wife's out of town and I thought maybe you'd like to catch a movie?"

Are you fucking kidding me? I became sick to my stomach. My blood ran hot but I hoped my icy response would turn his horny balls blue.

"I'm busy tonight. And I'm busy tomorrow night, too. Goodbye."

Strike two on the job search.

Dejected and disappointed, I replayed my interviews in Kent and Highline. *What's going on here?* Suddenly, I intuitively knew or at least suspected someone in Richland had shared the rumors about me during reference checks. Panic surged.

I called Jerry Lane, my friend and mentor.

"I think someone's talking, Jerry. I resigned for personal reasons and any mention of my private life based on rumors or even facts is inappropriate. Have you received any calls?"

Jerry assured me he had not and if he did in the future, he would never say anything to hurt my chances for employment. I believed him.

I then called Dr. Vandenberg, the personnel director.

"Al, someone's talking and you need to make it clear to everyone my personal life is not to be discussed. You know this is unprofessional. You also know it could be a lawsuit."

"I'm sorry to hear that, Gary. I've not had any such conversations. But I'll remind everyone at the next administrators' meeting that the law requires us to address only your professional performance. I'll make sure they stick to that."

I attempted to regain a positive frame of mind, wanting to trust things would work out even while fearing the discrimination deck had been stacked against me.

22

In mid-July, after I'd been in Seattle for less than a month, James suggested we become roommates. He owned a bed he could set up in the second bedroom.

"When your sons visit, they can have the bedroom and I'll sleep on the sofa," James said, trying to sell the idea. "Or with you," he added with a smile.

I considered the roommate idea from all angles.

Sure, it would be wonderful to pay less, especially with the job hunt not going well. And, yes, it would be great having the companionship of a friend with sexual benefits. But it also seemed potentially messy if James had romantic feelings for me. I wanted the freedom to date other men and worried our becoming roommates might jeopardize that freedom. In the end, I agreed to share the apartment, even with my reservations.

My sons visited a few times that summer. Colleen had recovered from her mastectomy, but sometimes, while she endured the horrible side effects from the radiation treatments, Eric and Ben stayed with me. That gave Dave a quieter house to tend to Colleen and a prime opportunity for me to take Eric and Ben around Seattle as well as to Vancouver, B.C., for the 1984 World's Fair.

In between my sons' visits, James introduced me to the Body Nautilus Gym, aka "Body-Naughty-Us"—a less respectful name for the predominantly gay gym. He taught me the correct way to lift weights and operate the machines. I enjoyed spending time with James but also looked forward to being left on my own while he fulfilled a three-week obligation in Joplin, Missouri. James had been hired to choreograph the flag corps of the high school's marching band. His amateur career as the lead rifle in two major drum and bugle corps had blossomed into professional teaching opportunities.

"Before I leave, Gary," James began, then hesitated before continuing, "I'm wondering if we can call ourselves boyfriends."

I was taken aback. First, he had convinced me we should become roommates and then, only a month later he wanted us to be boyfriends! True, we'd been sharing my recently purchased waterbed almost every night, but his proposal scared me. It was too much, too soon.

"I'm flattered, James. I like you, but I'm not ready for a boyfriend. I need the freedom to be single and date other guys."

Even though I felt sorry for James and uncomfortable being so direct and honest with him, I also felt proud of myself for standing my ground.

"I know," he whispered. "I was just hoping."

"Sorry."

"No, I understand. You should date and have some fun even though I wouldn't advise getting too deep into that scene. There are a lot of creeps out there. Besides, you won't find anyone better than me, so don't take too long!" he said, laughing.

While James taught color guard in Missouri and my sons were home in the Tri-Cities, I went out dancing with Lane and met an intelligent, articulate, muscular dude named Dana. It was fun but short-lived. After Dana and a lonely week sleeping in an otherwise empty apartment, I started pining away for James.

I committed to twenty-one consecutive days of weight training, eating lean, and drinking protein shakes. I wondered if it would make a noticeable difference and wanted to surprise James when he returned home.

My intention in doing so was unclear. Why did I want to impress a guy who already seemed smitten with me when, in truth, I remained unsure about him? Was I just lonely or afraid of living by myself? I felt rather lost as I drifted in the unfamiliar waters of single living.

Then, while working out one day, my new gym buddy, Don, noticed me gawking at the man on the bench press next to us—a biracial, Black-Asian man. He had a fit body and a handsome, almost pretty face. His brown hair, more straight than curly, had been cropped short on the sides and back but remained four or five inches long on top. He brushed the length straight up in a most unique style that would have looked silly on most people. On him it looked exotic. I couldn't take my eyes off him.

I'm sure he noticed me drooling but didn't reciprocate in any way. For some reason, his apparent lack of interest didn't deter me. The guy was simply too incredible to let escape without a good, old-fashioned try.

When he left the workout area to hit the showers, Don, always one with a flippant comment, remarked, "That guy stinks," referring to the fact he clearly wasn't wearing deodorant.

"No problem," I responded. "I'll scrub him down before I get started!" We laughed. Talking shit was half the fun of working out.

I didn't follow Mr. Exotic into the locker room or hunt him down in the showers or sauna, which I had learned to be the standard predatory practice at the gym. Instead, I continued my workout routine while also keeping an eye on the locker room exit.

When I saw him walk out in street clothes, looking hot and handsome, I went for him. He saw me coming but kept walking and exited the glass doors of the gym. I wondered if chasing him into the street would be required, but when I exited the glass doors myself, I discovered he had stopped to write something on a strip of neon-green paper in his small leather notebook. I waited for him to look up so I could introduce myself, not wanting to interrupt him while he wrote. To my surprise, he handed me the paper. It read, "Eugene," followed by a phone number. I smiled and looked up to see him smiling, too.

"I'm Gary," I said, totally charmed and already infatuated with this spectacular man.

"I guess that makes me Eugene," he said, laughing softly. We shook hands.

"And I will be calling!" I said with a nod.

"We'll see," he responded as we parted ways.

I called Eugene later that afternoon and invited him to dinner. As it turned out, he lived less than a block away from my apartment in that sixties motel-style apartment building I disliked.

We enjoyed a meal and a bottle of red wine at the Poor Italian restaurant in Seattle's downtown. The food tasted wonderful, the wine delicious, but the conversation . . . well . . . challenging. Eugene answered my questions and talked about his career as a model and now a modeling scout and agent. He told great stories about his work in Europe, New York, and Seattle, but an edge of arrogance seeped in, coupled with an occasional condescending tone.

After what seemed like an hour of Eugene-focused conversation, he finally asked me a few questions about my life. I already felt on guard, given his haughtiness, so as I shared, I also wondered if he was judging me or disinterested.

We finished the wine and returned to our common neighborhood.

"Would you like to come to my place for coffee or tea?" I asked, expecting him to decline the invitation and head home.

"Tea would be nice," he said.

Shocked, I led the way to my apartment where he sat on one of the cheap, blue foam chairs and looked at a magazine while I puttered in the kitchen.

"Or would you rather have a beer?" I asked, grabbing one for myself. This man made me nervous. I'd allowed his personality to shake my confidence and spin me into some kind of uncomfortable, low-level anxiety. But having his striking presence in my apartment left me feeling even more disoriented. I'd run out of conversation starters and the idea of initiating anything physical seemed too risky. I could just imagine his scoffing tone as he asked, "What do you think you're doing?"

He took me up on the beer offer, so I carried them into the living room and sat on the other foam chair. I had the chairs pushed together to give the impression of a short sofa—a very "Goodwill" look. As we drank our beers, he seemed to relax. He stretched out his legs, kicked off his shoes, and talked humorously about the photos in the magazine. Yes, it was all fashion-related, but I found it interesting. My impressions of Eugene shifted again as I listened with my heart instead of my ego.

I knew I was being unduly affected by his energy, but I seemed unable to stop it. When he displayed arrogance, I felt intimidated. When he relaxed, I became confident again. With him stretched out and his shoes off, I could suddenly sense the goodness in the guy. He seemed insecure for someone so stunning. In some ways, he also seemed angry and broken. My desire to rescue him blossomed. A loving, caring man like me might be just what he needed to feel better about his life.

He noticed I wasn't talking, just staring at him with a little grin on my face. "What?" he asked with an uncomfortable smile. "Why are you looking at me like that?"

"I like looking at you," I replied. "You're interesting and a very good-looking man."

He looked down, appearing remarkably innocent and vulnerable. Then he looked up. "You're pretty cute, too."

"Really?" I asked.

"Do you find that so hard to believe?"

"I just had no idea you thought that," I responded.

He chuckled in his soft, deep-throated way. "Do you think I give my phone number to everyone who looks at me?"

That hadn't occurred to me, but I'd heard enough. I leaned over and kissed him. He kissed me back. I wrapped my arms around him and did my best to gently lay him down on those ridiculous chairs. He didn't resist. He actually felt like warm putty as I ran my hands over him. We soon took it to the bedroom and my summer fling with Eugene began.

I saw Eugene only a few times over the next two weeks. As he left my apartment one evening, however, he came face-to-face with James returning home from his Missouri trip. James knew I'd been dating but didn't know I was dating a man named Eugene. And what I didn't know was that James and Eugene had attended the same high school. Furthermore, they didn't like each other—not one little bit.

"What are *you* doing here?" James asked in a rather shrill, bitchy tone.

Eugene looked at him with indignation, chuckled sardonically, then mimicked, "What are *you* doing here?"

James put his hand to his chest, struck an overly dramatic pose and said, "I live here!"

Eugene scowled as he walked away muttering, "Well, you don't have to be such a faggot about it."

James was aghast, I was confused, and Eugene was upset.

Pissed off at James, I let him have it as soon as we were both inside.

"Obviously, you living here is not going to work. I told you I was dating. You encouraged me to get out there. And now you act like this! What's the matter with you?"

James tried to play it off with a laugh.

"But I didn't know you were dating *him*!"

"It's none of your business who I'm dating," I said. "And if you're going to act like you own me, then you need to move out."

Still shrugging off the whole scene as funny, James responded, "Go ahead and date! Get it out of your system. But why do you have to date an asshole like him?"

Calmly I repeated myself, "James, you have a choice to make. Behave yourself no matter who I date or move out."

"Okay, okay . . . date a crazy creep. See if I care. My lips are sealed!"

Infuriated and done with the conversation, I got on the phone and called Eugene. He picked up on the first ring.

"May I come see you?" I asked.

That chuckle again. "Did the wife say it was okay?"

"Very funny," I laughed. "I'll be right down."

We talked about James' behavior. We talked about Eugene's use of the word "faggot"—an extremely derogatory word in the gay community. We talked about my lack of clarity—or perhaps lack of honesty—in the whole mess. When pressed, I admitted I liked James and wanted to see how our relationship might evolve. That was all Eugene needed to hear. My summer fling with Mr. Exotic was over.

Finally, I received a call from Seattle Public Schools, which, in 1984, remained the only district in the state of Washington to explicitly name sexual minorities as a protected group. I longed to work in a city and school district where being gay could not be used against me. I had grown tired of pretending, hiding, and being afraid.

My interview with the Director of Special Education for elementary positions was smooth and easy. He offered me a contract on the spot and told me to report back the following week for my placement. Relieved and grateful, I celebrated by sharing the good news with family and friends.

The next week, I returned to the personnel office and explained why I was there. The face of the staff member morphed from flat into concerned.

"I'm sorry. All of our elementary positions are filled."

After a brief moment of panic, I said, "I have dual certification. I can teach regular ed, too."

She shook her head. "All filled."

I couldn't breathe. I didn't know whether to faint or scream. Thankfully, I chose neither. I took a deep breath and gave her the name of the director who had interviewed me and quoted exactly what he said about being guaranteed a position. Without delay, she made a call, then, after a brief conversation, walked over to the boxes—literally dozens of cardboard boxes—holding hundreds of employee applications. I kept breathing, praying, and watching her with eagle eyes.

Finally, she pulled a folder and brought it to the counter, opened it, and read the documentation from my interview. "Your

folder was misfiled. Are you willing to accept a middle school or
high school position?"

My heart sank. I had no experience at the secondary levels—
none, zero, zilch.

"I have no choice," I said. "I need a job."

She nodded and wrote down three names and numbers. "I'm going to inform these principals you will be calling them tomorrow to
set up a meeting. It's not an interview. It's a meeting. After you've
met with them, call me at this number," she said, handing me her
card. "It's my private line. Just tell me which job you want. I am very
sorry your folder was misplaced. This is the best we can do."

I nodded and thanked her. On numb legs, I zombie-walked to
my car. Secondary special education. Shit.

The next morning, I made the calls. All three principals were
available to meet that afternoon. Two of the teaching jobs were
definitely not to my liking, both working with behaviorally disturbed high school boys. Fortunately, the third position was a
middle school math specialist, similar to my first job in Long
Beach but with older students, ages twelve to fifteen. Mr. Tom
Lord was the principal of Meany Middle School on the back side
of Capitol Hill, very near my apartment. I could ride my motorbike there in about five minutes. I really liked Mr. Lord and later
learned he was considered one of the most respected school leaders in the city.

Although I was anxious about teaching middle school, I
couldn't help but also feel blessed. I had my apartment and my
family much closer. I'd secured a fun summer job and a teaching
position in Seattle. My stars had begun to align.

As the sun dropped low at the end of that glorious summer
day, the temperature remained warm and seductive. I hopped on
my motorbike to putt about Capitol Hill and breathe in my good
fortune. Suddenly, as I traveled up Denny Way where it inter-
sected Olive Way, a rush of overwhelming joy came over me.

"Thank you, God!" I shouted with a smile as broad as my face
would allow. There had been very few moments in my life when
I had felt such bliss. I resided in God and God resided in me.

23

The summer was coming to a close and my new teaching job would start soon. So, with James out of town again, I decided to enjoy a night out on my own as a last hurrah. The thought of possibly meeting a man also had major appeal. I had felt uncomfortable, even guilty, wanting to date others while James was home, worried about hurting his feelings or dealing with possible drama. I seemed stuck in a situation of my own making and kept my dating on the down-low. Perhaps it was self-imposed nonsense, but such were my relationship skills at the time.

For my evening out, I gussied up and went to Neighbors to drink beer and dance. But the crowd was sparse, so I entertained myself by playing pool. Shooting both the solids and stripes guaranteed me a win. After a few games with no one asking to challenge me, I made my way to the dance floor.

From across the big floor, I could see a relatively tall, seemingly fit, dark-skinned Black man in a tight, light-colored, sleeveless T-shirt. His shoulders and arms were impressive even from a distance, but I couldn't tell if he was attractive.

I grabbed my beer and with a casual stride made my way around to the far side of the room where I could catch a better look. Standing two yards to his left, I focused on the dancers, not wanting to be caught checking him out. Then slowly, I cut my eyes to determine what I could see without moving, just tilting my head ever so slightly to catch a little more of his body. Gray canvas shoes, fantastic-fitting 501 Levi's, extraordinary athletic torso—not a bodybuilder, but more like a dancer or sprinter. I felt intimidated and tiny.

Sure, I'd already been with other attractive men, but standing next to this guy shook my confidence. Determined to see his face, I picked up my beer and took a drink. Then turning, as if interested in something behind me, I took a good look. Oh my Lord, the man was flawless. Shaved head, regal profile, chiseled features. Out of my league. Plus, he'd made no attempt to even glance in my direction, only staring straight ahead, expressionless.

Nevertheless, I decided to face my fear of possible rejection. I promised myself I'd ask him to dance when a good song came on, and by good I meant no disco, ABBA, or Copacabana. If he said no, I would survive. I had nothing to lose by asking a gorgeous man to dance.

My God clearly had a sense of humor in that moment, because as soon as I made the promise to myself, I heard the DJ mixing in some Chaka Kahn. I had to dance whether or not the man accepted.

"Excuse me," I said as I lightly touched the most alluring shoulder west of the Mississippi. I waited for eye contact and felt light-headed when his eyes sparkled with charm. "Would you like to dance?"

After a pause, a crooked smile appeared, exposing shiny white teeth that illuminated the otherwise dark club.

"Okay," he said in a deep, sexy-as-fuck voice.

I melted and his previous aloofness seemed to melt away, too, replaced by a softness I found most appealing. We danced. I flirted. He responded. We chatted. We went to my apartment. Even more remarkable naked, Lamott was really quite a sweetheart.

Over the next couple weeks, I learned Lamott was a Stanford grad. He'd been a running back on their football team, then modeled in Milan and had magazines with his photos to prove it. Although a working model in Europe, agencies considered him too dark for mainstream American magazines in the 1980s, so at the ripe young age of twenty-five he focused on work as a personal trainer. Lamott expressed concern that some people in Seattle found him scary with his shaved head, classic African features, and dark skin. I assured him I found him beautiful. He smiled.

I also learned, however, Lamott was not yet out. He was living a double life, hiding his truth from a girlfriend with whom he was sexually active. I explained as we chatted on the phone one morning why that wouldn't be acceptable to me, no matter how much I liked him. Having personally experienced the drama and shame of living a double life, I wanted no part of it. Unfortunately, I went a bit too far with my sass, trying to cover my disappointment with humor.

"This means, of course, you and I will not be having sex again."

Lamott got very quiet, then said, "Just let me pick you up for lunch. We'll discuss it over a glass of wine."

He arrived before I was ready, so I opened the apartment door and hustled back to the bathroom to finish with my hair. Lamott quietly entered the small bathroom and came up behind me while I stood in front of the mirror. He wrapped his yummy arms around me, his hot body pressed against my small torso and his erection crawling up my back. I pushed his arms away, spun around, and flicked his boner with my long rattail comb.

"Ouch!" he screamed, laughing and running out of the room.

"Keep that thing away from me!" I yelled and closed the bathroom door, locking it. "Lord, give me strength," I prayed to the mirror with a big smile on my face.

We walked up to The Deluxe on Broadway and had a tender talk over pasta and wine. He explained why he wasn't ready to come out and I explained why I couldn't be with someone living a double life. I could not be Lamott's secret slice on the side even if he was smart, kind, and sexy as hell.

It was all cool. Sad, of course, but an elegant ending. After hugging goodbye, we went our separate ways. I never saw Lamott again.

After my summer-dating experiences, I felt disheartened. In truth, I must admit, I didn't yet know how to date. I knew how to flirt, dance, drink, chat, and have sex. I didn't have the patience nor the sense of self to take it slow and develop a friendship first. My insecurities ran deep, and I hadn't even begun to scratch the surface of addressing them.

Shortly after I called it off with Lamott, James' friend Willie invited James and me to join him for a potluck at Golden Gardens Park hosted by Black and White Men Together, a group that organized social events. The potluck featured volleyball, croquet, and loads of delicious food. At one point in the afternoon, while James and Willie walked on the beach, I made eye contact with a man I found particularly attractive. He returned my smile and approached me.

Our conversation had just begun when he asked, "So where do you live?"

My face went as blank as my mind. I didn't know where I lived. I didn't know the city and I couldn't picture my residence. While a brief memory lapse may be normal, this felt different. The depth and darkness of the temporary amnesia frightened me.

"Could you excuse me a minute?" I said and walked away. He must have thought I was rude or crazy and the latter would have been an accurate diagnosis.

Standing by myself and breathing deeply, it took perhaps twenty seconds for my memory to return like a video-highlights clip. Finally, I could picture my Seattle apartment, which helped to center and calm me, even as the memory of the experience continued to feel disturbing. There I stood in the middle of a magnificent park, by all appearances relaxed and enjoying life, but clearly stressed out of my fucking mind.

You need some stability, Gary, I told myself. *Get your life settled.*

Later that month, James again asked me to commit. Given the false belief I needed a relationship to bring stability to my life, I settled for James.

There's nothing wrong with a sweet relationship with a fun guy, I told myself. *I love him enough to make it work.*

24

My first year teaching middle school math in the special education department started out rough. The mercurial teens pushed all my buttons, forcing me to learn new skills in communication and tough-love discipline. For the first few weeks, I became so exhausted I put my head down on the nearest desk during my afternoon prep period and fell fast asleep, only to be woken by the next bell fifty minutes later. Over time and with support from my teammates, I got the hang of teaching adolescents and my students responded.

By the end of that challenging year, I was confident enough to apply for one of the five upcoming openings for elementary principals in Seattle. I landed an interview, which I thought went very well. A week later, I met with a personnel analyst who graciously explained why I was not being selected.

"Your interview went great and we were very impressed. You have good experience, but the group just wondered, 'Who is this guy?' You're new to Seattle. Only Tom Lord knows you at the middle school level and nobody knows you in the elementary school ranks. We encourage you to find some ways to get yourself better known and apply again next year."

Although crushed, I kept my wits about me. "Can you give me some specific suggestions how I might go about doing that?"

"I suggest you discuss it with Tom Lord and also keep your eyes and ears open for district committee work," she offered.

Once back in my car, I let the tears silently fall. It seemed as if a deep shame remained that could only be healed once I'd regained a principalship—the position I believed best matched my talents.

Less than a dozen tears fell and less than a dozen minutes passed before I accepted the reality of the situation. With acceptance came a new determination to ask questions, listen for answers, and strategize a pathway to an elementary principal's position the following year.

Tom Lord suggested I meet with the superintendent to introduce myself and ask how I might assist him in furthering his goals and priorities. He also suggested I meet with Nyra Gray, a highly respected elementary principal.

I then shared an idea of my own.

"Tom, would you be open to me doing an informal administrative internship with you?"

Tom was agreeable but asked me to run it by the superintendent first.

I went about scheduling the meetings and gathering information. In short order, my three-part plan fell into place. I would engage in an informal internship with Mr. Lord, volunteer for a district curriculum committee drafting new elementary report cards, and research the transfer process in the hopes of being granted an elementary teaching job the following school year should I once again not be selected for a principalship.

My second year teaching middle school proved to be much more pleasant and reinforced my love of working in a school rich in ethnic, cultural, and language diversity. My internship with Mr. Lord consisted of committee leadership with a challenging staff and using my prep period to enforce student discipline.

Mr. Lord and I met regularly to discuss my internship responsibilities. He welcomed my questions and one day I asked, "Tom, in addition to Nyra Gray, who's another strong elementary principal working in a racially diverse school?"

"John Morefield, principal of Whitworth Elementary," he answered without hesitation.

I called John to set up a time to meet.

"Can you come today?" John asked. "I'll be supervising after-school activities in the cafeteria but track me down and we'll talk. Plus, you can get a feel for the positive school climate we have going here."

I spotted John in the lunchroom, which buzzed with students playing board games, reading to one another, and working with parent volunteers on craft projects. It felt wonderful to be back in an elementary school, even as a visitor. I found John delightful and his wise guidance most helpful. I believed I was optimally set up for a return to elementary education.

The previous year, all principal positions had gone to people of color, honoring the district's goal to diversify its leadership ranks—a goal I fully supported. A year later, the summer posting announced only three openings. I hoped I had a chance.

I applied, then engaged in my usual prep process, including rehearsing orally in front of the bathroom mirror, like an actor learning his lines. The preparations paid off. It was the best interview of my life. Although moderately nervous in the beginning, I soon found myself in the zone and turned on the charm. By the end of the interview, the team of ten principals and central office administrators were grinning and nodding. It had become a dance and we moved in tandem.

"Mr. Tubbs, do you have anything you would like to add before we conclude the interview?"

I considered this, then proceeded—taking a risk. "Well, I don't have anything to add, but I do have a question if that would be okay."

"Certainly."

With my sassy grin in place, I asked, "Is it possible for a White man to get a job in this district?"

Eyes darted around the room, but no one said anything. A few people seemed to be swallowing their laughs. Then Mrs. Louise McKinney, a talented principal and respected matriarch in the African American community, sat erect and spoke.

"We believe in hiring the most talented people to lead our schools, regardless of race."

I nodded and said, "Thank you. That's good to know. And thank you for your time today."

The following week I got an unexpected call in the evening.

"Hi, Gary, it's John Morefield. Can you come down to the central office?"

"Sure, when?"

"Now."

"Is there a problem?"

"No, there's no problem, but I'd like you to get here as soon as you can."

"Okay, I'll leave right now. I can be there in fifteen minutes."

"Great! Look for me in the auditorium."

I found John in the semi-crowded auditorium where the school board was holding its official meeting and sat next to him. He leaned over to whisper in my ear.

"They're about to approve you as the new principal of Whitworth."

I looked at John in shock. Whitworth was John's award-winning school. It turned out he had accepted a promotion and Whitworth had become open. John used his influence to have me assigned as his replacement.

In the very next moment, I heard my name being recommended. The school board approved my selection, and I was being congratulated.

On my solo drive home, stopped at a red light on Mercer Street, I gave out a scream, "Yes! Thank you, God!" I had not only risen from the ashes, but I was also overcome with joy, flying high on the wings of angels.

25

Being the principal of Whitworth, the largest elementary school in the city, was challenging. I often worked twelve-hour days plus evening meetings with community groups. The six-hundred students brought with them a fair number of academic, behavioral, and emotional difficulties. I had very little downtime.

My new salary, however, allowed me to significantly improve my wardrobe as well as buy a small house for $65,000. I'd become comfortable in my new city and in some ways, more comfortable in my skin. Being protected as a gay man at work was a huge weight off my shoulders.

While my professional life continued to thrive, my relationship with James grew stale after the first year. Little things started to annoy me—the amount of time he spent on the telephone, his almost constant attention to color guard, and his lying about quitting cigarettes. Even his laugh grated on me. I suggested couples' counseling so I could share my concerns with a therapist. I just knew he would help James see how he needed to change in order to save our relationship.

"So, James," Dr. Haldeman said, "I hear you saying you're comfortable with who you are and accept Gary for who he is. You're not needing him to change anything for you."

"That's right," James said.

"And, Gary, you're saying you're not happy and need James to make some changes if the relationship is going to continue."

"Yes," I agreed.

"Well, if James doesn't see the need to change or is not willing to change, how long will you remain in the relationship?"

"I'm not sure," I admitted.

"Okay, so what I'm getting here is that one of you, James, is emotionally healthy and relatively happy, while the other, Gary, is unhappy to the point of it perhaps becoming unhealthy. Do I have that right?"

James nodded. I sat, stunned.

Over the next year, I saw Dr. Haldeman on my own. He helped me see how I expected James to make me happy rather than seeking my own happiness. I was looking outside myself and trying to control my outside environment rather than looking inward.

James and I tried to make it work. He continued to be sweet and a lot of fun. I quit trying to change him and focused instead on activities I enjoyed doing. But I realized I wasn't really in love with James, and after our second year together, my old friend, fantasy, began visiting again, just as it had when I was unhappy in my marriage and unhappy in my relationship with Phil. The lustful dragon within awoke and I became more responsive to the attention and touch of other men, causing me considerable frustration and worry.

"James, we need to talk," I said one weekend when we had some quiet time at home.

"Okay, what's up?"

After getting seated at the kitchen table, I said, "I'm unhappy. This is not working for me."

"Why? What's wrong? What did I do?"

"You didn't do anything, James. It's not that. It's just that I don't love you the way you deserve to be loved and I don't want to be in this relationship anymore."

"But there must be something wrong. Tell me one thing that's wrong and then I'll be able to accept this," James insisted.

"Please, James, don't make me say things that might hurt your feelings."

"Hurt my feelings? Please hurt my feelings! I have a right to know."

"But you already know. I told you when we went to Dr. Haldeman together."

"Tell me again."

After a few deep breaths, I said, "James, you are constantly on the telephone, gossiping and talking about color guard. Everything is about you and I'm finding myself too often annoyed. Even your laugh is making me crazy. I don't want to live like this anymore."

"My laugh?" he cackled with the very laugh that made my skin crawl. "So basically, you don't love me anymore."

"Like I said, I don't love you in the way you deserve to be loved."

"Okay, okay, you're not *in* love with me, right?"

"Right."

"Were you ever in love with me?"

"I thought I was, but looking back, I'm not even sure."

The following week, James moved out.

I lived alone but kept so busy working, socializing, working out at the gym, and traveling to see my sons, I didn't feel lonely. That's not to say I'd faced my discomfort with living alone or being alone. I hadn't. In fact, I didn't yet fully realize those deep fears existed.

My weight training and aerobics created a body I didn't think was possible. It developed beautifully and proportionately. I felt confident, strong, and sexy. That led to new clothes to show off my muscles and paying three times as much for hairstyling. I bought a sporty, dark-blue BMW325i, used but in mint condition. I believed I had achieved my dreams—a high-profile position, a good salary, a muscular body, and lots of social connections. Yet I discovered that not everyone approved of my transformation. Over the course of one summer, I heard a variety of comments making that quite clear.

"Geez, your boobs are bigger than mine!" laughed my younger sister, Debi, squeezing my pecs.

"I know!" Colleen said, examining me. "I think you're getting too muscular. Lean is better than bulk."

"I think my son's becoming a snob," my mom told Nancy, who, for some reason, passed the comment on to me.

"God, those are some ugly shorts," Dad said, laughing at my tight aerobics outfit.

My trips to the Tri-Cities would have decreased had it not been for my desire to see Eric and Ben. I had otherwise become uncomfortable visiting where I no longer felt I belonged.

By contrast, the Seattle community embraced me. I sensed no attempt to keep me small. I was recognized and celebrated as an innovative educator and powerful personality. My closest friends encouraged and supported me without fail, and as a single, gay man, I finally felt free to experience the dating world and enjoy the attention of men like never before.

I still didn't know how to date in a casual, sensible way, however. And I must say none of my friends, straight or gay, were good role models in that regard. The only way for me to learn how to date was to practice. And I certainly didn't hesitate or hold back, even though in the mid-eighties, AIDS was making headlines and the identification of the HIV virus had altered my sexual practices. Fortunately, I tested negative and was one hundred percent committed to safe sex.

I started seeing Eugene again, then a millionaire named Jerome, who was absolutely husband material had I been ready, which I wasn't. Tony and I met playing pool, but I lost interest after a few weeks. I had playtime with a bodybuilder named Rich, met sweet, skinny Kevin, but soon got hot and heavy with gregarious Marv. Then, one evening at a bar called the Brass Connection while dancing with Marv, I bumped into Kevin, only to learn that Marv and Kevin were half-brothers who didn't know they'd been sleeping with the same man. Awkward.

Come July, and with a couple weeks of vacation time, I took a road trip to southern California. In San Diego, I danced with some muscle stud with whom I then had messy car sex in the parking lot. I spent an evening in Laguna Beach where I met a nice man, Monsel, from the island of Anguilla. In Long Beach, I met Quatario, who wined and dined me, then later flew up to visit me in Seattle. We had a steamy summer romance, but he scared me with the intensity of his affections. Soon I met Judson, the cutest man in the world, who was just coming out. Then Roberto, a very lighthearted date.

I spent time with so many men, sometimes several during the same time period, I couldn't remember who was from where or who had sisters and brothers. Things had gotten out of hand. I convinced myself my active social and sex life was all in good fun, making up for those lost years as a sexually repressed teenager and young adult. There was some truth in that but a deeper truth lay beneath the surface. I was lost and afraid, hiding behind a façade of perfection, all the while desperate to be accepted, adored, desired, and loved.

Later that fall, in the midst of me juggling men on my weekly calendar, my sister Debi called. "Hi, Gary, can you drive over this Friday?"

"I'm already planning to drive over for Ben's birthday. What's going on?"

"Well, Nancy, Dave, Colleen, and I are talking about holding an intervention for Dad. His drinking has gotten so bad that Mom's thinking about leaving him."

"An intervention's a good idea. Do you need me to do something?" I asked.

"Yes. Can you intercept Dad at the bar before he drinks anything, then bring him to the house?"

"I can try," I said, unsure of how to make that happen.

I left work early on Friday to make the four-hour trip and arrive at the bar Dad frequented every day after work. The place was empty except for the bartender and one handsome, dark-haired man sitting on a stool at the bar—my dad. Fortunately, he hadn't yet sipped the bourbon being set down when I walked up, surprising him. He took on a look of concern.

"Dad, can you come with me, please? I need to talk to you."

I looked at the bartender, who casually pulled the drink away as if she'd witnessed the same scene a time or two before.

The intervention was facilitated by an experienced counselor from Alcoholics Anonymous. As Dad listened to each of his kids share a loving memory, something seemed to release inside of him. I shared about our father-son day when he came to my softball game and bought me an ice cream cone afterwards. At first, he lowered his head, tears streaming down his cheeks.

"Archie, can you please look at your son while he's speaking to you?" requested the counselor in a gentle voice. "It's important, for both you and him."

Dad raised his chin and looked me square in the eyes.

I finished my story and concluded with, "I love you, Dad, and I want you to be happy and healthy again."

Dad did his best to grin as he blinked away tears. "I love you, too, Gary," he said.

The intervention was successful. Dad called his boss, and all was arranged for him to enter rehab. It was a remarkable example of our family coming together to do what needed to be done.

As part of that experience, the family received educational materials about the effects that Dad's drinking might have had on us. We were encouraged to participate in the organization Adult Children of Alcoholics. I attended a few meetings but didn't see how the information applied to me. My coming-out trauma had already forced me to face my fears of abandonment and rejection. I wasn't an alcoholic. Therefore, I was fine. There would be no need for an intervention or rehab for me. Famous last words.

26

The name tag of the new employee at the front desk of the Body Nautilus read "Jim." I'd seen him at a bar with his friends maybe three years earlier but not since. Still, who could forget such a tall, handsome, physically imposing man. Those long legs, I guessed, had run the high hurdles—and I would be correct.

"Hi, I'm Gary," I said as I signed in.

"Hi, Gary. I'm Jim. Have a nice workout," he replied, with a huge smile.

I thought that gap between his front teeth was just too darn cute.

I was too shy to actually converse with Jim at first, let alone flirt—although I definitely wanted to do both. Younger than me and much taller, I couldn't imagine him having any interest in a short, thirty-five-year-old man. But I passed him from time to time while he assisted someone with a workout, hoping to catch his eye and smile. Jim became my new lustful fantasy but without any serious hope of the fantasy coming true.

Over the next few weeks, his friendliness emboldened me. So, when I saw him walk into the locker room at the end of his workout, I waited a few minutes, imagining him getting undressed, then walked into the locker room myself. My heart pounded when I saw his huge bare back, and muscular legs and buttocks. I lingered at the drinking fountain until he made his way into the sauna wrapped in a towel. Taking my time, I stripped down, stored my sweaty workout clothes in the locker and joined him.

I chose an adjacent bench on the same upper level with a strategic view of his full body. No longer wearing his towel, but sitting on it instead, he sat upright, eyes closed, with his back against the side wall and those amazing legs stretched along the full length of the bench. After a few minutes, he bent up one knee then the other, pulling each knee to his chest in a stretch that gave me a revealing view of the merchandise. His eyes remained shut and mine were only open enough to peek without being too obvious.

Eventually, he shifted his position to bend his knees over the side of the bench and sit up with his eyes open.

"Hi! How ya doin'?" he asked.

"Good. How are you?"

"I'm good. Hey, someone told me James is your boyfriend, but I haven't seen him around for a while. How's he doing?"

"I think he's doing okay, but we're not together anymore, actually."

"Really? Sorry to hear that."

"It's okay. It needed to happen."

Another man entered the sauna just as I began to feel overheated, so I departed with a standard, "Take care. See ya later," and headed for the showers feeling pleased to have had the interaction.

Jim and I continued to be cordial when we saw each other at the fitness center, but nothing more developed. It was during that same July when James called me one evening to ask if he and his good friend, Donny, could move into my unoccupied upstairs. I expressed my apprehension of having my ex live in the house but considered it, since he and Donny were at least honest, nice guys, and agreed to pay a fair amount of rent. The extra cash would come in handy for updating the house. James had already had a short romance with another man, so I hoped he was over me.

"Okay, James, we can give it a try," I said. "But I'm dating now, so no drama like with Eugene, or you'll have to move out."

James agreed and within the next few days, he and Donny dragged beds and clothes upstairs to get settled.

With each of us busy working and running in different social circles, we didn't see each other often. Once we figured out the logistics of sharing a single, small bathroom, groceries, and one telephone, it looked like the arrangement could work.

A week or two after they moved in, the red light on my answering machine was blinking when I arrived home on a Friday afternoon. Jim had left a message for James, suggesting they meet for a drink at the Brass Connection later that night. Evidently James had given Jim the phone number within the past week or two. I found that surprising since they had previously only been gym acquaintances, not really friends.

James was out of town teaching color guard and wouldn't be able to meet Jim. But what if I "accidentally on purpose" showed up at the bar? It seemed a bit devious using James' message to my advantage. It also seemed like opportunity knocking.

I kept to my evening routines while mentally mapping out the details of my clandestine plan. I didn't want to enter the bar before Jim but also didn't want to arrive too late or he might be gone. A ten-thirty entrance seemed optimal.

After paying the cover at the door, I entered the club and took a seat at the bar. I intentionally did not look around, hoping to appear cool and relaxed rather than anxious. I ordered a draft beer and chatted with the bartender, wearing my best smile. If Jim was watching, I wanted him to see a friendly, easygoing Gary.

When my beer was nearly gone, I glanced around the room. Jim was seated at a table by himself, drinking a beer. I ordered another draft, took a deep breath to center myself and walked over.

"Mind if I join you?" I asked.

Jim looked up, surprised to see me, and gave me one of his huge smiles. "Hi!" he exclaimed. "Sure! Have a seat."

I pulled up a chair, then sat smiling, my mind totally blank. I hadn't considered conversation starters in my planning. Fortunately, Jim initiated a conversation and before long, I relaxed. I bought more beers and the easy conversation continued with a balance of laughter and substance.

The DJ mixed in Whitney's "So Emotional," and I invited Jim to dance. He accepted. My goodness, the man was tall—six-feet, four-inches it turned out. And on the dance floor he towered over my five-foot, five-inch body. Pulling him down by his muscular arm so he could hear me over the club music, I asked, "Does it bother you I'm so short?"

He shook his head, "No. Does it bother you I'm so tall?"

"No," I said. But that was a lie. Actually, no it wasn't. It didn't bother me that he was so tall. I admired his height. But I felt insecure in comparison—inferior perhaps—at least concerned that other people might be looking at us and laughing at me.

My lifelong insecurity was brought to fore with Jim's commanding presence. I had learned over time to compensate for being short in order to be heard and seen, but I had not learned to be honest about my underlying insecure feelings. This lack of honesty, this tendency to tell half-truths, had been a major theme throughout my life.

I had avoided direct honesty with my dad, fearing his disapproval. I didn't disclose to Colleen the full extent of my sexual desires. With Phil, I failed to be honest about our move to Long Beach. I pretended to love James when I knew I didn't. If I was going to break an old, unhealthy pattern, I knew I had to begin by being more honest with Jim. But since my size didn't bother him, I ignored my feelings for the time being and simply relished the experience of a fantasy becoming real.

After dancing and enjoying another beer together, I asked Jim if he would consider going out to dinner with me some evening.

"Sure!" he said again with that endearing smile. He wrote down his phone number on a tiny slip of paper with a golf pencil provided at the bar. I hugged him goodnight and found my way home, realizing my lust for Jim had evolved into romantic obsession as well.

It would be decades before I would understand how a pattern of lust and romantic obsession had wreaked havoc in my life. With Jim, I had already put him on a pedestal by considering him perfect—charming, physically impressive, and a terrific conversationalist. By doing so, I had also set him up to fall off and to fail. I idealized him before even knowing him, a classic characteristic of a love addict in the making.

For the next two days, I thought about Jim every hour, but resisted calling him. Where would we go to dinner? How formal? How relaxed? Was it a good idea to have sex right away? Maybe he didn't even want to have sex with me. *Shut up, Gary!* I admonished myself. *Just take it slow and easy!*

Finally, I gave myself permission to call him. No answer. I left a message. The next day when I arrived home from work, I had my karmic debt to pay for taking advantage of James' phone message. Back from his teaching gig, James had not only heard his old message from Jim about meeting at the Brass Connection, but also Jim's new message—for me.

"Are you seeing my friend, Jim?" James asked, sounding upset.

"Your friend?" I remarked with a chuckle. "You two hardly know each other and, yes, we're planning on having dinner. Why do you care?"

"I care because he's my friend and I think it's mean of you to go out with him when we just broke up a few months ago."

"James, you promised no drama."

"Well, I'm going to talk to him because I don't think this is right."

"Don't you fuckin' do anything to mess this up for me!" I screamed, as I hurled my briefcase—a gift he had given me the previous Christmas—directly at him. He dodged aside and it crashed into the sofa, then fell, unopened, onto the floor.

We both froze, stunned by my rage. Never before had I expressed such intense anger. Silence and stillness consumed the room.

Looking forlorn, James sat on the far end of the sofa, his face buried in his hands.

Then, with his voice soft and quivering, he said, "You must really like him."

"I do like him, James, and I'm sorry if that bothers you, but please don't say anything."

After a few silent moments, James said, "I guess this means we're not getting back together."

I said nothing as the truth revealed itself. James had manipulated his way back into my house with hope of a reconciliation.

After a few quiet moments, he said, "Okay, I won't interfere, but please don't bring Jim over while I'm here."

"I understand. That's fine for now. But you need to make other living arrangements as soon as possible." James didn't argue. He and Donny moved out a few days later.

It was during that same week that I picked up Jim for our date. Dinner was delightful. After our meal, we continued our conversation while we finished the bottle of wine.

"This has been nice," I said. "If you don't mind, I'd like to see you again."

"I'd like that," Jim replied.

We smiled and held the eye contact long enough for it to feel romantic.

"But before we take this any further," I said, "I need to open up to you about a few things."

"I'm listening," he replied.

"Well, I tend to move too fast, too soon. Before I even know someone or become friends with them, we end up having sex and then I can get far too serious. I like you and don't want to mess anything up by doing that."

Jim nodded. "Okay, so what do you propose?"

"Well, I've been thinking about how to do things differently this time. If we could go slow, like maybe have, I don't know, ten dates before we have sex? Something like that. Then, if we still like each other, well, hey, it's on!" I smiled.

Jim returned my smile. "That makes sense. I'm cool with that."

Then for the next hour, Jim and I shared about our past relationships, including my recent drama with James.

"Is it going to be a problem for you that James is upset with us dating?" I asked.

"No problem for me. But whether or not James and I hang out, I'll leave that up to him."

Over the next six weeks, Jim and I enjoyed walks in the park, movies, brunch, and dinner dates. We went out drinking and dancing and even had a double date with friends.

During our many conversations, I told him my life story, including my long-distance relationship with my sons, my brother's marriage to my ex-wife, and Colleen's ongoing battle with cancer—a battle that included surgery, radiation therapy, chemotherapy, and a few encouraging years of remission. Most recently, however, the cancer had shown up in her liver. Colleen had found a prayer of healing and asked her family and closest friends to recite it for her every day. For the past six months, I had done so without fail and shared the prayer with Jim.

I then made an effort to be honest about my concerns regarding our age and size differences. He was kind and promised not to tease me, although my tiny shoes made him chuckle. To him, my height was a non-issue. Whereas my insecurities, masked by a façade of perfectionism, would remain a debilitating issue for me.

Jim shared his own life story, including the emotional trauma he'd experienced as a little boy when forced to view the body of his beloved father. For weeks after seeing his daddy in the coffin, Jim didn't speak, causing great consternation for his family.

His mom, who described her deceased husband as a "rolling stone," raised Jim and his two siblings in a predominantly White suburb north of Seattle. They were among very few Black students throughout their public school years.

Jim was a track star in high school and a collegiate, possibly Olympic, hopeful until he faced the emotional challenges of coming out. He had most recently been in a long-term relationship with an older, wealthy attorney who, financially, had taken very good care of him.

"So, what happened between the two of you?" I asked.

"Well, he kicked me out," Jim laughed.

"He just kicked you out for no reason?"

"No, there were arguments. I thought he was being too controlling, acting like he was my father or something, and I got sick of it," Jim explained.

"So, you argued, and he just kicked you out? End of story?"

"Jeez, Gary! It's in the past, I'm not the same person so just leave it alone, okay?" Jim said, getting upset.

"Jim, we're building a relationship here. I believe you when you say you're not the same person and I'm not here to judge you. Just tell me what happened."

"Many things happened!"

"Give me one example."

"Okay, we went for a drive out Highway 2 toward the mountains. He kept challenging me about things. Going to the bars. Getting coked up and staying out all night. It turned into an argument. I screamed at him and told him to stop the car. I wanted out."

Jim acted like he was done talking.

"And then?" I prodded.

"He let me out and drove away. Now, end of story."

"He didn't come back for you? How'd you get home?"

"Hitchhiked and walked. I managed."

After a quiet moment, I asked, "Do you still use cocaine?"

"No. It's been over a year."

I wasn't sure what to think about Jim's story or his reluctance to be fully transparent, but I hoped we'd at least begun to establish a foundation on which to build trust.

Good night kisses later became make-out sessions on the sofa. But no sex. By date number seven, we got impatient. We wondered if meeting for breakfast then seeing a movie in the evening, would count as two dates. It was pretty cute how we both longed to make love. And remarkably, this man with whom I thought I didn't stand a chance, appeared to adore me.

For our ninth date in late September, we attended the Washington State Fair in Puyallup some forty miles south of Seattle. It was sweet and magical—a key moment in our developing relationship as we settled into feeling like boyfriends. The romantic evening was spectacular—a bedazzled, star-filled sky with temperatures in the seventies.

I found it funny that such a big man could be afraid of the Ferris wheel. Even though he agreed to ride it, he was giddy with fear, not liking the open seats with nothing to keep us from falling out. The first time we rode a full rotation and the seat tilted back a little at the crest, I thought he was going to scream like a little girl. I got the giggles watching him squirm and, of course, had to tease him without mercy.

On the ride home, we relaxed in my car's black leather seats and held hands. I queued up Anita Baker in the tape player so Jim and I could get "Caught Up in the Rapture" of falling in love.

We celebrated date ten with dinner and wine at a nice restaurant, recounting the progression of our relationship from the day in the sauna until the state fair. It was a loving and lighthearted conversation. Once we were back in Jim's apartment, we made love and the sex was good—very good. We discovered we were both versatile and playfully uninhibited. Jim encouraged me to express my creative self during our lovemaking. I didn't hold back and neither did he.

Jim had worked at the Body Nautilus only a few months when he resigned to accept a job at Nordstrom. It was a graveyard shift doing what he called "pulling tapes" in the data-processing department.

"It's only an entry-level position and not much pay at first," Jim told me, "but there's a definite career ladder."

"Cool, Jim! That's very exciting."

With Jim's graveyard shift, we didn't see each other during the week but tried to make the most of our weekends.

"Hey, Gary, how about we read the same novel and discuss it?" Jim suggested one Saturday as we walked up to Broadway from his apartment.

"Sure," I said, "but I'm not a fast reader and with all the reading I do for work, I'm not sure I can keep up with you."

"Well, we can just read a few chapters at a time. I was thinking about *Watership Down*. Have you read it?"

I hadn't and agreed it was a good idea. While on Broadway, we went to a bookstore and bought two copies. A week later we had our first discussion.

"I wonder if we aren't all like the smallest rabbit, Fiver, in that we each have a unique gift that can benefit others," Jim said.

"Yeah, I think that's probably true," I agreed.

"But then I think we're also like the other characters in these early chapters," Jim continued. "Sometimes it's best when we contribute by following and assisting. Other times we become afraid or resistant to change, even when it's in our best interest."

"Jim, you're quite insightful. Have you ever thought about returning to school?"

"What? You didn't think a big Black guy could be insightful?" he asked in a huff.

"That's not what I meant at all," I said. "I'm trying to compliment you here and encourage you to consider returning to school."

"Well, it didn't sound like a compliment to me, and I don't need you putting pressure on me to go to school. Everyone does that—my sister, my boss—and I'm tired of it."

"Sorry, I didn't know."

Silence.

"I'd like to admit something to you," I finally said.

"What?"

"I think of you as my miracle man."

"What do you mean?"

"Well, I never in a million years thought a man like you would be interested in a man like me. I mean you're tall, attractive, smart . . ."

"What are you talking about, Gary? You're a handsome school principal with a master's degree!" Jim insisted.

"Yeah, I know. I've worked hard," I said. "I'm not saying I'm stupid or ugly. I'm just saying I think you're exceptional and I'm smart enough to know that, intellectually, you're smarter than me. I have no doubt."

Jim didn't react or respond. I had shared what I believed to be true, but what I also did was unfairly project my own perfectionism onto him—another characteristic of love addiction. By doing so, I set myself up to be hurt and disappointed, thus putting me in a position to later blame Jim if he didn't fulfill my fantasies and expectations.

Even though Jim's temperamental personality could make me feel uncomfortable, I fell hard for him. He always greeted me with a big smile and a hug, sometimes picking me up and spinning me around.

"Put me down!" I would demand, even though I loved how it made me feel loved.

When I shared about my struggle with perfectionism—how I felt the need to be perfect, even compelled to maintain perfection in my living space with everything tidy and in its place, Jim chimed in.

"Do you think perfection is even possible?"

"No, but that doesn't stop me from trying to be like Mary Poppins—practically perfect in every way," I chuckled.

Jim's eyes lit up. Then he crowed with glee, "That can be your Halloween costume next year! We'll need to shop for a white frilly dress and big bonnet for you!"

"Shut up," I said, laughing in spite of myself.

Jim and I had been boyfriends for going on six months when I met him on the sidewalk outside the downtown Nordstrom where he worked. An elderly Black man asked us for spare change. Jim shook his pocket full of coins and snapped, "I don't have any change! Have I ever had any change for you?"

"Why did you say that to him?" I asked, feeling confused as we walked along.

"He asks me every day and he needs to stop!" Jim barked.

Then one evening when we went out for drinks, my colleague, Ron Jones, approached me to say hi and chat. Ron was a nice looking, African American man who adorned himself with gold rings and multiple gold bracelets. Jim had turned away to smoke his cigarette when Ron approached, so I gently took Jim's arm to get his attention.

"I'd like you to meet my friend, Ron."

"Well, I don't want to meet *him*," Jim snarled with a curled upper lip that reminded me of a threatened feral dog—a look I would come to fear. I was taken aback but ignored him and returned to my conversation. Ron was pretty drunk and appeared oblivious to the antisocial remark, but once again, Jim's abrupt behavior bothered me. Loving Jim was easy, but I began to wonder if being his boyfriend might not be.

27

"Mr. Tubbs, please report to the office. Mr. Tubbs, please report to the office."

As a principal, such an announcement was rarely good news.

"Your sister, Debi, is on hold."

"Debi? Thank you." A dark haze shrouded me. "Hello?"

"Hi, Gary. Colleen's back in the hospital and not doing well. You should probably get here as soon as you can."

"Okay. I understand. I'll leave right away."

I had picked up ten-year-old Ben the previous weekend when his school year ended and brought him to Seattle with me. Eric, thirteen, had chosen to stay in the Tri-Cities with his friends. Their mom's condition had deteriorated over the past six months, requiring several emergency trips to the hospital. The boys remained troopers and stayed encouraging, giving their mom lots of love even when she couldn't get off the sofa to physically return it. Nevertheless, Colleen's five-year cancer battle had taken its toll on everyone in my family. Dave was exhausted being the primary caretaker and living in constant fear of losing his wife.

Since Seattle schools were not yet on summer break, I took Ben to school with me. He enjoyed hanging out in Ms. Lynn's fourth grade classroom where she lovingly welcomed him to join in the field trips and fun activities she had planned.

After speaking with my sister, I got Ben from Lynn's class, then drove to my house to pack our clothes, including my funeral suit. I called to update Jim, locked the house, and drove east on I-90.

"So Ben, do you understand what's happening right now?"

"Mom's in the hospital again and she's really sick," he said, looking at me for confirmation.

I nodded. "Yeah. It looks like this could be her last day." I wanted to prepare him, if that was even possible. "I know it will be hard to see her, but I think it's important you say goodbye. Are you okay with that?"

He nodded.

"Of course, you know Dave and I will take care of you. And even though you'll miss your mom, we also don't want her to suffer."

"She's been sick so long. I think she's tired," Ben said.

"I think you're right."

Our four-hour drive seemed to take forever. We arrived at the hospital and met Debi and Eric in the lobby, then made the dreaded trip up the elevator to the Intensive Care Unit. My dad stood in the hall outside the elevator. He came up to embrace me, slumped over with his voice cracking, "Oh, Gary, she's so sick."

My mom expressed concern about the boys seeing Colleen.

I said, "She's their mother and they need to say goodbye."

My brother, Dave, paced outside of Colleen's room. "I can't go back in there," he said. "I can't just stand around and watch my wife die."

"You don't have to Dave. Just do what feels right. Wait for us here," I said. "We'll be out in a few minutes."

Colleen's mother Dolores, her dad Bill, and her cousin Darlene were at Colleen's bedside. Dolores was calm and loving as she told her grandsons it was good that they could say goodbye while their mom was still warm. Those words shook me. *While she's still warm.* Dolores held her only daughter's hand and rubbed her shoulder. Colleen was not conscious. She looked near death—very near.

I told the boys to touch her and tell her goodbye. They did, adding "I love you" all on their own.

Then, it was my turn.

I held her hand and let my tears flow. "Colleen, thank you for being such a good mom to our sons. Please know we'll take good care of them. I love you."

She made a noise. It could have been for any reason, but to me, it sounded desperate.

I spoke to her again, softly and up close. "It's okay. Don't worry about anything. You can go now."

A few hours later, she left us. June 21, 1989, the first day of summer, her favorite season. She was thirty-seven.

Colleen, my dear friend and first love, taught me to lighten up and laugh more freely. Her gentle spirit and radiant smile still visit me in my dreams from time to time. Although I will always miss her, I'm grateful sweet memories are everlasting.

28

Two days before I received the call about Colleen, Jim and I had decided to live together in my house. But I had to abruptly abandon that plan to focus on family. I negotiated a year's leave of absence from Seattle Public Schools so I could move into my former house with Dave and my sons.

Seattle's superintendent showed great compassion by generously granting me permission to find temporary employment during my leave of absence. He understood I needed a salary to help contribute to my sons' well-being as well as make my mortgage payments for the house I intended to keep in Seattle.

Each week, I cooked, cleaned, and took care of Eric and Ben, as well as supported my brother. On some weekends that summer, I drove to Seattle to be with Jim. Then, beginning in September, I taught twenty-four first-graders on a temporary contract and brought schoolwork home each evening to complete after the boys were asleep. It was a challenging time of adjustment for everyone in my family.

Later in October, Dave, the boys, and I traveled to Seattle for a weekend double date with Jim and Lynn, the Whitworth teacher who had taken Ben into her classroom. With Dave and Lynn's permission, I had set them up for a simple night out. Lynn's teenage sons watched Eric and Ben while the four adults went to a comedy club in Pioneer Square. It was a fun evening of drinking and laughing as well as a healthy escape from grief and stress.

During intermission, already high from the alcohol and environment, I made an off-the-cuff remark about possibly house-hunting with Dave in Kennewick. It was crazy-thinking and I didn't stop to consider how my words might impact the heart, mind, and life of the man I loved.

After the comedy club, we picked up Eric and Ben at Lynn's house, then drove to Jim's apartment, where he wanted to host me and the boys and prepare a special breakfast for us in the morning. Dave dropped us off before heading to a friend's house to crash.

Eric and Ben got settled into their sleeping bags in the living room at one end of the apartment, while Jim and I went to the bedroom at the other end. The bathroom, kitchen, and foyer separated us. I had just crawled into bed and leaned my head on Jim's chest to cuddle when he asked, "What's this about you buying a house with Dave?" The annoyance in his voice caught me off guard.

I looked up to see his lip twitching, that feral look beginning to appear. "It's just an idea. I'm sure it won't happen. I need to explore all options to make sure my babies are taken care of."

He bristled severely and pushed me away. "Well, then take your babies and get the fuck out of here!"

It was after midnight on a chilly, rainy October night.

"Are you serious?" I asked.

To demonstrate his seriousness, he gave me a sharp push out of the bed, folded my suitcase with clothes hanging out, and carried it to the door of the apartment. As I followed him in disbelief, I glanced at my sons who lay motionless in their sleeping bags. Jim opened the door and tossed my suitcase into the hall then slammed the door with a thunderous bang. He stomped his muscular frame back into the bedroom, with me trailing and attempting to appease him in a calm voice. He spun around and grabbed my arms, then forced me out of the bedroom and slammed that door, too.

Trembling with fear, I tried to breathe and think clearly. My first thought was to get my sons someplace safe. I called the number Dave had given me earlier. "Please come get us as soon as you can. We'll meet you outside."

I thought surely Eric and Ben had been awakened by all the noise, but they appeared to be sleeping.

"Eric, Ben, wake up," I said, shaking them gently. "We need to leave. Get dressed and roll up the sleeping bags. Get your coats. It's cold outside."

They didn't ask any questions.

As they packed up, I rushed to the hallway to grab the clothes I'd been wearing earlier, including the jeans with my wallet in the back pocket, and shoved my other clothes into the suitcase. I then hurried the boys outside, down the two flights of stairs and into the rainy night. We waited for Dave, huddled in silence beneath the overhang of the adjacent building to keep from getting wet.

Finally, safe in Dave's car, I broke down and cried as silently as possible.

"What happened?" Dave asked.

"Jim got upset. I'll tell you about it later."

Dave dropped us off at my Seattle house where the boys and I crawled into my waterbed and finally got some sleep.

The next morning, I felt drained yet clear. My one-year relationship with Jim was over. While I was sad, I also experienced a sense of solace. I could focus exclusively on my family and not concern myself with maintaining such a volatile relationship.

Back in Kennewick, Dave and I made time for a private conversation about next steps. He had been doing a lot of thinking about his future. Only thirty-three years old, he did not see himself living with me and the boys long-term. He intended to remarry at some point and have children of his own. We decided the boys should stay in Kennewick for the current school year, then move to Seattle to live with me. When we shared this plan with the boys, Ben accepted it. Eric argued against it—not wanting to leave his friends. But Dave was firm and told Eric to prepare himself to move to Seattle.

I arranged for a realtor to sell my house in Seattle, which I had decided would be too small. In the meantime, I didn't want the hassles of renting it nor the expense of keeping it. Before

November ended, the house had sold with the proceeds tucked away in savings and my possessions secured in a storage unit. To keep from missing Jim, I stayed busy until I was exhausted and could finally fall asleep.

Then, one morning, the month after the incident at Jim's apartment, I heard Dave shout, "Gary, telephone."

I came to the phone to see him grinning at me with his eyebrows raised. "Hello?"

"Hi," Jim said.

Silence.

"Can I come see you?" he asked in a soft voice. "My sister said I could borrow her car."

"Why?" I knew I should say no, but for some reason I couldn't.

"Gary, I love you. I'm sorry and I want to make things right."

I was powerless. My miracle man wanted me in his life. And doesn't everyone deserve a second chance?

"Okay, Jim," I said. "I'll see you Saturday."

When Jim visited, we talked things through. He apologized again for his aggressive action. I apologized for my insensitive remark at the comedy club and assured him I would not be house hunting with Dave. We then agreed to take turns traveling to see each other. To support that happening, I purchased a reliable used car for Jim.

He kept the car but not the agreement—that being the only weekend Jim came to the Tri-Cities. When I brought it up, he confessed his discomfort staying in the house I shared with Dave and the boys. Trying to be more compassionate, I let him off the hook. I started driving to Seattle every weekend, putting the full responsibility of seeing each other onto my shoulders while my boyfriend, a bright, capable, twenty-six-year-old man, happily let me do it.

Each Friday, I prepared to drive directly to Seattle from my teaching job. Dave and other family members cared for Eric and Ben while I was gone. I never felt rested. Instead, I kept moving, taking care of everyone except myself.

To save money, Jim had moved in with his friend, Mike, in West Seattle. I arrived at their apartment around 7 p.m. each Friday to be greeted by Jim with a hug, a kiss, and a soft bed in which to rest. It was a tiring routine but pleasant enough.

One weekend, Jim had made plans for us to join Celeste and Alise, two lesbian friends of his, at a women's bar in the Eastlake area near downtown Seattle. It was a new experience for me, and I enjoyed the club's energy and music. Very few men were there, but as Jim and I walked around searching for his friends, I noticed a tall Black man, smiling at me from the other side of the dance floor. He looked rather sexy in his tight, white Levi's, but I was already with my miracle man, so I just smiled and looked away.

Nevertheless, I was flattered by the attention. No handsome man had ever flirted with me from across a room before. I suppose Mando did, but that was only after I stood searching the bar like a lonely, desperate man. I had been the one to approach Phil and James. I had been the one to track down Eugene, Lamott, and almost all the others, including Jim. So having this man's attention on me was novel. I liked it.

The evening turned out to be a lot of fun and shortly before one a.m., we called it a night. All was quiet as Jim drove toward the freeway entrance, but he seemed tense. His hands clenched the wheel with his shoulders hunched forward, his face tight.

Once we entered I-5 heading south, he blurted, "Why'd you flirt with that man?"

"What man?"

"You know what man . . . when we first got to the bar. Black guy, white Levi's."

"Oh, him. I wasn't flirting. He smiled and I smiled back." I suddenly worried I had done something shameful for having enjoyed the man's attention.

"Gary, you were flirting. I saw you!" Jim insisted, getting louder.

"It's okay, Jim," I said, trying to help him relax. "I was just being friendly."

"Stop lying!" he yelled.

"I'm not lying and stop yelling at me!" I yelled back, fear pumping through me.

By then we were on the high-level West Seattle bridge. Jim, rigid with rage, hit the brakes and brought the car to an abrupt halt on the shoulder of the road.

"Get out!" he screamed, glaring at me with contempt.

"What?" I gasped, "Are you crazy?"

"Get out!" he screamed again and reached across me to push open my door. When I didn't move, he unlatched my seatbelt and gave me a powerful shove. I hit the cold pavement. Only my feet remained in the car, but I pulled them free when Jim stepped on the gas—passenger door open, passenger expelled.

In shock, alone at night on an empty freeway, one hundred and fifty feet above the Duwamish River, I felt terrified of the enraged man who had just driven away. I checked for my wallet and keys. *Should I head toward town or walk the mile to Jim's apartment where my car is parked? Yes, going back to my car would be best.*

Almost as soon as I started walking, I saw Jim's car backing up on the freeway. *Should I run? Cross the freeway barrier to escape?* I stood motionless until the car stopped next to me. After a quick, internal debate, I opened the door, sat in the passenger seat, and remained silent for the ride to his apartment. I stayed as far away from Jim in bed as possible, and after very little sleep, got up at sunrise, gathered my belongings, and left without a word.

Over the next twenty-four hours, I replayed the evening over and over in my head. Jim's extreme reaction was certainly unacceptable, but when I looked at it from his perspective, I started to doubt myself.

Did I flirt? Then lie about it? Was this, in some way, my fault?

I became so confused I completely lost sight of the fact that Jim had violently ejected me from his car on the fucking West Seattle Bridge at one o'clock in the morning.

So much for second chances.

An apologetic Jim called a few days later.

29

I ended up blaming myself for the incident on the bridge as much as I ignored Jim's violence. Then I took it upon myself to rescue our relationship, as if its very survival depended on me doing more, trying harder, being perfect. Whatever I believed Jim needed me to be, I would strive to become that. My perfectionism wouldn't allow me to lose Jim, be left alone, and fail at yet another relationship.

With Jim in agreement, and Dave's support, I decided to move back to Seattle and find an apartment with Jim if the Seattle School District had a position for me. Living in Seattle would also provide me with an opportunity to search for a house for when Eric and Ben moved over. Until then, I would drive to Kennewick each weekend to be with them.

In early January, Seattle's superintendent offered me the principalship at Beacon Hill Elementary beginning the first of February, just three weeks away. I accepted the position with the kind support of my Kennewick principal, who then hired an experienced substitute teacher to take my first-grade classroom. Jim and I rented a comfortable ground-level apartment on Queen Anne Hill just north of downtown. Excited to finally live together, we enjoyed a couple months of what seemed like relative bliss.

I soon discovered that although most of the housing market was out of my price range, a new housing development in south Seattle offered good terms and the ideal floor plan—a master suite on the main level and two bedrooms, a full bath, and a family room in the daylight basement. Construction was underway and the house would be ready for occupancy in the spring.

By April, the energy in the Queen Anne apartment became mysteriously toxic. Jim stomped around, easily irritated over the smallest things.

"What's going on, Jim?" I asked. "Are you concerned about the new house or the boys moving over?"

"No, why do you ask that?" he snapped.

"It's just that you seem upset. Is everything all right at work?"

"I hate it. It's so boring!" he exclaimed. "My supervisor told me I need my degree to qualify for promotions, but I don't have the money for school right now."

Jim had been given a lateral change in position, working days rather than graveyard, but turned down for promotions.

"What about student loans?" I suggested.

"I want Nordstrom to pay for it! They say they want to promote diversity, so they need to put their money where their mouth is."

"That'd be great. Do you think they might?"

"We're having discussions, but they keep putting me off," he said, exasperated.

"Hey, if you get your degree, I'll treat you to a trip to Europe," I offered.

"You think I need a bribe to get my degree?" he asked. "I'm not one of your students you can treat to ice cream for good behavior!"

After a minute of silence, I tried again. "I'm sorry. That came out wrong. I know you can get your degree without an incentive. I would just be so proud of you and would love to celebrate your accomplishment with a big trip. That's all."

"Well, that's not what you said, so just forget it. I'm not interested in your help."

Seeming to put that misunderstanding behind us, we packed our gym bags and walked up the hill to the neighborhood fitness club. Jim pretty much ignored me but was all smiles when some young men admired his huge biceps. We left the gym and bought takeout for dinner, then walked home to relax for the evening. But evidently, tensions remained, and an invisible spring had tightened to the breaking point. Jim started stomping around the bedroom, making growling sounds like a frustrated, trapped animal.

"Jim, I don't understand what you're upset about. What's happening here?"

"Just get out!" he shouted, then physically forced me out of the bedroom and locked the door.

Although his aggressiveness frightened me, I was less afraid than I was sad and angry. I had tried so hard to be supportive and keep our relationship alive. But now I felt done, depleted. I wanted out.

I stayed awake all night planning my escape, and I must admit, a fair share of vengeance. Walking around the apartment in the middle of the night, I took account of what was mine. I already had packing boxes and tape on hand. When Jim's alarm clock buzzed at 6 a.m., I lay motionless on the sofa with the blanket over my head until he left for work. Then I went into action, following the step-by-step list I had composed, including calling my secretary, reserving a U-Haul truck, and making an appointment to view a furnished studio apartment. By the time Jim returned home in the late afternoon, I'd be gone with my possessions stored in south Seattle near the construction site of the new house.

I wrote a note and left it on the floor of the now empty dining room where he would see it when he got home. I don't remember what it said. It wasn't mean. Just honest. The rent on the Queen Anne apartment had previously been paid for the month. Beyond that, Jim could manage on his own, or not. I didn't care.

I signed a week-to-week lease on the studio apartment, knowing the new house would soon be ready for occupancy. The tension in my stomach never eased until I saw the smiling faces of the children at work or had the weekend for my drive to see Eric and Ben. After two weeks of living on my own, however, I decided it was cruel not to at least check on Jim. Of course, what I called compassion was in reality my own unhealthy attachment.

I phoned and Jim wanted to meet. I agreed. We met at a coffee shop where I would not have to worry about being shouted at or grabbed. The sweet man I had fallen in love with appeared for the meeting. He wanted us to try again. I insisted any attempt at reconciliation was contingent upon counseling, individual and for us as a couple. He agreed, giving me renewed hope.

Jim and I moved into the new house in mid-May. I then relocated the boys to Seattle and enrolled them in school. I hoped they could make friends before summer vacation began. The house was ideal. The schools were hit or miss—a hit for Ben but a big fat miss for Eric. He did fine at South Shore Middle School in the spring, but struggled as a freshman, mandatorily assigned to Rainier Beach High School. I fought the assignment but was unsuccessful.

Eric did his best to cope with and adjust to being one of only a handful of White students. He played football, made a few friends, and had a part-time job. But it wasn't enough to help him feel centered in his soul. He shut down and it frightened me.

After eight months in Seattle, Eric asked to move back to the Tri-Cities. It tore me apart seeing him so distressed. Therefore, I supported his request, and in collaboration with Eric and Dave, arranged for Eric to live with Bill and Dolores, his maternal grandparents. In my farewell letter to him, I wrote, "You will make your own path by walking on it. I support you, knowing you will find your way."

Ben's experience in Seattle was very different. He did well in school and had a terrific group of diverse friends, including a girlfriend. But three years later, as a freshman in high school, he also asked to return to the Tri-Cities. He tried living with Dave and Dave's new wife, Sai, but that didn't work out. Bill and Dolores then welcomed Ben into their home. One grandson moved in and another, Eric, almost eighteen, moved out—on his way to Denmark as a foreign exchange student.

While Ben's request to move away hurt and confused me, I reluctantly supported his wishes. Many years later, he told me his anxiety about my sexuality had become more than he could handle. He worried the kids in his high school might discover I was gay and make an issue of it.

With my sons no longer requiring my daily attention, I hoped Jim and I could make our relationship work. We engaged in individual and couple's counseling, but our dysfunctional pattern continued—basically, a period of smooth sailing followed by building tensions, always culminating in a dramatic explosion.

Our good months consisted of fun with friends, family activities, romantic moments, and passionate sex. Jim enrolled at the University of Washington and did well. His career at Nordstrom advanced. I also thrived at work and was rewarded with promotions.

On the surface, our life together looked calm and routine. But for one reason or another, an unforeseen circumstance would arise, and Jim would explode. I walked on eggshells after each of Jim's outbursts, but when verbally attacked, I no longer fell silent. Instead, I started to express myself in ugly, accusatory ways, like shouting, "You're fucked up!" or complaining, "It doesn't matter what I do, you'll still find a reason to yell at me." Even during our good months, I too often behaved like a critical nag. My buried resentments had come to the surface, while I remained unskilled in expressing them. Dr. Freed, the couple's counselor we'd been seeing, provided us with new tools of communication as we tried to mend our dysfunctional relationship.

"How are things going, guys?" he asked.

"Well, all right most of the time," I said after Jim remained quiet. "As long as things keep improving or staying at least ninety-percent good, I think that's okay."

"Ninety-percent, huh? Do you agree with that, Jim?"

"I think things are going good. We have little conflicts from time to time, but that's normal, isn't it?"

"There's no normal here. Every couple establishes what works for them. Gary, is there a resentment you need to share with Jim today?"

"Yes. Jim, I resent doing all the shopping and cooking. Even though you stop at the grocery store almost every evening after work, you walk in the house with only a six pack of beer and a pack of cigarettes."

"Good," said the counselor. "Jim, could you hear that? And how might you like to respond?"

"Yes, I hear you, Gary, but I don't know what food to buy and I'm so tired at the end of my day I have no energy to think about it," Jim replied.

For each resentment we voiced or issue we brought to the table, Dr. Freed guided us to a plan of action. But in practice at home, nothing changed. Jim got annoyed if I reminded him of our agreement, then I'd get angry at him. It didn't matter if the subject was shared responsibilities or healthy communications. We just spun our wheels.

In one of our last sessions before we agreed to abandon couples' therapy, the counselor asked me, "Gary, are you afraid of Jim?"

I lied. "No, I'm not afraid of him. I hate it when he yells or grills me like a prosecutor, but I'm not afraid."

The truth should have been spoken. *Yes! Sometimes I'm so fucking afraid of him I'm even afraid to tell you I'm afraid of him for fear he'll get mad at me later!* But that level of truth was not possible then. I hadn't even admitted it to myself yet.

When our couples' counseling failed, I awakened to the reality that I had once again trapped myself in a relationship with little chance of happiness. I don't know if Jim's individual counseling was helpful to him, but mine proved to be the pathway I needed to learn about myself and to be supported by a skilled practitioner.

Dr. Haldeman helped me see my unhealthy emotional reliance on Jim's approval—a behavior Dr. Haldeman called codependence. When Jim was happy, I was happy. When Jim was worried,

I tried to solve the problem. When Jim was mad, I appeased him. I had trouble staying true to my own feelings, which had become increasingly difficult to even identify. The deep emotional work I needed to do in order to recover from my codependency would be near impossible to accomplish while in a hostile environment.

"Gary, thinking back to your childhood," Dr. Haldeman asked during a session, "what age stands out to you?"

"Five," I replied.

"Why five?"

"I remember everything about being five. I was expressive, creative, full of life. Happy."

"And are there specific memories that stand out to you?"

"Yes, I remember acting out skits for my parents in our living room. And I remember playing in the mud one day when I had an unforgettable spiritual experience."

"Tell me about that."

"It was a really hot day—like over a hundred degrees. Mom had sent me outside to entertain myself because I kept whining about being bored no one to play with me. My older sister was at school and my younger sister and brother were napping. I ended up playing with the hose on the side of the house and making a muddy mess in a dirt patch. Eventually, I sat down in the mud—no shirt or shoes—intently focused on making perfectly round, smooth mud cakes. All of a sudden, my body got quivery, and it felt like something was turning my head to look up into the sky toward the sun. It was incredible! I couldn't stop smiling— feeling so much joy, like God was washing love over me."

"That's a powerful story and potentially very important. I'm quite certain that five-year-old still lives within you. Do you have a sense of that?"

"Yes actually, I do. I've always felt connected to God. Not necessarily religion or church, but I've always believed God was with me."

"Then I'd like you to consider your five-year-old self when things get difficult. Take care of that little boy and protect him.

Remind him that you accept and adore him, just as he is. Perhaps your love for little Gary will help you show more love for this adult version of Gary."

Dr. Haldeman's wise counsel stayed with me, even though the process of actualizing it was very slow in developing, as evidenced by my final years with Jim. There were repeated incidents of emotional abuse I didn't even label as abuse at the time.

Jim once convinced me we could experiment with a three-way, just for fun. I was scared and resistant, then agreeable and excited, at which point he called me disgusting.

"Do you really think I'm the kind of person to have a three-way?" he roared.

When I accused him of "mind-fucking" me, he grabbed an expensively framed print and threw it across our bedroom. I had it repaired.

Twice he dug through my private box of memorabilia and found something to spark jealous rage. When he discovered my collector's edition of a book of famous homoerotic etchings, he set it on my bed pillow with a note reading "This goes or I go!" I tossed the book in the trash. And when he found a glossy headshot of an old flame, he put his fist through the wall. I patched it.

On another occasion he pinned me to the floor so I couldn't move, forcing me to listen while he scolded me. Months later, I knew the violence had escalated when he stopped just short of punching my face.

Several times, I sent him away. After a week or two, he knocked on the door with an apology or red roses in hand.

Then, an evening came when I sensed his anger building. He stomped around and his lip began to twitch. I ignored him. As I went downstairs to check on the laundry, I wondered if he would lock the basement door. He did.

I wasn't bothered. In fact, I shook my head and thought: *Here we go, Gary. But don't worry. I'll take care of you.* It was in that moment when I knew the relationship was over and I would never, couldn't ver, go back. This time was different, as if resolve had locked into place. I took a deep breath and with my exhale, I let go of Jim, watching him float away like a helium balloon I'd been grasping. I felt alone but resolved, distressed but determined, with no inclination to cling, control, fix, or react in any way.

Once downstairs, I checked for my wallet and keys. My wallet was in my back pocket, but I'd left my keys on the kitchen counter. I grabbed a hooded sweatshirt from the dryer and walked out the exterior basement door into the backyard. The glorious November day embraced me with clean, crisp air and blue sky. The few remaining leaves on the lone maple tree lit my way forward with their stunning yellow.

When I found the front door also locked, I walked down the hill to the bus stop and waited for the 106 to Capitol Hill. My shoulders relaxed, my breathing deepened, and the knot in my stomach loosened. I already sensed a level of freedom I had forgotten was possible.

The bus driver's bright smile welcomed me aboard and reminded me of all the good in the world. The repetitiveness of the bus stopping every few blocks with the whooshing doors opening then closing became a comforting pattern—as if being reminded over and over that a chapter in my life had ended and new possibilities sat on the horizon.

I discovered myself relishing the experience of watching the passengers board the bus to chat with their friends or sit alone in silence. It was as if my experience was brand new—not unlike the joy of my first ride on a city bus as a child.

After the forty-minute bus ride, I sat down to a dinner of pizza and wine, followed by friendly games of pool at a neighborhood gay pub. I then rented a room at the nearby bathhouse for a short night of sleep.

How was it I had stayed in and repeatedly returned to such a relationship? In most areas of my life, I was strong and courageous, never a weak victim. When kids were bullied, I spoke up. When teachers were incompetent or unfair, I challenged them.

When anyone demonstrated racist behavior, I intervened. But when it came to romance, I had become disabled.

The next morning, I enjoyed a latte and biscotti on my bus ride home. As I walked up the hill from the bus stop to my house, I was at peace with my decision to end the relationship. I harbored no will to fight regardless of what happened when I walked in the door.

"Where have you been?" an agitated Jim demanded.

Silence. I felt no compulsion to answer but went to the kitchen to get water and aspirin for my hangover.

"I bet you went to a bathhouse, didn't you?"

Silence.

"Since you're not even denying it, I bet it's true."

Silence.

I walked to our bedroom and closed the door.

Later that afternoon, a calm Jim asked if we could sit down in the living room to talk. I sat on the sofa and waited.

"I've spoken with my therapist, and he suggests we consider a six-month trial separation," Jim said as his soft, gentle self.

Giving him as much eye contact as I could manage, which wasn't much, I said, "What good will that do? After six months, we'll just circle around to this same place. Nothing will change. Let's just be done."

"Is that what you want?" he whispered.

I nodded and then sat motionless. Soon, he got up and walked away. Later that week, he moved out. The seven-year roller-coaster ride had ended.

On that day, I freed myself from my toxic relationship and pledged to focus on family, friends, and career. This love and boy-friend bullshit . . . fuck it.

30

After my breakup with Jim, I went through a difficult period. My brief feeling of freedom was replaced by sadness and pain—a form of withdrawal. There was no temptation to return to the relationship, but I did grieve the loss of it. Rather than risk becoming melancholy during the Christmas season, I suggested to Eric and Ben, who were now nineteen and sixteen, that we enjoy a Costa Rican vacation together. It was a trip I couldn't really afford, but escaping Seattle and the family festivities of Christmas became the priority over any concerns about credit-card debt. With their agreement, we were off. I could be a single dad on vacation with my teenage sons, but also a single gay man in a gay-friendly country.

After a long day of traveling, we had dinner at the hotel on our layover night in San Jose. We got settled in our room, and after first checking with my sons, I found my way to a gay club. The club was conveniently located within a ten-minute walk from our hotel. My pledge to not have a boyfriend did not, for one minute, mean I intended to deprive myself of the company of men. Heaven forbid!

The sparkling lights and loud music of the huge and happening club set the mood for me to enjoy a beer at the bar and flirt from a distance. I had my eye on an adorable man in his twenties who had returned my smile. As I contemplated my next move, a man closer to my age, perhaps forty, approached, introduced himself, and attempted a conversation. He seemed to notice my attention was elsewhere and soon excused himself with a courteous smile.

Happy to see him go, I homed in on the cute, young man who kept looking my way. I picked up my beer glass to toast him from across the room, then signaled for him to join me. He did.

After introductions, I offered to buy him a drink.

"Sí, gracias," he said. Then in English, "Today my birthday."

"Oh, really!" I laughed, assuming he was feeding me a line. But he pulled out his ID to prove it. So I bought him two drinks instead of one.

"I come to your room?" he suggested after our drinks.

"Sorry, my family is with me."

"It's okay. I know a place."

I followed him to a cheap but clean hotel near the club where I just knew he could help me feel better about my life. After an hour of play, I did not feel better and returned to the hotel room where my sons slept.

The next day, we flew in an eight-passenger plane to a delightful resort in the spectacular Costa Rican cloud forest. After two days of relaxation and a nature hike to see our first sloth, we survived a treacherous thunder-and-lightning storm on our flight to Quepos on the Pacific Coast. There, we had a full week to unwind and celebrate a quiet Christmas before returning to Seattle.

Our room at the Quepos resort was much smaller than I had anticipated, but we decided the cramped quarters would be fine, given we had no intention of hanging out indoors. After all, we were in a tropical paradise with white-sand beaches and our own pool. We took long walks along the beach and throughout the adjoining national park. Later, we caught the resort's little shuttle into town where we enjoyed new foods, shopping, and, of course, cerveza, which Eric was legally allowed to drink.

Midway into our holiday, we learned of an event happening that evening. Once a week, the citizens of Quepos turned the community center into a nightclub and encouraged tourists to join the locals for drinking and dancing. We decided to give it a try.

As the sun began to set we made our way to the venue located just a five-minute taxi ride away. By 7 p.m., the place was already starting to hop. Eric and Ben joined some new friends they had met at our resort, while I joined the adults hanging around the bar and dance floor.

The atmosphere was friendly, informal, and very comfortable. Everyone seemed relaxed and ready to have fun. I bought a beer and enjoyed watching the Latin style of dancing. The rhythms were staccato and quick-paced, the dance steps colorful with dramatic intricacy. I subtly but unsuccessfully tried to emulate the joy-filled dancers as I stood off to one corner of the floor.

"Hello! It's good to see you again!" I looked up in surprise to see a man's smiling face. I shook the hand being extended but didn't recognize the face.

Reading my confusion, he reminded me, "I met you at the bar in San Jose."

Oh my goodness. He was the friendly man who had approached me in San Jose when I was distracted by the cutie.

His name was Juan Carlos. He managed the restaurant at a resort hotel called La Mariposa. He regularly traveled to San Jose to purchase restaurant supplies and transport them over the mountains to the hotel. The more Juan Carlos and I chatted, the more I liked him. It was delightful having a relaxed conversation in English with a local resident. He took an interest in my life and asked about my family and profession. When we discussed our respective relationship status, he told me he was single and I told him about my recent breakup with Jim. I was touched by his compassion and kind heart.

"Tomorrow, I would like to show you La Mariposa where I work. It's on top of the hill just outside of town and the view is very beautiful."

"That sounds nice," I replied.

"And then," he continued, the timbre of his voice warm and rich, "I hope you will join me for dinner at my favorite restaurant."

"That would be lovely, Juan Carlos. Thank you."

His face lit up with delight.

As we continued our chat standing next to the dance floor, Juan Carlos became more flirtatious, casually touching my hand or shoulder as he spoke and holding me hostage with his big, brown eyes. A drink or two later, he invited me to his house for coffee and dessert.

"Dessert?" I chuckled. "Is that what you call it in Costa Rica?"

He joked back, raising his eyebrows. "Come to my house and you will see."

"Let me check with my sons. I can't just leave them," I said.

"I can get them a taxi," Juan Carlos suggested.

Eric and Ben were fine with the plan, so I introduced them to Juan Carlos, who then spoke to a taxi driver standing outside the venue. I rode with Juan Carlos in his little two-seater car as we followed the taxi to the resort. Once I was assured that Eric and Ben were safe with the room key, Juan Carlos and I drove another five minutes up the road.

While I admired his humble wooden house, Juan Carlos fixed the coffee and put homemade chocolate cake on plates for us— literally, coffee and dessert. We sat in his spotless little kitchen at a table pushed up against the wall next to the stove. The setting was so relaxed and quaint, I envisioned myself living there. But such thoughts were out of the question. Juan Carlos seemed like a great guy, but I wasn't ready for Mister Right, only Mister Right Away.

After my cake and coffee, I asked if I could relax in the hammock slung across the wooden front porch.

"Make yourself at home!" he said with a smile.

I felt special, given his attentiveness and enthusiasm to host me with such kindness.

While Juan Carlos puttered in the kitchen, I made my way outside and relaxed in the hammock. I breathed in the subtle, floral scent that was floating in the air and enjoyed the sensual warmth of the evening, grateful for the moment as I gazed at a sky full of stars. The gentle rocking of the hammock was like a comforting, soft blanket.

When Juan Carlos finished in the kitchen, he joined me on the porch. "Would you like something more to drink? I can open a bottle of wine."

"Oh, I think I've had quite enough, thank you. Any more and you might take advantage of me."

"I would never take advantage of you," he reassured me with a smile.

"But what if I want you to take advantage of me?"

"Then it would be my pleasure."

We laughed.

"Is this hammock big enough for two?" I inquired.

"I don't know. I've never tried it before."

"Yeah, right! Never?"

"No, really! You don't believe me?"

"I don't know you well enough to believe you or not. But, okay, I'll believe you if you tell me it's true."

"It's true," he said, looking at me with soft eyes.

"Let's try it."

I did my best to make room in the hammock. We shimmied and balanced, scooted and squirmed, until both of us were relatively comfortable.

He held me in his arms as I lay my head on his chest near his shoulder. Cuddling led to soft kisses and the buildup of passion, but I soon sensed the hammock experience would result in disaster. Laughing at how silly we must look, we ceased our hammock play and carefully climbed out without incident.

Once he was standing safely again on the porch, Juan Carlos wrapped his arms around me. His delicious kiss lingered and his heat rose against mine.

"Sit down in the hammock," he whispered, guiding me to sit sideways with my legs over one side. He then helped me onto my back. "Just relax. Let me take care of you."

I melted, feeling tears well up. Oh, how I needed to relax and be taken care of—to simply receive tenderness from a kind man without effort or concern.

Juan Carlos pulled up a chair between my legs and sat down. Massaging my thighs then moving his hands up my jeans, he took his time unbuttoning my Levi's, one button at a time. His hands were soft and warm as he found his way under my briefs and lifted my dick into his mouth. My eyes rolled back in ecstasy. The smile was still plastered on my face when I climbed into my twin bed in the little room of the Quepos resort where my two wonderful sons slept peacefully.

The next morning showed every indication of being another magnificent day. The boys and I ate breakfast and shared our individual plans. We were only three days from departure and in total vacation mode. They weren't interested in souvenir-shopping with me, so we agreed to meet for lunch, but otherwise would each do our own thing. Ben wanted to join his friends on the beach and Eric, pining away for his new girlfriend, Beth, wanted to write in his journal and read a novel. I informed them of my dinner date and the likelihood I would again go to Juan Carlos' house and stay until late.

It was still daylight, perhaps 5 p.m., when I took a taxi up the hill behind Quepos village to La Mariposa Hotel overlooking the gorgeous Pacific coastline. As I walked into the lobby, the reception staff greeted me with big smiles and didn't seem surprised when I told them I was there to meet Juan Carlos.

"Yes, Mr. Gary, we will call Juan Carlos for you. Please have a seat. May we get you a welcome drink?"

"Yes, thank you."

After a short wait, a smiling Juan Carlos greeted me in his sharp hotel uniform and walked me around the finely appointed dining areas and meticulously landscaped grounds of the resort. We then drove a few miles to his house so he could shower and change his clothes. His brown skin looked particularly rich against the bright blue-and-yellow of his pressed, patterned shirt. I also noticed how his jeans fit him just right. Juan Carlos was becoming more handsome the more I got to know him.

The sun had just set as we got back in his car.

"Now I will take you to my favorite restaurant," Juan Carlos announced.

In short order, we arrived at what appeared to be a simple wooden structure painted in bold primary colors and perched on the side of a hill. Its welcoming presence was enhanced by big hellos for Juan Carlos from some of the staff. They bustled around him to shake his hand and speak to him in rapid Spanish. He smiled at me and translated. They had assured him his favorite dishes were on the menu. A smallish, middle-aged man with a huge smile, the owner I was told, came rushing up to shake Juan Carlos' hand and then mine. He escorted us through the interior of the restaurant, then out the back to a tri-level deck, each level down a few steps and extending farther out over the cliffside. The restaurant's simple wooden exterior had disguised its true elegance.

The owner escorted us past at least twenty candlelit tables, all occupied by other diners, and down to the last deck. There, centered against the far railing and featuring an unobstructed view of the Pacific coastline, sat our vacant table. The spectacular sky full of stars could only be upstaged by the full moon spotlighting our entrance.

Wine, please! I need wine! This was too much. I had to pinch myself to believe my good fortune. And, as if he read my mind, Juan Carlos nodded to our server that yes, he would have his usual wine. Red, of course. Dry, of course. My favorite, of course. And I hadn't uttered a single word. We toasted the unforgettable evening and like a soothing bubble bath, I let the bold wine and warm evening caress me as my date, Juan Carlos of Quepos, Costa Rica, ordered his favorite foods for us, always checking with me first, refilled my wine glass without being asked, and engaged me in delightful conversation.

There may have been no space in my life for a serious relationship, but a romantic dinner with a charming man fit just fine. It was my pleasure, later in the evening, to give him everything he desired.

I didn't feel codependent with Juan Carlos. I didn't fantasize or dream of a future life together. I simply stayed relaxed, present, and grateful. It was as if I had finally learned how to date in a normal and healthy way without slipping into romantic obsession.

After the boys and I returned home from our trip, Juan Carlos and I corresponded and enjoyed a couple of expensive conversations on the phone. But within a few months, our communications ended—not unusual for two people living four thousand miles apart. I would always remember Juan Carlos as a godsend, a healing salve, and a hero. He reminded me I was worthy of kindness and adoration. Meeting him taught me that someday I would be ready to experience a healthy balance of giving and receiving with a loving partner. Before that day could arrive, however, I had more lessons to learn.

31

After Costa Rica, Ben returned to the Tri-Cities and Eric returned to the house in Seattle's University District that he shared with other college students. I lived alone in a house too big for one person and didn't handle it well. I turned to workaholism during the day and romantic fantasy at night to comfort myself from the stress of my loneliness and new financial concerns.

Without Jim's monthly contributions to the mortgage and utilities, I needed to rent out the downstairs bedrooms for additional income. I'd been promoted from school principal to central office administrator, which provided a significant raise, but it wasn't enough to keep me solvent. Fortunately, the house was designed so that those living on the lower level had their own bathroom and door to the outside. Everyone enjoyed enough privacy while also sharing the kitchen and laundry.

Instead of continuing my therapy and doing the inner work so sorely needed to address my mental health, I sought men who wanted to spend time with me—or at least spend time with my body. Almost every weekend, I danced at the Timberline, a downtown gay bar housed in a century-old performance hall, where the drinks were served at a classic country-style bar sitting atop the former stage. At first, I danced on my own or with friends, then later, with whomever caught my eye. Occasionally I went home alone, but most of the time I hooked up, with lots of uninhibited safe sex, no strings attached. Call me wild. Call me a slut. I couldn't give a shit.

I had shut down my heart, becoming emotionally detached, much like my dad did during his heavy drinking days. It was the late seventies, before my coming-out, when Dad and I had sat at the kitchen table together having a bourbon. Peggy Lee's depressing song, "Is That All There Is?" came on the radio.

Dad slurred along with the song. He looked miserable. "Sometimes I think about that," he said. "I mean, is this all there is? Is this it?"

Fifteen years later, I was having similar sentiments, but instead of breakin' out the booze, as the song suggested, I had turned to lust to soothe my sorrows.

After a year of meeting a new man almost every weekend, I returned to therapy knowing I was using men like a junkie used drugs. It was time to face my fears and learn more about my codependency, which I worried could be planting the toxic seeds of sex addiction in me.

Dr. Haldeman assured me I wasn't a sex addict. I wasn't having multiple partners in one day or even one week. I wasn't going to bathhouses or having sex in parks or public places. I wasn't engaging in unsafe or degrading behaviors. No, I wasn't doing any of those things. What I was doing, however, was working like a crazy man Monday through Friday, then drinking and hooking up on the weekends, sometimes obsessing over a man I had just met. Very normal, single, gay behavior it seemed to my therapist. Perhaps he was correct, but my promiscuity was not making me happy. I felt no sense of contentment, satisfaction, or fulfillment. Only more emptiness.

When one of the bedrooms downstairs in my house became available, Eric asked if he and Beth (soon to be his fiancée) could move in. I was happy to accommodate their budding romance. A few months later, however, while paying the bills, Eric saw me stressing out and reinforced what I had already been considering. "Dad, you need to simplify your life." Within weeks of his wise counsel, I told the household I was putting the house up for sale. It sold later that month.

My rather impetuous action pissed off my housemates, including Eric and Beth, who I then helped settle into an apartment a floor below my own small apartment. I was moving fast and not looking back.

Selling my house and being out from under the high monthly expenses gave me the money and opportunity to travel to Europe with my longtime friend Larry. Unfortunately, the intended slowing of my sexual escapades got usurped by the excitement of being overseas and anonymous. I cared less about the cathedrals and museums than I did about the hottie in London, the blow job in Paris, and the hookups in Amsterdam, including a former "Mr. Leather" and a married couple named Frank and Frank, who treated me to drinks, pot, and my very first three-way, culminating in an unforgettable, earth-shattering orgasm.

I was out of control, pretending I was having fun, all the while feeling sad and lonely.

"What's the longest you've been alone?" Dr. Haldeman wanted to know. "And by alone, I mean no wife, boyfriend, roommates, or one-night stands."

I had to think long and hard. From Colleen to Phil to James to Jim—one right after the other. Then, all those men and, most recently, a house full of people.

"I think two or three months," I finally said.

"Do you think you may have a fear of living alone and being alone?"

"Even the thought of that terrifies me," I admitted.

As is the nature of synchronicity, it was about that same time when John Morefield, my colleague and now friend, introduced me to a retreat series sponsored by the Center for Courage and Renewal. The retreats were based on the work of Quaker and educational leader Parker Palmer—work that focused on spiritual and social change. John knew I had been struggling with personal issues and encouraged me to attend an introductory retreat, where I volunteered to participate in what the Quakers referred to as a "clearness committee."

John came to my cabin at the mountain retreat center to explain what I was about to experience.

"You'll sit facing the other retreat participants, who will listen deeply and with compassion to whatever you share about the issue you are facing, or whatever may be blocking you. You'll share for ten to fifteen minutes. They will not interrupt you. Their job is to hold a safe and loving space for you."

"I can't imagine talking for that long," I said. "I'm not even sure what my issue is."

"Don't overthink it, Gary," John advised. "Remain open and allow your inner teacher to guide you."

"You mean like my higher self or my connection with God?"

"The Quakers refer to it as the voice of truth, that voice within that guides us to discover our own wisdom. The other members will take notes while you are speaking and later ask you open and honest questions. The entire process will take close to two hours. Everything is confidential. In fact, they will give you their notes at the end and not speak to each other or with you about what you shared, unless you initiate the conversation."

Once seated in front of the twelve or so other retreat participants, I spoke from my heart and resisted any inclination to censor myself.

"I grew up believing there was something wrong with me," I admitted, my hands and voice shaking as I shared my deepest fears with strangers. "I know I was not the son my dad had hoped to have. I faced job discrimination for being as God created me— a gay man—and felt cast out of my hometown. I want to move forward as a spiritual person, but I'm not sure how. I want to be loved, but at this point, I'm not sure I even love myself, which probably keeps me stuck in unhealthy relationships and patterns."

By this time, my knees were pulled up to my chest with my arms wrapped around my shins. My head was bowed, my voice barely audible, and tears were rolling down my cheeks. After speaking, the listeners asked questions, then shared affirmations and nonjudgmental observations.

"Gary, if you were to paint a picture of the life you want, what might that picture look like?" one member asked.

"I noticed when you shared your desire to be a more spiritual person, you raised your chin and took a deep breath," said another.

At the end of the two-hour clearness committee, my soul felt nurtured and my eyes started to open. I began to understand how becoming a spiritual person was for me different from being religious. My spiritual path was unique to me, and between me and my God, not dictated by dogma. Over time, my routines changed dramatically. I read books to help me better understand codependency and how to overcome my fear of aloneness. I learned to meditate, started journaling, and spent a high percentage of my time outside of work by myself. I attended yoga classes and continued therapy. To help me stay focused on my personal and spiritual growth, I went without TV or newspapers. No men were in my bed for months at a time, even though the dragon within constantly tempted me.

Ignoring those temptations often required white-knuckling it until the compulsive thinking dissipated. While I still enjoyed the Sunday Tea Dance at the Timberline, I almost always arrived *with* myself and left *with* myself—a very different state of consciousness than feeling alone and *by* myself.

One year of living alone turned into two with more books, videos, retreats, and workshops to guide my developing spiritual practice. All the inner work eventually led me to Seattle's Center for Spiritual Living, which became my church home for many years.

The work to better know myself, love myself, and forgive myself was soul-enriching and heart-opening. I felt solid enough emotionally to discontinue therapy. But, in truth, stepping into my full authenticity was very slow in developing.

32

One Sunday at the Timberline, I shouted over the loud music to my friend, "Hey, Larry, I need you to tell me if a guy is cute. It's too dark in here and I don't have my glasses."

The bar was packed and the music was pumping. With Seattle's short summers, there was always a vibrant energy on clear, warm nights with sunset delayed until almost 9 p.m.

I'd been single for more than two years, and after my wild past, I'd become far more mindful about meeting new guys. I felt no urgency to get involved with someone but remained open to the idea as long as I could refrain from returning to unhealthy habits and obsessive attachments.

"What guy?" Larry asked, intrigued.

"Okay, well, don't turn around, but he's right behind you. Black guy, maybe five-foot-eight, athletic build, tight haircut."

Larry took off and returned a few minutes later.

"Yep. Pretty darn cute," he reported.

"Good to know. Thanks. Wish me luck! I'll track you down later."

"Okay, I may be outside," Larry said, which meant smoking a cigarette or a pipe full of pot. Larry never left home without his little box and a small pipe.

"Hi, may I meet you?" I asked the man in question.

His quick smile and little laugh were charming. It was impossible to tell how old he was, but he was clearly younger than me.

"Sure, you can meet me," he said.

"I'm Gary." I held out my hand as I admired each curve of his face: high cheekbones, naturally sculpted eyebrows over twinkly eyes, and a rather narrow, turned-up nose.

"I'm Thomas."

"How ya doin'?"

"Alrighty, alrighty," Thomas replied with a distinct southern twang.

"Wanna dance?"

"I don't really like this song," he said.

"Well, if you hear a song you like, just come join me."

I smiled and walked away, consciously acknowledging my personal growth. The old Gary might have abandoned his desire to dance in order to cling to Thomas' attention.

On the way to the dance floor, I finished the beer I'd been drinking and tossed the red plastic cup into the rubbish bin. Then, gratefully, I let the music take me away. I wanted to see if Thomas was watching me, but resisted looking his way.

One song ended as Cheryl Lynn's "To Be Real" mixed in. I looked up to notice Thomas dancing near me. Our eyes caught. We smiled and I moved a little closer.

Our dance movements were in total sync, and before the song ended, we were dancing pretty sexily together. Thomas giggled and moved a few inches away, appearing shy over the sexual energy we had generated.

Given my years of therapy, I'd armed myself with enough information to observe when I was starting to slip into a behavioral pattern of love addiction. I caught myself already wondering if Thomas would be my next boyfriend. I had allowed the lyrics of the love song to take me on a five-minute, dizzying ride of romantic obsession.

My eyes were open, even as I observed myself stepping onto a minefield.

Larry showed up on the dance floor to signal he was going outside to smoke. I held up a finger to let him know I'd be out in a minute.

"Do you like pot?" I asked Thomas.

"I love pot!" he replied.

The way he said "love" instantly caught my attention, reminding me of my dad the night I came out to him.

"You like this stuff, don't you?" I had asked him as we sipped our bourbons.

"I love it," he admitted, with so much passion I had no doubt he meant it literally.

And now my sexy dance partner was telling me he loved pot. *We shall see*, I told myself. *We shall see.*

"Well," I said to Thomas, "my friend, Larry, is outside smoking. Shall we join him?"

We found Larry on the side deck in the shade where I introduced him to Thomas. The deck was packed with men drinking, smoking, and laughing—a joy-filled, party atmosphere. Larry pulled out his little wooden box with the lid that slid to one side, revealing robust buds of potent Seattle pot. He filled the pipe and took a good hit before passing it along with the lighter to Thomas, who relit the pipe and sucked on it like he'd been stranded in the desert and someone had offered him water. His eyes bulged as he pulled the smoke deep into his lungs. Being a lightweight, I then took my little hit before standing in line to buy more beers while Larry and Thomas got stoned.

It turned out Thomas, twelve years younger than me, had just moved to Seattle two weeks prior, having driven cross-country from Virginia to escape an unhealthy, long-term relationship. He had rented an apartment and was starting a new job in downtown Seattle the following day.

Over the months that followed, I got to know Thomas much better and we quickly became friends. He was smart, kind, funny, and honest. He was also a competitive, softball-playing jock who could watch sports on TV, carry on witty conversations, and beat your ass at pinochle all while getting progressively more stoned. Yes, he was a serious pothead, but he was the most functional pothead I had ever met, never missing a day of work at his downtown office job.

I managed to get Thomas naked a few times, even though he said he didn't care much about sex. Against my better judgment, given his love of pot and disinterest in sex, I became enamored. Thomas was happy to date me and cuddle in bed, but he made it clear he wasn't interested in anything serious for at least a year due to his messy breakup experience.

"Well, that's actually good for me," I admitted. "It's difficult and frustrating, but good. And to be honest, I can't really see myself in a long-term relationship with someone who loves pot as much as you do. No offense."

"Well, let me know, because I have no intention of ever quitting," Thomas said flatly.

"It's not a problem right now, but if it gets to be one, I'll be sure to let you know."

And with that, Thomas and I continued to date and eventually hang out together almost every day. We talked openly about everything, laughed a lot, cooked food together, and played pinochle every week at Larry's condo.

I spent a full year spoiling Thomas rotten to win him over, including sending flowers to his office on the twenty-second of every month—"22" being his softball uniform number and his birthdate. Instead of simply letting June 22 be his birthday, I made June his birthday month and gave him a small gift every single day. I started helping with fundraising for Thomas' softball team and keeping the stats during games. One thing led to another until I spent practically all of my spare time focused exclusively on Thomas and Thomas' hobbies.

He admitted I made him feel special—a feeling he had never before experienced. But I wasn't acting like a mature, spiritual man. I had once again become codependent, falling in desperate love with a brilliant, witty addict. So when the one-year anniversary of our meeting came around, I was compelled to push the agenda.

"Thomas, I think it's only fair you let me know where I stand. I'd like us to be boyfriends and live together. But if you're not ready, then I think you probably never will be ready, at least not with me."

"So what are you saying, Gary? Is this an ultimatum?" Thomas said, smiling.

"Well, kinda, sorta," I said, keeping it light. "If you want me, I'm yours. If you don't, I have a right to know and we can still be friends—but without benefits. So what do you think?"

"Mmm . . . I think . . . okay." He grinned.

"Okay, what? Just tell me what you're thinking and stop acting like you're shy because you are not shy." I laughed.

"Okay. Here goes. Gary, you mean a lot to me. I do love you and I've loved you for a long time. So, yes, we can be boyfriends and rent an apartment together."

I was over the moon with happiness and gave him the biggest squeeze possible. To celebrate, I made his lifelong dream come true by paying for two Final Four college basketball tournaments—women's in Kansas City and men's in St. Petersburg, Florida.

My two years with Thomas were almost always entertaining. I never doubted my love for him nor his for me. But I progressively lost myself to be whatever I thought Thomas wanted me to be—his caretaker, his assistant, his chauffeur, his loyal comrade. My life outside of work, church, and family was all about Thomas: softball, pinochle, sports on TV, and pot.

Thomas lit up first thing each morning, just before brushing his teeth, then smoked pretty much nonstop when he wasn't at work. At first, it didn't bother me, but when he pressured me to buy pot for him during our time away in Florida, I got a different perspective of how dependent he was on his drug.

I had tried to be everything for Thomas, but not once did he take me on a date and pay for it. Not once did he give me a gift that wasn't related to his own hobbies. Not once did he initiate sex. I didn't blame him. Thomas had shown me who he was from the very beginning.

"Gary, you've done it again," I said out loud to myself. "You got what you wanted and now you're unhappy." Such was the insane nature of my love addiction.

My lack of mental health haunted me one day while I walked the halls at work. I experienced a rapid shift in my psyche and felt like a fuzzy bubble had shrouded me. Nothing about my life seemed real or important. My colleague, Clara Scott, a certified counselor—and earthly angel—noticed my heavy energy and asked me what was happening. After describing my symptoms, she said, "Gary, it sounds like you're functionally depressed."

That description sounded correct. I showed up for work early as always, went through my daily routines, then headed home to fix dinner, only to lie on the sofa with absolutely no desire to get up.

The day after my talk with Clara, I told Thomas how I was feeling and informed him I had made an appointment with my therapist. Dr. Haldeman suggested I get a limited prescription for a low-dose antidepressant from my doctor. I hated the idea of meds but followed through and started taking what the doctor prescribed. Within two weeks, I received the clarity I needed to move out of my depressed bubble. It was as if the drug had jump-started my brain and helped me view life from a slightly different angle, sharpening my focus.

My new clarity revealed that my relationship with Thomas did not provide enough emotional nourishment. In fact, it had depleted me. I hadn't gone as deeply into codependency or love addiction as I had with Jim, but I needed out and I immediately told Thomas—a sad but necessary conversation that happened without anger or drama. I had learned to be more honest about what served my spirit and what did not. The journey to authenticity and my true nature required a three-hundred-and-sixty-degree examination of my life, and sometimes, even loving relationships had to end.

33

The twentieth century came to a close just prior to my breakup with Thomas, and as the new year gained momentum, Eric and his now-wife, Beth, dropped in unexpectedly at my work. Although pleased and surprised to see them, I had to sit down in shock when they showed me an ultrasound with not one, but two penises in the picture! I was delighted but also thought: *How can a med student and mother-to-be prepare for two bundles of joy at once?* As it turned out, bed rest, hard work, and student loans got them through with great success.

The new millennium also birthed in me a renewed calling to a more spiritual life. When a little house in Seattle's Beacon Hill neighborhood became available for two years while the owner taught school in Japan, I decided it could serve as a much-needed sanctuary for me. I returned to a life without TV or a boyfriend, a life of spiritual practice and calm. Over time, I experienced a healthy shift away from my usual busy-ness and workaholism. I became more present and peaceful—less driven by any false sense of urgency, worry, or self-imposed nonsense.

Suddenly, I was bombarded with information ·from outside sources. Eric gave me a copy of an ancient Chinese text, the *Tao Te Ching*, meaning "the way." It blew my mind. Then, he mentioned Joseph Campbell and *The Hero's Journey*. A woman I had just met through a mutual friend opened the trunk of her car and handed me a copy of Eckhart Tolle's book, *The Power of Now*. A colleague mentioned a Larry King interview with the spiritual leader, Neale Donald Walsch, which led me to purchase even more books to guide my journey.

My studies at the Center for Spiritual Living intensified, including New Thought and metaphysical teachings. We studied the works of great philosophers and mystics from many of the wisdom traditions and integrated the cutting-edge discoveries of quantum physics. All the while, I was guided by my instructors to follow my own path to Higher Consciousness, to God. I should listen to and follow that which resonated within me. Forgiveness work, setting intentions, and affirmative prayer greatly enriched my spiritual practice. In many ways, I became a new man.

When Clara Scott had suggested I might be functionally depressed, she also asked me the best possible question. "Gary, what is it you want?" She knew depression could sometimes be linked to a person not achieving their dreams. I didn't have an answer to Clara's question at the time, but later, after contemplation, I shared with her the thought that had stuck in my mind and refused to leave.

"I want to create a soul-centered school," I told her.

The concept of a soul-centered public school had never been discussed or attempted, at least as far as I knew. Certainly, in my nearly thirty years of educational leadership, I had never encountered such a notion. Character education and social-justice curricula danced around the edges of the work I felt called to do, but a soul-centered school was something more. What "something more" meant, I wasn't yet clear. But I believed by daring to state my intention out loud—an intention that sung in my heart—clarity would arrive.

Not more than a month after my conversation with Clara, I received a group email from the superintendent that announced an opportunity for a standing principal to lead the creation of a new school. The project would be endowed for a minimum of ten years by private philanthropic funds and begin in September of the following year—2002. Pre-kindergarten education, small-class sizes, and an extended school year were all planned components of the school's program offerings.

My heart leapt. The email seemed like more than coincidence. In fact, I no longer believed in coincidence. I believed that by stating a clear intention, mysterious and miraculous forces then created new opportunities to support that intention. What if the philanthropist and superintendent would support a soul-centered school? The only way to know was to act. After serious consideration, I composed a reply.

"Hi Joseph. I have a million questions and a million ideas regarding this proposed project. I would be very interested in having further discussions with the appropriate people. Thanks for letting me know about this exciting, innovative adventure!"

I wrapped up necessary tasks at my office and went home knowing I needed to get busy clarifying a vision and mission for my dream school. Should my inquiry lead to an interview, I needed to be prepared. The ideas spinning around in my head generated a lot of energy, opening up channels of creative thought well into the night. Finally, after a brainstorming session, I made my way to bed feeling the need to rest my mind, only to have a new thought bubble up. I jumped out of bed to jot down the idea at my desk on the other side of the house. Then I brought the notepad and pen into the bedroom and set it on the nightstand.

After a few hours' sleep, I woke with renewed clarity and a dozen more ideas. I had become a vessel through which information was flowing. I could hardly write fast enough to collect all the ideas springing up. My soul-centered school would focus on guiding children to understand the power within them: the power to learn, face challenges, overcome obstacles, and contribute to solutions. We would practice loving kindness and creative expression through music, art, and dance. Each morning, we would sit a few minutes in silence and honor our bodies with healthy foods and fitness. The staff and parents would commit to the idea of "being the change we wish to see in the world" so that we might be role models for the children.

Three principals were invited to interview for the position of leading the project. I was among them. All three hour-long interviews were held on a Saturday in October. The interview team was comprised of prominent Seattle educators, the philanthropist, and members of his foundation's board of directors. Most of the questions were predictable and I quickly fell into a comfortable flow, carefully weaving in my ideas for making the school unique, including specific examples of program offerings, such as mindfulness practice, yoga, and weekly spirit assemblies for children to creatively demonstrate their learning through visual and performing arts.

But one question stumped me. "Gary, in looking over your resume, I see your experience has been predominantly with elementary school students. Why did you choose elementary schools over, say, high school or the university level?"

The question was posed by the philanthropist. After hearing his question, I realized I didn't have an answer. Nothing was coming to mind and my face scrunched, perplexed. I wasn't afraid or embarrassed. I was mystified by why I didn't have a response.

Perhaps ten seconds of silence ensued until I said, "I need to think about that a moment."

"That's okay," he interjected. "I was just curious."

But I couldn't leave the question unanswered. I needed to know for myself as much as for the interview team. I also believed the answer resided within me.

"It's a fair question and I want to answer it. So if I could have a moment of silence to consider it more deeply, I would appreciate that opportunity."

I smiled and waited for a general nod of approval. With that, I looked down and closed my eyes, breathing deeply as the room became silent. I went within and wordlessly asked: *Why elementary kids?* It was a deep dive that took only a few seconds as my mind recalled my first-grade classroom, greeting the students on the opening day of school.

Returning to the present in the interview room, I smiled again. It was clear. "It's been my practice in life to follow my joy. Little kids bring me joy."

There were smiles all around.

Only my closing statement remained, for which I was well-prepared. "I know some of my ideas are unorthodox. Should you be too uncomfortable with what I'm proposing, then I will understand if you need to select a more traditional candidate. However, I believe the creation of a soul-centered school—one that honors the separation between church and state, yet also honors the spirit in each child—is a novel-enough idea to draw positive attention and community interest. I believe it is the right thing to do and for me, what I feel called to do. So my question for you is, 'Do you want to cause a ripple or make a splash?' Thank you."

On Monday, I received a call from the Director of Personnel for Seattle Public Schools. I had been selected. Did I accept? Yes! Yes!! Yes!!!

At the semester break in January, I was relieved of my other administrative responsibilities so I could focus exclusively on co-creating The New School @ South Shore—the name I had decided to give the school. This gave me from January to September to plan, market, and open a nonexistent school—a task that seemed impossible. I had no staff, students, furniture . . . not even a pencil. But I knew the daunting job before me wasn't about what was humanly possible. It was an opportunity to let go and let God—time to put my five years of spiritual practice to work.

Each morning I found myself wide awake at 4 a.m. Initially, I fought it. Then I made a conscious decision to accept it as an opportunity to quiet my mind and remain open to new information. Clearly, something mysterious and marvelous was happening.

Stay out of the way, Gary, I would remind myself. *This is not about you. There is a Higher Power in charge. Just pay attention and do what is before you to do.*

The vision statement fell into place: "Together, we will create a loving community of purposeful learning that honors the whole child: body, mind, and spirit." The idea of an affirming yellow button for each child, parent, and staff member surfaced: "I am a bright spirit on a magnificent journey!"

A talented and diverse staff came on board. Parents flocked to the enrollment center, resulting in the longest waitlist in the city. The student population beautifully reflected the natural diversity of the neighborhood. The teachers and I visited each family in their home, bringing a children's book of affirmations along with the yellow button to remind the kids of who they already were.

Almost every family attended our welcome-to-school barbecue the weekend before the first day. The evening was lovely—a clear sky with a soft, warm breeze caressing our new community. One of the guests approached me with a big smile. "You've created a little utopia right here!" she exclaimed. She was right. It was magical—a gift to us all.

After The New School's impressive first year, I opened myself to the possibility of a cabin in the woods where I could spend twenty-four hours each week in silence and solitude. I believed such a practice would further expand and enhance my spiritual journey. So, heading home from a weekend of camping near Mt. Index, an hour northeast of Seattle, I started noticing For Sale signs along the way. I pulled the car over and wrote down a few phone numbers. Once I got home, I checked my savings and determined what I could afford as a down payment and monthly mortgage. It wasn't much.

Before calling the numbers, I imagined what would be optimal in terms of my ideal cabin: cozy but not too rustic, private, naturally beautiful surroundings, charming, and comfortable. Only one person answered the phone when I made my calls. Dan was exceptionally experienced and knowledgeable about real estate in the Index area, as well as a cabin owner himself. His positive energy convinced me to meet with him on the weekend to look at a few properties.

The third cabin he showed me sent a joyful vibration through my body. It felt like a Yes!

"This is perfect, Dan, but I may not be able to afford it."

"Well, tell me what you can do. You just never know what's possible."

"I can comfortably put $5,000 down and pay $600 a month."

"That won't be enough for a bank loan, but I'll check with the owners to see if they're willing to sell on contract."

Dan made the call and all unfolded with ease. The next weekend, I was on my way back to the cabin to sign papers. Once I had the keys in hand, I asked how soon the previous owners would be removing the furniture, TV, dishes, pots and pans, etc.

"Oh, everything stays. Didn't I tell you?"

What? Unbelievable! No, he hadn't told me, but I expressed my delight at what seemed miraculous and got busy cleaning and re-arranging to my heart's delight. The late afternoon sun filtered through the large, surrounding pines as I worked up a sweat sweeping the back deck that overlooked the immaculate Sky-komish River. I stopped for a glass of cold tap water but wished I had a beer. I opened the refrigerator to find it empty except for a tub of margarine and three ice-cold, pale ale beers. *Eureka!* Laughing with joy, I praised God, not knowing how life could get any better.

My life was unfolding with grace, mystery, and abundance. Professionally and spiritually, I knew I was in the flow of Spirit. My relationships with family were healthy and positive. Both Eric and Ben, now in their late twenties, had returned to Seattle and lived in their own residences. My daughter-in-law Beth had become my daughter-in-love—given our spiritual connection. And my three-year-old twin grandsons, Sam and Holden, were bright, beautiful, and entertaining. Still, I remained a man wanting to love and be loved: a sexual being who desired a healthy relationship. I started to wonder if I might be ready to open myself to the world of dating and romance once again.

34

Out to dinner one night with Rose, my good friend and former teaching colleague, I saw Reynaldo walk through the dining room on his way to the restroom. I had met Rey a few years prior when he played on Thomas' softball team and found him kind and gentle. He was a handsome, fit Filipino man, soft spoken, and very sexy. I told myself, *If he notices me and smiles on his way to his table, I'll ask for his phone number.*

Rey exited the restroom, immediately caught my eye, and smiled.

"Hey, Rose, do you have a pen?" I asked. She did not. "Excuse me, I'll be back in a minute."

I found Rey on the bar side of the restaurant where he had rejoined a group of five or six men.

"Hi! How are you?" he said when he saw me standing next to him.

"I'm good, Rey," I replied. Then, leaning closer to speak more privately, "May I ask you a personal question?"

"Okay," he said with some hesitation, eyebrows raised.

"Are you single?"

Laughing softly, he told me yes, he was single.

"Then may I have your phone number?"

He told it to me, I repeated it and said, "Thanks," before returning to my table with a big smile.

"I need a pen!" I announced with pretend urgency.

Just moments before Rey caught my eye, I had been telling Rose how I was feeling ready to meet someone special. When I returned to our table with a smile, she laughed out loud, knowing

I had scored a phone number. She then stopped a waiter to borrow his pen so I could write down the number on a paper coaster.

I called Rey the next day and we agreed to meet for a drink, which led to honest sharing. He had just broken up with his longtime boyfriend and wasn't ready for dating.

"That's cool," I said. "I understand."

"But if you twist my arm," he continued, "I might be interested in something casual with no strings attached."

I smiled, gently twisted his arm, and our new fuck-buddy relationship was born. This wasn't going to be the romantic relationship or spiritual partnership I had envisioned, but having a sex-only relationship with Rey drew me in without hesitation. I convinced myself it wasn't contrary to my spiritual path. In fact, it was refreshingly honest, convenient, and safe.

The sex was amazing. Once every week or two over the next year, Rey and I couldn't get enough of each other. Sometimes we didn't even make it to the bedroom—totally wrapped up in the passion of the moment. It was wild, fun, and uninhibited. So incredible, in fact, I decided I wanted to date Rey and get to know his mind as well as his body. He agreed we could date and see if the relationship evolved.

I discovered Rey to be sensitive, nonjudgmental, smart, and respectful. He seemed like the perfect man, except for one critical detail. I wanted a soul-enriching partner with whom I could deeply discuss life, love, and Spirit. Rey was not that. My attempts at such discussions went nowhere. Rey squirmed and struggled for words, clearly outside of his comfort zone.

I knew enough about codependency at that point to realize my trying to control, change, or rescue someone would be unhealthy and futile. However, I ignored that truth because I really liked Rey and felt compassion for what I perceived to be his inability to express himself. He seemed emotionally blocked and afraid. I thought I might be able to heal him of his shortcomings. Yes, I was a spiritual man leading a soul-centered school, but I had fallen into the all-too-common trap of becoming spiritually arrogant.

Over the next two years, my relationship with Rey remained drama-free and sweet but also shallow. When he asked for an open relationship, I knew it was the beginning of the end. And because he couldn't actually talk to me about his desire to play with others, he broke the news via online chat while I was at my cabin.

His request stunned me. I reacted with classic codependent behavior—denying my own feelings and agreeing to an open relationship (with Rey's assurance he would not participate in unsafe sex). The agony of what felt like Rey's rejection, along with my fear of being alone again, loomed larger than I realized—greater even than my ability to be true to myself. The dragon within then reminded me I was free to use sexual play to self-medicate the pain of not being enough for Rey. Although acting out sexually was tempting, I worried it could lead me back to promiscuity and derail me from my spiritual path.

As a compromise, I decided to engage in massage exchanges with other gay men. My intention—or so I told myself—was to enjoy bodywork and the "natural flow of erotic energy" without it turning sexual. It seemed like a good idea at the time, but the massages almost always resulted in sex of some kind. In fact, one of the men I massaged was Rey's type—Caucasian, tall, and athletic. Wanting to please Rey—another classic codependent trait—I suggested a three-way between Rey and my massage partner, both of whom were more than willing.

The experience was initially friendly and relaxed, with everyone having fun. At one point in the play, however, our guest wanted to mount me from the backside.

"The condoms are right there," I said, pointing to the nightstand. I rested on my stomach and heard him tear off a condom from the strip, only to later learn he hadn't used it. Rey watched the man enter me unsafely and didn't say anything.

"What the fuck!" I yelled.

"Don't worry, I didn't come," the man said.

"And you think that's safe? It's not! Rey, you just watched him do it?"

"I thought you knew," Rey said, shamefaced.

"Have I ever once been open to unsafe sex?"

I left the scene and locked myself in the bathroom. My head swirled with anger, fear, and shame. It would be a long three months waiting to get tested for HIV. I knew I had to do better. I knew I had to reconnect with my true spiritual nature in some way. But how? Taking at least a short break from Rey and Seattle seemed like the right first step, and Bali had come on my radar.

When I accepted the position as principal of The New School, I'd committed to only three years. I knew I could retire at fifty-five with thirty years' experience in Washington's retirement system. Having fulfilled that commitment during The New School's successful expansion years, I retired in June 2007, feeling grateful and blessed. A very generous colleague had offered me a two-month stay in a Bali townhouse as a retirement gift. Needing a break from Rey, I headed to the small Indonesian island.

I felt safe, relaxed, and comfortable in Bali. Unexpectedly, I also discovered myself of average height—quite a new and delightful experience. I traveled to many parts of the island and fell in love with the smiles and the friendliness, not to mention the natural beauty of the volcanic mountains and verdant rice fields. Bali seemed very spiritual with its daily rituals and frequent religious ceremonies. It seemed the ideal environment to support my spiritual practice by guiding me to more inner peace and fewer unhealthy obsessions.

However, the gay bars and gay beach club in the tourist town of Seminyak were an unexpected surprise and distraction. I didn't realize Bali was quite so gay-friendly. Many of the young men were extremely forward, even toward older men. Apparently, my desire to achieve more peace and less lust while in Bali would be challenging.

Many spiritual leaders have written how being challenged, even tested, is often part of the spiritual path. Gary Zukov wrote in *The*

Seat of the Soul, "Did you think authentic power would be so easily achieved?" Since I did want to become more authentic and lead a more spiritual life, I accepted that tests might be a part of my journey—not tests by a judgmental old man in the sky or temptations by some devil figure. No, I believed life would provide me ample opportunities to build spiritual muscle or be humbled when I fell short. It didn't take long for me to feel tested in Bali.

"So, how many men have you been with so far in Bali?" a hunky Indonesian man in his thirties asked me one night at the bar. I'd been in Bali for a month and had noticed the man several times before. He was always smiling and joking around with his friends or chatting it up with a Westerner.

"Actually, no one," I replied, curious about the question but enjoying the attention.

"No! Really?" he said, laughing. "That's not possible."

"Well, it's true."

"Then, my name's Jay. Maybe I can be your first," he suggested with a seductive grin.

"Hi Jay. I'm Gary. But, sorry, I'm not staying in Seminyak."

"That's okay. Right next door is a small hotel, not expensive. We can go there."

His invitation reminded me of a similar conversation in San Jose, Costa Rica, but that thought was quickly drowned out by my dragon roaring: *You're in an open relationship! Jay's sexy. He's nice. It's been a month already!*

Before the clock struck twelve, the deed was done. Pandora's box had been opened and lust had been released. Then, for the next few weeks, like an unsupervised kid in a candy store, I sampled so many treats I got a belly ache. The staff at the bars and beach club knew my name as did many of the regulars. I took men to dinner, bought drinks, got invited to parties, and danced my ass off.

My spiritual practice had gone out the window and my ego had me by the balls. However, my workout routine increased exponentially—swimming, jogging, pushups, and sit-ups—not to be healthy but to attract attention and lure my prey. Being a man in his fifties but acting like a horned-up frat boy was exhausting and insane. Clearly, I had failed my Bali test. But life doesn't just grade the paper and walk away. Nope. Life provides as many opportunities as it takes for humans to learn and grow. Evidently this human named Gary needed multiple smacks upside the head.

When I arrived back to Seattle, I unpacked, then drove directly to my cabin to detox and regain my balance. I knew I couldn't survive in an open relationship with Rey. Even though my HIV status remained negative, I had to settle down with one man in a healthy, committed relationship. I believed the only way for that to happen was to turn to Spirit. So, I wrote an affirmative prayer along with a clear intention: "I am open to my perfect partner. In divine, right time, I will know true love with an amazing man who is head over heels in healthy love with me and I with him. Thank you, God!"

Sharing my intention with Rey, I explained how my perfect partner was what I wanted and needed to be happy.

"It would be great if he turned out to be you," I said to Rey, "but that would require a deep, spirit-based relationship which we presently don't have."

Rey pulled his eyebrows together. "I have to admit, I'm not so comfortable with your spirituality."

It impressed me that Rey could articulate his feelings and I tried to keep the conversation going. "So, is our relationship—the way it is right now—enough for you?"

"It's fine," he said.

It annoyed me how often Rey said "it's fine" to my questions about our life together, but in truth, Rey was content with what we had. I wasn't. It didn't feel healthy and I definitely wasn't thriving. Still, I believed in miracles and I tried to imagine a miracle for Rey and me. But after a few additional months, our relationship hadn't shown any depth or expansion—only stagnation. I broke it off.

My perfect partner had yet to manifest.

35

After breaking up with Rey, I took stock of my life and revisited the idea of split-living between Seattle and someplace else in the world. Contemplating my options, I considered returning to either Bali or Costa Rica. Both locations met my criteria in terms of climate, safety, and cost of living. But Bali also had a spiritual energy I found appealing. So I began planning an itinerary to visit the Island of the Gods once again.

I decided to rent a bungalow in Seminyak for two months and live as a new resident rather than a tourist. In that way, I would have a better idea if Bali was the right move.

Independent living in a foreign country brings many questions to mind: How to secure accommodations? Costs? Internet access? To get answers to these and dozens of other questions, I needed locals to educate me. Chatting with men on Gay Romeo, an online social and dating site, proved not only a good way to gather valuable information, but a fun way to make contact with potential men to date once I arrived.

Most of the chat was with men who saw my profile and asked to meet me. They provided helpful information about living in Bali, even though almost all were too young to date. I had a rule about dating anyone even close to my older son's age. (Eric was now thirty-two.) But when a man's second question was "Are you a top or a bottom?" I immediately eliminated him from perfect-partner contention regardless of age or attractiveness.

But one man was different from the rest. His name was Adi.

"Hi. How are you? I hope you enjoy living in Washington. I have read about it and have always been curious." There was no photo, just the message and his interest in having a real conversation with me.

Adi and I started chatting daily, even though his curiosity turned out to be about Washington, D.C., rather than Washington State. The conversations stayed casual, mature, and interesting. We became "cyber-friends," and soon our discussions turned spiritual. I was intrigued.

Adi was a middle-aged, college-educated Christian living in a predominantly Muslim country and residing on the Hindu island of Bali. His love for Jesus was innocent and pure, founded solely on loving kindness, compassion, and forgiveness.

He didn't quite understand my "New Thought" spirituality, but he also didn't judge or challenge it. Adi was clearly special and regardless of whether or not we dated, I wanted to meet him when I arrived in Bali.

Eventually, I asked him to please post a photo and when he did, I just stared at it. He had a big, warm smile and sparkly eyes, along with a fit, athletic body. There was something about him that felt deeply soulful to me. Natural. Yes, that was it. He was leading a beautiful black horse and smiling directly into the camera. The whole scene said, "Natural Man," as in authentic, real, and healthy. Or maybe I was just making all that up as part of some new romantic obsession.

Adi and I agreed to meet sometime after my arrival in March. However, I was reluctant to contact him right away, knowing my long history of unwise relationship decisions. I could just imagine myself falling for a guy, then moving halfway around the world before even knowing if I wanted to live in Bali. Therefore, before meeting Adi, I needed clarity about the island of Bali itself.

I busied myself getting acclimated to my bungalow located in a busy tourist neighborhood. I shopped for groceries and a phone, then signed up for Indonesian language classes. For the first few days, I also got caught up in going to the bars and beach club. I loved the attention of being welcomed back to the island, but that got old in a hurry.

I then slowed down my island life, created a financial spreadsheet to see if split-living was feasible, and focused on my spiritual practice: reading, praying, journaling, and meditating. Jogs on the beach and yoga also became daily routines. In an effort to learn as much Indonesian as quickly as possible, I created hundreds of flashcards and spent hours doing my homework for class.

During the second week in my new residence, as I walked up a bustling side street of small tourist shops filled with souvenirs and sarongs, I became acutely aware of how relaxed I felt. So relaxed, in fact, I couldn't remember if I'd ever been so content. The man I observed myself becoming in Bali seemed very different from the man I had been in Seattle. And I really liked this new, evolving Gary.

It was in the very next moment when an extraordinary level of clarity stopped me in my tracks. *Yes! I will try living here.* I didn't know for how long. That wasn't important yet. If I split-lived, I would need to work approximately three months per year in Seattle. If I sold my properties and lived full-time in Bali, employment wouldn't be necessary and I would still have enough income to fly home whenever I wanted or needed to. Either way, I would make Bali at least one of my homes.

That being settled, I decided it was time to text Adi.

"Hi, Adi. I'm in Bali now. It would be nice to meet you."

A few hours later I received his reply. "Hi. Yes, that would be nice."

I didn't know what to make of the terse response. Maybe he was upset with me for not contacting him earlier. Maybe he wasn't really interested. I made up all sorts of stories.

Then I counseled myself. *Gary, don't obsess. Don't attach. If you're meant to meet him, you will meet him.*

The next day, Adi was back on my mind. I wanted to meet this guy who seemed so soulful and different. I sent another text message, "Hi, Adi. Hope you are having a great day. Maybe we can have dinner some evening when we're both free."

"Sure, that would be nice," he replied.

Is that all you can say? I thought as I scowled at the phone.

What was I expecting? He replied in a timely and friendly manner. But I selfishly wanted something more. Maybe I wanted him to pursue me or at least show more interest, something less passive.

The next day, March 17, 2008, to be exact, after completing my little bit of grocery shopping, I crossed the busy street filled with taxis and tourists to enter the alleyway leading to my language class. I ran my vocabulary homework through my head as I approached our little classroom space but stopped to read a small sign on the door, "Teacher ill. No class today."

I turned around to walk back to my bungalow. Adi came to mind again.

"My Indonesian class is canceled," I texted. "Are you free to meet me for dinner tonight?"

A reply came within seconds, "Sure, that would be nice."

I smiled and shook my head in amusement, then sent a new message. "Want to meet at 6 p.m.? I stay at Puspa Bungalows just off Jalan Double Six."

"Okay, I will find you."

I got myself ready in anticipation of Adi's arrival. My bungalow was tucked away, not visible from the street, so a few minutes before six I walked out to the main road. With helmets, visors, black hair, and smallish body types, dozens of men looked similar to my Western eyes as they zipped along. But shortly, a motorbike approached. The driver had pushed up his visor, exposing a big, bright smile—the same smile I'd admired in the photo. And, as he got nearer, I locked onto those sparkly eyes. Who was this guy? I felt like I had known him forever—and weeks later, he told me he felt the same way.

"Hi! So nice to meet you finally!" I said, extending my hand.

"Nice to meet you, too," he said.

"My bungalow is down this alley and hard to see, so I was out here where you could see me," I babbled.

"Yeah, thank you. I recognized you right away."

"Well, not too many little White men standing around," I joked and he politely laughed. "I was thinking we could have dinner on the beach. Is that okay?"

"Sure, I can give you a ride. I am so sorry I didn't bring a helmet for you."

"No problem. I don't need a helmet. We're not going far."

I hopped on behind him, sitting close but not so close as to disturb him—or me. I put my hands on his trim waist and as we traveled the three minutes to the beach, I took a quick inventory: nice butt, broad shoulders, muscular arms. *Oh, my.*

We ended up at the Blue Ocean Grill where seating was only available at the bar, giving us an opportunity to sit close and carry on an easy conversation. His English was good but his accent sometimes made it difficult for my "fresh off the plane" American ears to understand. Still, the essence of our conversation was delightful and quickly moved into discussions of beliefs, values, and God.

I was impressed and quite taken with this humble man. My earlier intuition appeared accurate. He did, indeed, seem natural and authentic, very comfortable with who he was while exuding what I sensed to be a gentle energy of deep soulfulness and inner strength.

After dinner, the balmy night air and clear sky beckoned us to walk barefoot on the deserted beach. The experience quickly felt loving. We held hands and talked like dear friends, finally reunited after a long separation. It was effortless, as if a spiritual shift had occurred and my fragmented life had suddenly aligned.

After our walk, we rode the motorbike back to my bungalow where Adi politely walked me to my door. We stepped inside for privacy.

"May I kiss you?" I asked.

He smiled, "Sure, why not?" We kissed. And kissed again.

Adi and I saw each other almost daily over the next few weeks. My feelings for him grew and every minute remained as comfortable as lounging in my favorite slippers. Such a relaxed feeling was foreign to me. I was familiar with romantic obsession, drama, and feelings of insecurity. With Adi there was only ease and joy.

One night, as we were hugging and kissing goodnight, I silently thought: *I feel like God has answered my prayer and sent this man to me.* At that exact moment, Adi said out loud, "I feel like God sent you to me."

It freaked me out! It felt both eerie and miraculous that we should have the same thought at the same time. Adi was the most amazing man I'd ever met, but it was all happening so fast, and given my history, I got scared. My stomach lurched. I didn't know if I was going to vomit, shit my pants, or both.

"Adi, I'm not feeling well. This is happening so fast."

"Okay, okay, we'll just take it slow," he sputtered.

"But it's too late to take it slow, it's already moving very fast. I need a few days to think about this," I said, ushering him to the door. "Sorry but my stomach is sick. I need the bathroom. I'll text you later."

I could see the worried look on his face but he respected my wishes and left with a little hug, wishing me a quick recovery.

After a long time on the toilet, I stripped and curled up on the cool, tile floor. *Is this what true love feels like? Okay, okay, don't panic— just breathe. Clarity always comes when you get out of the way and remember the truth of who you are.*

Finally, I felt relieved enough to get dressed and make my way to bed. I sent a series of texts to Adi. "I'm so sorry I needed to send you away, Adi. I feel a little better now."

"I'm happy you feel better."

"My feelings are strong for you, but I must be careful. Too many times I have made the mistake of moving fast and we have only known each other a short time. I hope you understand."

"Okay, I understand. I will bring you *soto* tomorrow at my lunch break. It's Indonesian chicken soup."

The next day I continued to suffer physically while also remaining unsettled emotionally. A morning message arrived checking on my condition, and at noon, Adi knocked on my door with the promised chicken soup.

I took the soup but did not invite him in. "Thank you, Adi, I will try to eat some of this. I have to rest until I feel better, okay?"

He looked dejected but I would not be deterred. This was about me taking care of myself and making sure I did not repeat my codependency patterns of the past. Clarity must come first. For the next two days, Adi respected my wishes and showed only love and compassion. Each day, he sent a couple of text messages and dropped by with soup.

By the end of the third day, I was clear and healthy again. I was calm, at peace, and full of joy. This was truly a special man. A gift from God. And I was going to let myself fall head over heels in love if that was to be in the cards. I would let it play out naturally without forcing, controlling, or manipulating. No obsession or drama. Instead, I would simply express gratitude that my perfect partner and I had possibly found each other.

When Adi arrived that evening, I invited him in with a big smile and long hug. We talked deeply and honestly about our feelings for each other. We shared our hearts and then we shared my bed. The kissing was sweet. The touching, electric. Then, as if a switch got flipped, Adi took over. The quiet, humble man pressed his muscular body against mine and left me breathless.

After, as he gently held me, he said, "I have nothing to give you but my big heart."

I smiled to myself. *Enough. That's enough.*

By the end of my two months in Bali, split-living no longer made sense. I wanted to be with Adi and only Adi. Like in the movie, after Harry met Sally, he discovered he wanted to be with her for the rest of his life. So, he wanted the rest of his life to begin as soon as possible.

Fourteen years later, as of this writing, I have never regretted my decision. Unfortunately, the same cannot be said for Adi.

36

I returned home for a month to sell my property and spend time with my family—the highlight being the joyous wedding of my younger son, Ben, to the lovely Akela. It had always been Ben's dream to be a family-man, and he certainly achieved that without delay, because also in attendance was their handsome, six-month-old son Caden. I now had three grandsons along with Eric and Beth's precocious twin boys, Sam and Holden, already eight. But I would only have to wait another eight months until Ben and Akela gave me my only granddaughter, the beautiful Chloe—who unbeknownst to everyone was in early embryonic development on her parents' wedding day! I missed Colleen more than ever on that day and I'm sure I wasn't the only one. She would have absolutely loved being there—and perhaps she was. Who knows?

A few days after the wedding, I headed back to Bali, packed to the max. Adi met me with a happy hug, then took me to the traditional brick house he had rented for us while I was away. I was pleased to see he had set up the kitchen but even more impressed with our bedroom. He had purchased a new mattress, lovely sheets, romantic mosquito netting, and sweet-smelling fresh flowers to welcome me.

Adi worked six full days each week at an equestrian resort, leaving me on my own during those hours. Over the next two months, I shopped for housewares and bamboo furniture in the local neighborhood, kept to my spiritual practice, and puttered around the house—organizing, decorating, and doing the necessary domestic chores. I even found temporary satisfaction in ironing clothes, but that didn't last long and I soon discovered how inexpensively I could get our laundry done professionally for only a few dollars.

After riding on the back of Adi's motorbike, I started to understand the Indonesian rules for driving. What initially seemed chaotic actually had a sensible flow. That's when I found the confidence to take his mountain bike onto the busy roads and ride twenty minutes to a supermarket, where I could shop for Western products and fresh meats.

It was during these bicycle trips into town that I decided to enjoy a reflexology foot massage at a spa close to the grocery store. I loved a good foot massage, and in Bali, the prices were incredibly low. The young man massaged my feet and calves with good pressure, just the way I liked it. I could sit back, relax, and listen to the soft, healing music.

"Your pressure is strong. Do you do body massage?" I asked.

For years, I had treated myself to massages in Seattle, but what cost a hundred dollars in the U.S. cost about five dollars in Bali.

"Yes, you want body massage?"

"One hour would be great!"

The massage swept me away. There had been a fair amount of stress, albeit positive, with moving to a new country and into a new home with a wonderful man I had only known for a few months. My body relaxed as the lightly scented coconut oil was massaged into my muscles.

I made it part of my weekly routine to ride the bicycle into town, get a massage and groceries, then pedal home. The foot massage followed by a body massage was a rejuvenating two-hour treatment. However, after three or four sessions, the massage shifted. The therapist's hands crept closer to my genitals, arousing me. And because I didn't object, in fact moved my body to indicate pleasure, he progressed from a deep stomach massage down to the pelvic area, repeatedly brushing my cock. Before long, I orgasmed. At first, I felt embarrassed and then ashamed, knowing I would have to tell Adi.

When Adi got home from work, I told him what happened, apologized, and promised not to return to that spa again. But something inside my brain wouldn't let the erotic experience fade. I had been so sure my desire to play sexually would disappear as soon as I was with my perfect partner. The erotic massage had me questioning that assumption and revealed the dragon within had been sleeping in the shadows all along.

Fantasies of erotic massage began haunting me day and night. My heart wanted Adi and only Adi, but the dragon within wanted more. I resisted by staying focused on healthy living with the love of my life. I prayed and meditated daily. Eventually, the fantasies and cravings calmed down.

Adi and I decided to take a big step forward in the progression of our beautiful life together by investing the money from my Seattle properties into land where we could build a simple house. After more than a dozen considerations, we settled on a one-third acre of gorgeous rice-field land near Tanah Lot Temple, twenty minutes north of our leased house and farther away from the noisy tourist areas.

I suggested Adi resign his position at the equestrian resort since there was so much involved in securing the property, hiring workers, and beginning construction.

"I think I can resign at the end of August," he told me in July.

I was curious as to why he didn't want to resign immediately, since my pension was enough for us to live simply yet comfortably. But I respected his decision and didn't press. What I learned later was that he had two bills to finish paying. One for his motorbike and the other for medical expenses incurred when a pack of dogs on the beach had spooked a temperamental horse he was riding. Adi ended up in a pile of concrete rubble with broken ribs. His employer wouldn't pay the medical bills and even docked his salary for days missed. We both were grateful when he could resign from the equestrian resort.

Over the next year, our humble two-story brick, teak, and ironwood house was constructed in the middle of rice fields,

244 · GARY TUBBS

giving us views of both sunrise and sunset. Six of seven mornings during the construction period, Adi and I drove to the worksite to assist the crew with the endless tasks involved in converting rice-field land into a residential property with ponds and gardens. During this time, I also built up enough confidence to drive the motorbike. I enjoyed putting around the quiet village roads near our property. Eventually, I felt comfortable driving into town to run errands.

On Sundays, the work crew took the day off and Adi and I often headed to the beach to walk, jog, and splash around in the Indian Ocean. It was on one of these Sundays, with our construction project more than half completed, when Adi ran into a middle-aged European man he knew named Billy. Billy then introduced us to his young Indonesian boyfriend Arie. They invited us to their apartment in Seminyak for drinks and dinner, at which time we learned Arie was a massage therapist. They had recently converted their extra bedroom into a very pleasant massage studio and Arie was in the early stages of trying to get his business going.

The following week, I scheduled a massage session with Arie. He was quite skilled, but without my encouragement, began touching me erotically. It took every ounce of willpower I had to keep my promise to Adi.

"Please don't," I said. "I don't want that."

"Okay," he said. "But I need to come."

It surprised me a professional massage therapist would even suggest such a thing, but I kept quiet. Arie quickly stripped, then leaned himself over the massage table to rub his erection against my thigh while masturbating. He orgasmed then cleaned up the mess with the sarong he had been using to drape me.

I didn't tell Adi about Arie's orgasm nor did I share my temptation to return for another massage. I knew what was right to do, but instead I kept those secrets to myself. A common adage in the world of recovery is, "We are only as sick as our secrets." I was becoming sick.

So, as my fifty-seventh birthday approached, I told Adi I was going to treat myself to a massage and scheduled it with Arie.

"Before we get started, Arie, I want to show you my boundaries so you understand what is okay to do," I explained.

"What do you mean?" Arie asked.

"Well, I think it will make more sense if I show you. Are you willing to get on the massage table?"

"Okay, you can massage me. Should I take my clothes off?"

"Fine with me," I said with a smile

Arie stripped and got on the massage table. I demonstrated and explained the limits I would allow: Down the butt cheeks and crack, fine. Under the upper legs to the groin, wonderful. Deep stomach and pelvic massage, nice. But no dick or ball action. No orgasm. Of course, I was getting my jollies by putting my hands on the young man's body, but I justified it since there was no touching of genitals.

I had just finished my demonstration and was trading places with Arie when a man yelled, "Arie!" I thought it might be Billy yelling, even though he had said he was leaving to run errands. I worried he was ill or hurt, his voice sounded so urgent. Not for one second did it occur to me that he was outside the room, standing on a chair, and spying on us through a small hole in the wall.

Arie was startled. "It's Billy! He's been watching!"

"Fuck!" I said. "Fuck! Fuck! Fuck! Adi is going to break up with me."

I quickly got dressed, and as I left the apartment, I saw Billy in the courtyard.

"I'm so sorry, Billy. It's all my fault. Don't blame Arie."

I'm not sure why I said that, but it didn't matter. My primary concern was for Adi and how he would react once I'd told him what happened.

The motorbike ride home was a very long forty minutes. When I reached our construction site, I saw the crew milling about the property, but I couldn't find Adi. I ventured to the very back boundary of our land and saw him sitting alone on the ground, something I'd never seen him do before.

"Adi, I need to tell you something," I said.

He looked at me with glassy eyes. "Billy called me. I already know," he said.

My tears came immediately. I could not stop crying. Adi's sadness, my shame—our trauma together—was so desperately disturbing.

Adi's trust in me was bruised if not broken. And I was faced with the very real fear that I was spinning into behaviors I seemed incapable of controlling. I was with my perfect partner, building our dream life together and still facing acting-out challenges I thought would be resolved once I was in a healthy relationship.

A few weeks later, it seemed Adi had worked through his sadness. His smile returned, along with his sense of humor and sweet affections toward me. He then suggested we discuss other ways to address my desire for erotic massage. We agreed to try engaging in three-way massage from time to time. There was no need for secrets and we found security in being together.

Then, over the next three years, Adi and I met other couples in the Bali gay community, only to discover the incestuous nature of many social groups, particularly those with expats from Western countries. There were polyamorous relationships, open relationships, and "don't ask, don't tell" relationships. Many young Indonesians happily engaged in secret play or even full-blown affairs. It often didn't matter if their sex partners had boyfriends or not. Endless opportunities revealed themselves. Adi and I got caught up with a rather promiscuous crowd and occasionally experimented together with safe, sexual adventures involving others.

The play was only thrilling in the short-term, not at all satisfying. Even though we continued to feel secure in our love—never jealous or threatened in any way—we eventually agreed to stop all outside play. We knew it was not contributing to a healthy, sustainable relationship.

Adi told me that maintaining monogamy was not an issue for him. But it had become increasingly challenging for me. The dragon within had loved its opportunities to be unleashed on occasion. It was willing to rest for a while, but never slept for long and certainly was not tamed. It craved getting sexually high, achieving a temporary state of euphoria, which convinced me the high was what I wanted and needed. The outside play, even with Adi, was like playing with fire and I had set myself up to be burned. What Adi could discontinue doing with relative ease had become a dangerous habit for me.

I loved the flow of erotic energy—even more than the sexual release. Like my dad and Phil loved bourbon and Thomas loved pot, I craved the hit erotic energy gave me. I wanted Adi to give me permission to occasionally receive erotic massage—which he wisely did not give. Instead, he said, "I would rather be on my own."

I became convinced I could not live without my drug and started to act out with flirting, online chat, and fantasizing. I reassured myself: *It's no big deal. Just do this but not that. A little bit is no problem. Once in a while is okay.*

However, during our fifth year as a couple, I began to spin out of control—touching, gay massage, and even sex with a friend. The shame, guilt, and pain kept building, but I couldn't stop. I had become powerless.

Adi's integrity and authenticity made me want to be a better man. I wanted to be for him what he was for me. To do that, of course, I had to be honest and faithful. Instead, I covered up, snuck around, and withheld the truth. I wrapped up my shit in a pretty package with a lovely bow, attempting to make everything—including myself—appear perfect.

Convinced I had adequately hidden my indiscretions while also knowing I loved Adi with all my heart, I mentioned to him that we could get married in Washington State, since same-sex marriage had been legalized. He initially made no response and I let the subject drop. But weeks later, Adi softly said to me with his eyes downcast, "You talked about getting married—but I'm not so interested." He looked so sad and yet so strong.

I knew Adi well enough to understand what he was really saying. He couldn't trust me. I had to agree with him, because I couldn't trust myself and saw no escape from my powerlessness. I remained quiet. I could only look to the floor and nod my head in shame as I sadly accepted that the day would come when Adi would have no choice but to leave me.

37

When Adi informed me he wasn't interested in marrying me, I was crushed. I lay awake that very night with him sleeping beside me, trying to wrap my head around my inability to remain monogamous. I was not feeling codependent or off balance with romantic obsession. Adi was clearly my life partner. We were best friends and had healthy sex together—present with one another, intimate and vulnerable, safe and free to give and receive. I searched and searched for something to explain my acting-out, but I kept coming up empty.

Having reached the conclusion that I was trapped in my insane behavior, I decided my only choice was to surrender. I fell asleep having given life permission to play itself out, even if that meant the end of my relationship.

Then, in the dead of night, my soul cried out in such terror I sat straight up in bed, gasping for breath. I felt trapped in a dark, dank place with no escape. Within seconds, however, light flooded my mind, illuminating a vivid recollection of a recent email I had received.

Without disturbing Adi, I immediately went downstairs to open the email from my friend, Kevin, in Seattle. In it he had courageously shared his participation in SLAA meetings. SLAA was a twelve-step recovery fellowship, Sex and Love Addicts Anonymous.

When I first received Kevin's email, I was curious about why he attended such meetings. What was happening with him? And the use of the word "addict" in the group's title disturbed me. In my biased thinking, sex addicts exhibited severe behaviors, like my therapist had counseled me years ago. I wasn't engaging in any of the behaviors that stereotypically identified a sex addict. I did admit, however, I no longer felt in control. Even with every reason in the world to stop acting out sexually, I no longer seemed able to do so.

I certainly didn't want to be a sex addict and I wasn't yet convinced I was. Nevertheless, by taking a broader, more compassionate, less judgmental view of addiction, I was at least willing to seek any help available to save my relationship. That was my primary motivation on that night of terror—I was desperate to save my relationship.

I googled SLAA and took the forty-question survey for self-diagnosis. The survey asked questions, such as: Have you ever tried to control how much sex to have? Do you get high from sex and/or romance? Do you crash? Have you ever had a serious relationship threatened or destroyed because of outside sexual activity? I was shocked at how many times I answered yes to the forty questions.

There was no denying the fact that I needed to investigate SLAA. And by the grace of God, there was a fellowship meeting in Bali. It seemed miraculous such a group could exist on a small island in the middle of the ocean.

First thing the next morning, I shared my discovery with Adi. He showed his love and support by agreeing to drive me to the town of Ubud, an hour away, for my first meeting. He waited outside the meeting space which was located in an open-air room above a small restaurant. Before climbing the stairs to the meeting space, my fear-based thinking led me to wonder who would be present. Would I feel welcome? Would I be uncomfortable with the people in attendance given what I believed to be true about sex addicts?

My fears were for naught. The group was small and friendly with everyone appearing and behaving remarkably normal—actually abnormal, in that everyone was charming and attractive.

Two of the women were professional models, one an Australian actress. The men in attendance were sensitive and non-threatening. The meeting format explicitly identified sexual orientation as being irrelevant.

The individuals in the SLAA fellowship varied in their personal journeys and acting-out behaviors. Many had a history of alcohol or drug use before realizing that love and/or sex addiction was their core issue. Some were addicted to pornography, masturbation, or hooking up with prostitutes. Some suffered from romantic obsession while others had such a fear of romantic relationships they had become sexually anorexic. Like me, however, every person in attendance at the SLAA meetings shared a historical pattern of dysfunctional relationships.

I learned that sex and love addiction is an intimacy disorder— not really about sex or love at all. It had never occurred to me that my acting out was directly linked to intimacy and vulnerability. I wanted to know more. And as people shared, I could see they were demonstrating vulnerability by speaking openly and honestly in a safe space. Throughout my life, being honest about my mistakes had too often been met with judgment. What a breath of fresh air to share without fear, and in return, receive only compassion and acceptance.

I attended meetings for months, then felt ready to work with a sponsor in setting "bottom lines." Setting bottom lines involved self-identifying behaviors from which I had to abstain in order to recover. Not breaking those bottom lines was referred to as sobriety, while breaking one was called a "slip." To slip repeatedly and spin out of control was to relapse. My bottom lines were no sex outside my marriage, no fantasy, no gay massage, no flirting or sexual innuendo, including online chats.

As I diligently worked through the twelve steps with a sponsor, layers of shame peeled away, revealing a new level of self-trust and integrity. I was definitely on the road to recovery—completely sober and monogamous for a full year.

Piece of cake—easy as pie—or so I thought.

On December 17, 2014, I proudly received my "One Year chip" for maintaining bottom-line sobriety. I then asked Adi to marry me and he accepted. I was a happy man and quickly got busy announcing our engagement and planning a June wedding to be held at my brother's house in Kennewick. In the meantime, I continued to attend meetings and began to sponsor others in recovery.

My relationship with Adi was like putting together a mysterious, thousand-piece jigsaw puzzle over a seven-year period. It went smoothly in the beginning. Then, there were periods of great challenge when it didn't look like the pieces were going to fit. Finally, the complex puzzle shaped up into a thing of beauty with only one piece missing. But a jigsaw puzzle with nine-hundred, ninety-nine pieces linked together is still not complete. Marrying Adi was, for me, like putting the last piece in place. I felt whole and humble that this wonderful man was able to forgive me, then honor me with his hand in marriage on a record-hot day, June 27, 2015.

My entire family attended our ceremony wearing the Indonesian batik shirts, blouses, and dresses I had purchased. My best friend, Rose, and her husband, Geoff, served as officiants, while my six-year-old granddaughter, Chloe, charmed us as the flower girl and seven-year-old, Caden, carried the rings. Grandson Holden, almost fifteen, played a classical piece on the accordion and Rose's daughter, Isabelle, sang John Legend's beautiful lyrics to "All of Me."

A hundred guests later arrived to celebrate with us. My dear Aunt Patty gathered us in her arms and said, "This is such a beautiful love fest." I agreed and felt blessed to know such joy.

38

Being free from all bottom-line behavior for the eighteen months prior to my marriage to Adi gave me the feeling of having accomplished something wonderful. I had not slipped once, nor had I become severely tempted in any way. It had all been so easy: read the text, work the steps, attend meetings, pray, meditate, and keep communications open with my sponsor.

Rather than remain in a place of gratitude and humility, however, I became overconfident. I thought: *Perhaps I'm special, not like the true addicts in my meetings. Maybe I'm like an alcoholic who can enjoy non-alcoholic beer without it causing a problem. I think I can safely play around the edges as long as I don't have sex with anyone.*

With that mindset, I gave myself permission to fantasize and masturbate on occasion—beginning only a few months after my marriage to Adi. Later that year, when I was contacted online by a young man who seemed to have a crush on me, I played along—just for fun. My ego loved it. Yes, fantasy and online chat with sexual innuendo were behaviors not allowed according to my bottom lines, but what could be the harm in dabbling once in a while?

Well, the harm soon became evident. An addict doesn't stop after a little bit of "harmless" behavior. I started negotiating with myself. *I'm strong enough now to enjoy an occasional gay massage as long as I don't have a happy ending. And chatting online or even meeting up with this young man is okay as long as there's only flirting but no touching.*

But one broken bottom line led to two. One gay massage led to several. Relapse was inevitable.

Two years later, I had become a walking, talking, bullshitting mix of multiple messy metaphors. I had dug myself out of a rabbit hole only to be sliding down a slippery slope onto thin ice while playing with fire. Evidently, recovering from addiction was not a piece of cake or easy as pie.

Adi sat me down and said, "I don't want to ask questions. I want you to talk to me and tell me everything. Be honest so we can walk through this, hand in hand together." He then sat, waiting.

It was my day of reckoning. While my fear and shame overwhelmed me, I knew it was time to step away from the pain of deceit and into the healing power of truth. "I'm too afraid to speak out loud," I said to Adi. "You deserve the full truth. Please let me write it out so I can say all that needs to be said."

I fully disclosed everything from small flirtations to close encounters to erotic massages. I had not had full-blown sex outside my marriage during my relapse, but the obsessive-compulsive pattern of inappropriate online chats and sexual massage had unleashed the addict within me. The downward spiral of acting-out behaviors had once again convinced me at a base level that I was living the life I wanted.

I sat quietly as Adi read the disclosure. During the silence, I breathed deeply and turned inward. I accepted all that was happening and trusted God to light the way for us both. If Adi wanted to separate, I would accept that and financially support him forever.

"I'm not angry," Adi said. "I am just sad."

"I'm so sorry," was all I could say.

"This started soon after we got married?" he asked.

"Sadly, yes," I nodded.

"That makes me regret getting married," he said in a voice so soft it was almost a whisper.

Hearing that, I closed my eyes as the tears squeezed through. What had I done? How could I have ever hurt this sweet man again with my unfaithful behavior?

Almost every day during the next four months, I wondered if Adi was preparing to leave. He never smiled and rarely spoke except to answer a question with a soft, concise reply. There was no touching and an ocean of bed between us at night.

Each evening, I wrote him a note to share what I was feeling and to remain honest about my day. Were there any fantasies, unhealthy thoughts, or temptations? I sat at the table while he read my notes and waited to see if he had any questions or comments.

"Thank you," he would say. Rarely anything more.

So much had been destroyed by my diseased choices. If our marriage could be rebuilt over time, I knew it depended on my ability to recover—truly recover.

I remained free from all acting out during those months, but worried I might still be ill-equipped to maintain sobriety forever, even with the support of my twelve-step fellowship. I decided to seek treatment at a rehabilitation center and shared my decision with Adi.

"But you go to SLAA already. If that didn't work, why do you think rehab will work?" he asked.

"First of all," I replied, "SLAA works. I relapsed, but that doesn't mean SLAA doesn't work. It's not unusual for addicts to relapse at least once. I'm not sure what to expect from rehab, but I want to do everything possible to recover. I want to save our marriage, if that's possible, but first I need to save myself. I can't live like this whether or not we're together."

"Where will you go?"

"Chiang Mai, Thailand. It's a twenty-eight-day treatment program. They have a three-day program for family members. I hope you'll go, but I'll understand if you can't."

So, in late January 2018, with Adi at my side, I checked into The Cabin Rehabilitation Center. My clear intention for being there was to learn as much as possible and go as deep emotionally as I could.

Adi attended the family program where he found support from the loved ones of other addicts and learned valuable information about addiction. He joined me for lunch but otherwise had to remain offsite. On his third and final day before flying back to Bali, he wrapped me up in his big, strong arms. It was a hug I hadn't felt for months.

"I am so sorry you have this disease," he said. "I now understand how hard this is for you. I love you and support you."

"Oh! Thank you!" I said, feeling relief and gratitude as tears streamed down my face. "I love you, too, and thank you for your support. It makes all the difference."

During my first weeks of rehab, I learned how my family's multi-generational history of alcoholism was worth noting. The staff at the rehab center taught me there was little difference between the addict brain of substance abusers (drugs and alcohol) and process addicts (sex, gambling, compulsive eating, etc.). It is believed the addiction occurs because of a malfunction in the brain's reward system. Normal people have a stop system to avoid risky behaviors, but with addicts, this stop system effectively deactivates.

After Adi left, the real work began and I soon knew rehab had been the right decision. There were top-notch counselors and a balance of traditional and holistic treatment methods, including progressive techniques to free old trauma energies—the results of shaming, bullying, and emotional abuse.

I learned how my lack of healthy emotional boundaries had dramatically impacted my life. My perfectionism, for example, caused me to be impatient and judgmental. Always feeling under pressure, albeit self-imposed, I judged myself and others harshly. I covered up my discontent with the soothing behaviors of romance, love, erotic energy, and sex. The dragon within (my addict mind) repeatedly convinced me I would feel better, even though it was always the same dead end.

I came to understand, through introspection, the roots of how my addiction started and why it had found such fertile ground in me. Yes, there were hereditary factors, exacerbated by my upbringing and coming out. But the deepest root of the most toxic weed wasn't what my dad thought about me or what society thought about me. It was what I believed to be true about myself. My addiction developed in an effort to mask the unbearable pain of believing I wasn't enough. Not boy enough. Not tall enough. Not quite smart enough or talented enough or good enough, which all equated to not being lovable enough.

I thought I had hit bottom once before when I woke up in terror and recalled my email from Kevin about SLAA. I found the Bali fellowship meetings and stayed clean for more than a year before asking Adi to marry me. In hindsight, I can see I was determined to win Adi. My focus was on the marriage (goal-oriented), not on my true recovery (soul-oriented). I hadn't completely surrendered to my higher power, still thinking I was in control. As a result, I lost my moral compass and broke Adi's heart. In recovery, I became committed to spending the rest of my days—one day at a time—striving to be the husband Adi deserved and the person I knew myself to be.

39

"I'd like you to consider implementing semi-weekly check-ins," recommended Dr. Piper, the couples' counselor Adi and I started seeing upon my return from Thailand. "You each pick a day of the week to initiate the conversation, sharing how you are doing emotionally, physically, and spiritually. Gary, you should also share if you have had any challenges to your bottom-line recovery."

Dr. Piper had been recommended by a counselor at the rehab center in Thailand. Adi and I felt comfortable with her and also felt blessed to have such a talented and insightful therapist available to work with us in Bali.

Two months later, in addition to our check-ins, we started giving each other weekly foot massages as a show of intimacy. We also agreed to schedule a regular date for sex. If one of us was unable to show up for the date, it became that person's responsibility to explain and set another time—no surprises, no disappointments.

These practices kept us in communication and in touch with each other, providing a safety net to catch any insecure or troubling feelings one of us may have been experiencing. The multiple connections each week provided me, as the recovering addict, with the assurances I would be heard, touched, and loved.

My first year after rehabilitation was relatively easy in staying free from acting-out behaviors. I had no desire to flirt or chat online. When fantasy tempted me, usually when I was tired or alone, I changed my thinking or meditated to stop thinking altogether. If all else failed, I grabbed a good book, even if it was 2 a.m. I still loved massage and had regular, safe massages. But even

safe massages could sometimes feel triggering, which informed
me to withdraw from all massage for at least a month. Any temptation to have sex outside my marriage had dissipated.

I gave myself permission to be a work in progress rather than
a work of perfection, resulting in less defensiveness and a return
of my sense of humor. I became more humble, strong yet compassionate, more relaxed and patient, although patience remained
a challenge. I was on a delightful path to inner peace, self-
acceptance, and self-love.

Year two after rehab was different, however. Many of my old,
unhealthy habits remained inactive and my relationship with Adi
continued to strengthen and mature into a solid experience of un-
questionable love. But my desire for erotic massage grew intense.
I fought fantasy and caught myself waiting for an opportunity to
act out. I shared these temptations with Adi during our check-in
time and brought them up in our continuing counseling sessions
with Dr. Piper. I was particularly concerned about a trip Adi had
planned to visit the island of Java for a family reunion.

"Adi, how about you take my motorbike key with you so I'm
not tempted to drive into town for massage?"

"This is your issue, Gary. You need to take care of it without
involving me," Adi replied.

Adi was correct. His direct statement helped me become absolutely honest with myself. I could see how I had mentally
planned and schemed. First I had used fantasy to lure myself. I
had already imagined each step, each action for getting a hit. All
the dominoes were lined up. If the first domino was tipped, by
scheduling an erotic massage, there was a good chance I would
keep the appointment rather than cancel it, then binge on more
massages, resulting in a relapse.

Instead, I created a plan to keep myself safe. I asked the SLAA
fellowship to support me with phone calls and I locked my motorbike key at the very bottom of my little house safe. Having it
out of sight and not easily accessible made all the difference I

needed. I cancelled all appointments that would have taken me into town and kept my phone and laptop shut down, except to check for important messages once a day. Finally, I busied myself with healthy, top-line activities: reading, baking, swimming, gardening, meditation, yoga, and walking the dogs.

After the first day of Adi being away, my shaky, fear-based thinking subsided then vanished. I felt solid and relaxed again—clear, wise, and powerful. I knew I was being guided into right action, letting go and letting God, which resulted in building spiritual muscle and authentic power. By God's grace, I made it through the week without acting out on any bottom-line behaviors.

After a friend suggested it, I enrolled in a ten-day Vipassana silent meditation retreat to be held in the mountains of Bali. I hoped the experience would support my recovery by grounding me more deeply in Spirit and teaching me to better quiet my mind. Without phone, laptop, books, or even paper and pen, I was with myself and my thoughts in silence. All eye contact with others was to be avoided, including at mealtimes.

A 4:30 a.m., the gong called us to a large meditation hall where thirty men and thirty women sat on opposite sides of the room. Before we began our first hour-long meditation period, we were given instructions in meditation posture and breathing. The experience quickly became an inward journey—a deep and intimate time with self. Over the first few days, I was challenged by the discomfort of multiple meditation periods per day. I questioned my decision to be there.

But then, each subsequent day became more pleasant. By day six, I was at peace. On day nine, I had a profound meditation experience known as a free-flow. Subtle vibrating sensations emanating from the crown chakra at the top of my head spread without delay or distraction, out, down, and through every cell of my body. It was extraordinary—like a warm shower on a chilly day, only with super-slow, effervescent micro-bubbles washing over me. The sensations grew progressively stronger over the course of several minutes. I sensed myself vibrating as if my body's subatomic particles were expanding, detaching, then dissolving—a "Beam me up, Scotty" type experience that was both euphoric and foreign. My eyes were closed, so I couldn't witness what was physically happening, but when it felt as if my hands were levitating, I became startled. Rather than simply observe, as I had been instructed, I got distracted, thus ending the experience.

I later learned in private counsel with the teacher (when conversation was permitted) that what I experienced happened from time to time, but could not be chased or desired. I was advised not to cling to the memory or crave for it to reoccur.

I also learned my blissful experience, although short-lived, may have cleared a pathway for my body to release negative emotional imprints (fears, beliefs, thoughts) that had been repressed over the years from tragedy, trauma, and shame, for example. If my body felt ready and safe to allow the unpleasant imprints to surface, I should observe without reaction. I was not to search for stories or reasons. I was not to analyze, judge, or struggle. It would be a time for me to simply observe with focused attention, allowing the negative imprints to be released.

At the end of day nine, the teacher informed us the silence requirement would be lifted after our morning meditation period on day ten. In anticipation of heading home, I enjoyed a final, peaceful night's sleep.

The morning gong chimed for day ten and our session began as usual: enter in silence, sit comfortably and motionless on our cushions, close our eyes, and focus our attention on our breath and the vibrations in our body. Midway through the meditation period, however, instructions were given for a different form of meditation, known as "metta." During the metta meditation, we would send loving thoughts to ourselves. After a few minutes, those loving thoughts were to be energetically and silently shared with the others in the room, then out to the village, and eventually blanketing the whole world with loving kindness.

I'd experienced metta meditation before and always found it enjoyable, often deeply moving. During the final meditation of my retreat, however, I was experiencing unpleasant feelings in my lower abdomen. I recalled the teacher's instruction to not participate if we felt in any way negative. So I turned my palms up, welcoming loving support from the others in the room.

I then reminded myself: *Simply observe. Don't be afraid. Don't make up stories about what is happening. Instead, stay with what is actually happening and follow it as deeply as possible.*

The physical discomfort intensified. While everyone else was presumably sending out vibes of love and compassion to the world, I was slowly and silently doubling over. My eyes remained closed and I wasn't sure I could open them if I tried. I concentrated on maintaining a calm breath and allowing my body to feel and release whatever was optimal in the moment, without question or comment. My mouth contorted. I remained in a half-lotus position but my body became severely hunched, with my head approaching the floor.

The teacher's forewarning that negative imprints might be released after my strong free-flow helped me accept what was happening, even to be grateful. I had been told to keep my full attention on the current moment, but my mind briefly recalled the time, eleven years prior, when I had purged fear-based toxins. Adi and I had just had the same thought at the same time, *I feel like God has sent you to me.* The Vipassana experience was similar in some ways, but the abdominal pain was unique. I wasn't nauseous. My intestines weren't cramping like before. I didn't feel faint. Instead, the pain brought up deep feelings of shame mixed with sadness. Grief tinged with regret. I wondered if I might cry but no tears came. My job was to observe, not judge or become emotionally attached. Simply observe.

Suddenly, the meditation hour was over and the other participants silently exited the meditation hall. I started hearing voices outside in the yard. The silence requirement had been lifted. I wondered if any of the other sixty participants had remained in the meditation hall with me, but then I remembered to stay present with myself.

Finally, the discomfort eased. My breathing became more re-laxed and regular. My eyes still didn't want to open but I forced them to do so. That's when I noticed a woman watching me with soft, gentle eyes. When she saw I was okay, she silently exited.

Okay, Gary. Time to get up now, I told myself. I unfolded one leg, which went into a full cramp as if it were plastered stiff. A full ten minutes passed before I finally decided, *Enough!* I used a chair to pull myself up, then hobbled slowly until some life returned to my cramping leg.

Still limping, I exited the meditation hall and made my way to my room so I could be alone. I wasn't ready to engage with others while the profound experience still remained so vivid in my mind and body. I worried I would break down, but only a single tear of relief fell. Then, after splashing cold water on my face, I took a few deep breaths and prepared myself to meet my fellow retreat participants. I expressed gratitude to God for the experiences of the silent retreat, believing I had been miraculously cleansed of deep-seated emotional scars.

The Covid-19 pandemic struck just as I entered my third year of recovery. With everyone required to stay home, I admit I had a few wobbly weeks of low-level panic, which I shared with Adi during our check-ins. My fear of aloneness had resurfaced, trig-gering me in a disturbing way. I temporarily felt off balance.

The sleeping dragon within saw an opportunity to rear its vi-cious head and attempt a sneak attack, but I was prepared and it didn't work. When sexual videos started to circulate on social me-dia and a few of my more sexually adventurous former friends reengaged in online chat, I quickly recognized what was happen-ing and kept myself in check. Then, fortunately, my discomfort around isolation, along with any temptations, dissolved by grace into nothing. Literally *no-thing*. Thank you, God! I knew I re-mained an addict in recovery and vigilance would be forever required. Even a tamed dragon is unpredictable. But I had finally become a man who could honor his marriage and love and accept himself as perfectly imperfect and good enough.

I felt a shift in my consciousness and sensed an opening for something new to reveal itself. But what? A course of study? A social cause? A creative outlet? Like so many times before, I knew to stay out of the way. *What is mine to do?* I asked in silent prayer, knowing the information would come.

Later that week, while riding on the back of Adi's motorbike, an exciting idea came to mind: Compose short stories based on childhood memories to give to my mother for her birthday. The idea, clear and powerful, was like a divine spark. It seemed as if my level of recovery was directly linked and commensurate with the awakening of my soul's creative nature—not unlike cleaning a grimy window to allow the light once again to shine through. In that light, I noticed a willingness to move into a new area of creative expression: narrative writing.

Writing became a new hobby, a healthy, life-enriching activity, a new, top-line behavior. Eight months after the idea was born on the back of Adi's motorbike, my illustrated collection of eleven short stories titled *A Boy Like Me* was published and distributed with love to two hundred family members, friends, and educational colleagues. Most importantly, my beloved mother received the very first book for her ninety-fourth birthday.

Writing *A Boy Like Me* led to investing in a narrative writing course with a coach, a writing cohort, and critique group in order to acquire the skills and support I needed to tackle a memoir. But my decision to write such a personal account of my life also raised concerns.

"Dr. Piper, completing my memoir feels important to me, but I don't know about publishing it. I would be putting myself in a very vulnerable position," I admitted during our therapy session.

"Can you tell me what frightens you about publishing?" Dr. Piper asked.

"Well, I don't want to hurt anyone, of course. But there will be some who will be surprised or maybe disappointed in me.

Some might judge me and think it a mistake to air my dirty laundry in public."

"Gary, it's pretty much guaranteed those closest to you will have the strongest reactions to your story. But I also know many, many families are dealing with addiction, infidelity, abuse, and dysfunction in one way or another. Every human being has challenges. Some people are addicted to alcohol or food or compulsive stealing. But others are addicted to judgment, anger, control, or negativity. Once you release your memoir into the world, you will have literally let go of your story. If others feel the need to judge you, that's about them. It will have nothing to do with you unless you take it on."

I took Dr. Piper's words to heart and decided to publish if that opportunity came about naturally. As it turned out, my developmental editor, Jeanne, encouraged me to publish. She believed the book would be helpful to others. She pitched my memoir to a publisher, who then asked for a book proposal and subsequently sent me a contract. All unfolded with ease and grace.

It looked like my creative nature was leading me to become a writer in my golden years. But I had learned to believe in infinite potentiality and what I heard calling me was not only creative expression through writing, but using writing as an avenue to expand in consciousness. My passion to awaken in consciousness—to awaken in Spirit/God—resonated deep within my being.

Awakening in consciousness comes with many gifts—all miraculous. The most profound gift I'd received to date occurred as I drove my motorbike one gorgeous Bali afternoon. I had just left my fellowship meeting in town and completed a few errands. Midway on my thirty-minute drive home, the "veil of illusion" suddenly lifted, enabling me to see how all earthly matter was not solid, but more like a hologram or dreamlike in nature. I saw the motorbikes putting along with me and people driving them. I saw small shops edging the shoulders of the road, dogs sleeping in the sun, and Bali's volcanic mountains in the distance. But everything appeared as if pixelated with space between the particles. I later likened it to images on an early-model, large-screen television or an up-close view of a Georges Seurat painting composed of only tiny dots, yet appearing as solid figures.

I remained present and awake—detached and without fear—simply an observer of a world in which we reside but to which we are not bound. No ego. Perhaps no self. Maybe just soul. What I knew for certain, however, was the blessed nature of the brief experience—one I would welcome again with an open heart. As amazing as the experience was, I couldn't call it joyous. It simply was.

I'd heard the expression before, "veil of illusion." But I never related to it. After my experience, I understood what it meant, even though I remained unable to fully describe it. In Buddhism, it's characterized as realizing emptiness—being in the void. Deepak Chopra wrote about it in his book, *Meta Human*: "Physics dismantles every quality of a tree—its hardness, height, shape, and color—by revealing that all objects are actually invisible ripples in the quantum field."

My brief time observing "ripples in the quantum field" revealed that while the dramas and tragedies of the world represent important occurrences in our earthly lives, they do not matter in the big scheme of things. They do not change spiritual reality nor the omniscience, omnipresence, and omnipotence of God.

So it was in that spirit of being-ness, I AM-ness, I started each day in prayer. Before making my coffee or saying good morning to my loving husband, I made my way to the upper deck of our house and faced east at sunrise. With arms outstretched and breathing in the fresh morning air, I claimed my good in intimate partnership with my God: *Awaken! Awaken to love. Awaken to peace. Awaken to truth and beauty, wisdom and health. Awaken to creativity, power, compassion, and abundance. Command my life that I might remember all that I already am! Thank you, God. And so it is! Amen.*

ACKNOWLEDGMENTS

First and foremost, I would like to thank the One Life in which I live and move and have my being—the wise voice and gentle hand that guides me always.

I also want to express gratitude for the earthly angels who supported me along the way:

My friend, Ebon Therwanger, engaged with me in this project for a full year. He critiqued my work and challenged me in healthy ways to become a better writer with a more natural voice. Ebon helped shape the storyline with his insightful questions and wicked intellect.

My coach and developmental editor, Jeanne Rawdin (rawdinjeanne@gmailcom), taught to my growing edge, appreciated my sense of humor, and helped me gain confidence through constructive suggestions. She then encouraged me to publish and pitched my memoir to Lisa Dailey at Sidekick Press. Without Jeanne, it's unlikely you would be reading this book today.

Author and owner of The Narrative Project, Cami Ostman, who accepted me into the project and provided the forum, loving environment, and instructional format to get this book done! If you've always wanted to write a book, check out thenarrativeproject.net and sign up for a free book planning session.

My writing cohort in The Narrative Project (Martha, Jean, and Eve). These beautiful women demonstrated the compassion and encouragement I needed to keep going.

My Bali friend, Bob Campbell, retired Australian publisher, editor, and writer, whose advice and ideas got me unstuck along the way.

My BFF, Rose Palmer, and my sister, Nancy, who both read the first manuscript and gave me honest feedback, helping me reframe the narrative in a few places.

And finally, I would like to thank everyone who purchases this book and/or encourages others to purchase it. Your support of the LGBTQIA+ community is greatly appreciated. We are one human family and only move forward when we love and support one another.

ABOUT THE AUTHOR

Gary Tubbs is the author of *Mindful Messages for Children* (2016), and *A Boy Like Me* (2020). A former Seattle school principal, Gary is blissfully retired and residing in Bali, Indonesia.

CPSIA information can be obtained
at www.ICGtesting.com
Printed in the USA
JSHW021942100822
29116JS00004B/19